The FAQs of Pool & Pocket Billiards

Frequently Asked Questions for the Casual & Regular Player

First Edition

Allan P. Sand
PBIA Certified Instructor

ISBN 978-1-62505-001-4
PRINT 8.5x11
ISBN 978-1-62505-532-3
eBook format

First edition

Copyright © 2011 Allan P. Sand

All rights reserved under International and Pan-American Copyright Conventions.

Published by Billiard Gods Productions.
Santa Clara, CA 95051
U.S.A.

For the latest information, go to: http://www.billiardgods.com

Other books by the author ...
- Why Pool Hustlers Win
- Table Map Library
- Safety Toolbox
- Cue Ball Control Cheat Sheets
- Advanced Cue Ball Control Self-Testing Program
- Drills & Exercises for Pool & Pocket Billiards
- The Art of War versus The Art of Pool
- 3 Cushion Billiards Championship Shots (a series)
- Carom Billiards: Some Riddles & Puzzles
- Carom Billiards: MORE Riddles & Puzzles
- The Psychology of Losing – Tricks, Traps & Sharks
- The Art of Team Coaching
- The Art of Personal Competition
- The Art of Politics & Campaigning
- The Art of Marketing & Promotion
- Kitchen God's Guide for Single Guys

Table of Contents

WELCOME	1
GENERAL FAQS	1
Laws of Pool	1
What is a pre-shot routine?	2
Do you perform a post-shot routine?	3
How can your game go wrong?	4
Can you achieve "perfect" position?	6
When do you play a safety?	7
What are the different types of safety shots?	8
What is the purpose of safety/defensive play?	9
What happens when applying English to the cue ball?	9
What is this "killer instinct"?	10
What is an A, B, and C level shooter?	11
How do energy cycles affect my game?	12
What are some good excuses for missing?	13
Can a guy mix family life with pool?	14
How does age affect skills?	15
You are addicted to pool if	16
What is the real secret to winning?	17
Why do you love pool?	18
How do you know when you are good?	19
What is the "Zen" of the Green Game?	20
What are some bad habits to avoid?	21
You are obsessive about pool when…	22
Why is luck (good & bad) such a big part of pool?	22
How do people get hooked on pool?	23
Where can you play pool?	24
Got any pool jokes?	27
GAMBLING FAQS	28
What about gambling?	28
Should you gamble?	28
What are some gambling handicaps?	29
What is a comfortable way to handle gambling?	31
PLAYING SITUATIONS AND CIRCUMSTANCES FAQS	32
How do you respond to a beaten opponent?	32
Can a losing match be turned around?	33
How can you warm up for a competition?	34
How can you get used to another pool table?	35
What can you expect in a handicapped league?	36
Can I do a restroom break during a match?	37

What can be eaten while competing? 37
What are the different tournament formats? 38
How can you stop missing cut shots? 39
Why do you play badly against a lesser skilled opponent? 39
When breaking, should you inspect the rack? 40
How do you calculate the odds on a shot? 41
What do you need to know about one rail banking? 42
What is "pocket speed"? 42
Why do you choke on the game ball? 43
How do you analyze a lost match? 44
How can you play for long periods of time? 45
How do you handle a bad 8 Ball break? 46
What can give you an edge? 47
How much fair play is fair? 48
Can you get hurt playing pool? 49
How can you play a better bar table game? 49
What are recommended breaking positions? 50
How can you get over a slump? 51
How can you learn ball speeds on different tables? 52
Does drinking mix with pool? 53
How can you keep score with coins? 53
What are the different ways to keep score? 54
How does someone concede a game? 55
How can you handicap 9 Ball with a friend? 56
How can you handicap 8 Ball with a friend? 57
How can you play while nervous? 57
How can you rack for 9 Ball to make it easier or harder to run out? 58
What is a well-racked set of balls? 59
Do you play the opponent or play the table? 60
How can you evaluate your playing skills? 61
What is sharking? 62
How can you stop someone sharking? 62
How do you handle an opponent who is a poor sport? 63
What if your opponent is an ass? 64
How do you handle an angry opponent? 64
How can you make an accurate 1 cushion kick? 65
What are the different kinds of break shots? 66
How can you improve side pocket shooting? 67

PRACTICING FAQS 68
What does it take to reach the top tier of players? 68
When I do practice, what should I do? 69
How can you get more practice time in? 70

How do you move up to the next level?..72
How can you gradually improve your game?..73
How long does it take to fix a bad habit?..73
How do you plan to run a table layout?...75
Will exercise help improve your game?...75
How do you find a good instructor?...77
How do you practice with a friend?...78
What kinds of drills can improve your game?...79
How do you use the tangent line?...81
How can you shoot accurately with cue ball side spin?..83
How do you video tape yourself?...83
How much practice does it take to become an "A" player?.................................85
What is "playing the ghost"?..86
How can you practice 1 Pocket alone?..87

EQUIPMENT FAQS..**88**
How do you clean your personal pool balls?..88
Do you need cue insurance?..88
How do you ship cue sticks?..89
How should you pack cue sticks for airline baggage?...90
What are the dangers of lending out your stick?..91
How can you get stains out of table cloth?...92
How do people abuse pool equipment?..92
Should you own your own set of pool balls?..94
Why are bar table cue balls different?...94
What do you consider in a used pool table?...95
What are dead cushions?...97
How do you take care of a pool table?..97
What are the different pool table sizes?..98
Why should you own your own table?...99
What should you consider when buying a cue?..100
Should you buy a custom cue?..101
Do you need a jump cue?...102
Do you need a break cue?..102
Do you need a shooting glove?..103
What about using those screw-on cue tips?...104
If you are tall, can you get a longer cue stick?..104
How can dings be removed from a cue shaft?..105
How do you clean the cue shaft?...105
Why is chalk necessary?..106
What sizes and shapes of cue tips are available?..107
Why does a new cue tip flatten after a few shots?..107
When should you change cue tips?...108

What kinds of cue tips are available? 109
What cue accessories are useful? 109
What is a cue extension? 110

TEACHING & LEARNING 111
What is the ghost ball aiming technique? 111
Are you right eye or left eye dominant? 112
How do you use a mechanical bridge? 113
Should you use an open or closed bridge? 113
How does an instructor use a video camera to help you? 114
How to check your stroke for flaws? 115
What are the fundamentals of a stroke? 117
How do shoot one-handed? 118
How do you stop from jumping up on a shot? 119
What is a good stroke? 120
How can you improve your break shot? 121
What are the different hand bridges? 121
How can you reduce miscues? 122
How do you shoot a straight stroke? 123
How do you do a controlled draw shot? 123
How do you do a half-table length draw shot? 124
What makes a smooth stroke? 125
How do you learn to play opposite handed? 126
How do you play a cue ball on the rail? 127
How do you teach children? 128
How do you help a beginning player? 129
How do you coach a new player on a team? 130

QUICKIE TIPS 131
Watching your betters 131
Twirling your stick 131
Talc powder 132
Standing on a pool table 132
Speed kills 132
Reduce choking (failure by fear) 133
Recommended bridge lengths 133
Time to practice 133
An easy way to stop jumping up on the stroke 133
MP3 player use 133
Home table room sizes 134
High humidity problems 134
Check for cue straightness 134
Cue stick lengths 134
Cue ball jumping 135

Clean chalk from clothing 135
Buy your own balls 135

GAME RULES SIMPLIFIED 136

14.1 Continuous 136
Straight Pool 137
Speed Pool 138
Rotation 139
Pool Snooker 141
One Pocket 142
Kelly (Pea) Pool 143
Fargo 145
Equal Offense 146
Cut-throat 147
Golf (simplified) 148
Cribbage 149
Cowboy Billiards 150
Chicago (rail version) 151
Chicago (carom-scratch) 153
2 Cushion Pool 153
Bowliards 154
Bottle Pool 155
Bank Pool 157
Any Eight 158
9 Ball (Back Pocket) 159
9 Ball 160
8 Ball (standard) 161
8 Ball (coin-op table) 162
8 Ball (Chinese) 162
8 Ball (bar rule notes) 163
8 Ball (1-15 side) 163
7 Ball 164
6 Ball 165
3 Ball 165
Basic Pool Playing Rules (BCA/World Rules) 166

POOL TERMINOLOGY 167

A 167
B 167
C 170
D 175
E 177
F 177
G 179

H	180
I	181
J - K	182
L	183
M	185
N	186
O	187
P - Q	188
R	190
S	193
T	197
U-V	198
W-X-Y-Z	199

Welcome

This is an unusual book. It is designed to provide a single source for any player who wants to learn more about the basics of the sport of pocket billiards, also known as pool. Included are various FAQs, simplified game rules, and a "pool dictionary" that describes the common terminology used by pool players around the world. It is useful for anyone who has ever picked up a stick.

General FAQs

Laws of Pool

These apply to just about everyone. It is nearly impossible to avoid these laws and their consequence. They don't apply every time, but when they do, it is a personal intervention from the hands of any one of the many billiard gods.

- The more balls you make in an inning, the easier it is to miss an easy shot.
- On a 9 Ball hill-hill game, if you make the 9 ball, the cue ball will scratch.
- The better you play, the easier you can be beaten by a lesser player.
- The better you get, the worse your luck.
- If the game is very competitive, the louder the music will be playing.
- The longer you have to wait before your match, the greater the chance of losing.
- If the planned cue ball path goes within 6 inches of a pocket, it will scratch in perfect center pocket.
- If you make a difficult shot and the next one is easy, if there is any place on the table where you will not be able to make it, the cue ball will go there.
- If you make a successful bank shot, your next shot will also be a bank shot and it will not be successful.
- If you have others, add them to this topic.
- If you get perfect position on a shot, the chances of missing go up immensely. And, even if you make the shot, your next shot will be out of position.
- The importance of making the shot indicates the greater chances of a miscue or doing something stupid.
- The more difficult the successful shot is, the fewer people there are congratulate you on your success. On the other hand, when you miss

the easiest shot with money or pride on the line, there will be dozens of witnesses.

What is a pre-shot routine?

A pre-shot routine means exactly that - all of the little activities you do from bending over the table up through the final forward stroke to hit the cue ball. When you perform these steps properly, you get consistently good shooting results. When you skip individual actions, or are not attentive, you get poor results.

You want most of the elements of the pre-shot routine to be part of a semi-automatic checklist. A perfect example is using a hammer and nail. When first learning, a lot of little actions are consciously done, one after the other. The consequences of not doing so are painful. After a few thousand nails, most of these become routine.

The more experienced players have their routines so automated that absolutely no thought goes into the actual setup for the shot. The only thoughts that do cross their mind are related to the tactical considerations.

A thinking player compares the results of his shot to his intentions. Any variation between actuality and the plan are mentally reviewed. Mental modifications are done to ensure the next opportunity matches his intentions.

Too much thought about all the muscles involved leads to brain overload. Consciously thinking through all of the necessary adjustments turns a 10 second shot into two minutes. Some people cannot let the back brain take over common actions.

When you first start including a pre-shot routine into your playing habits, a basic checklist helps:

1. On making the shot choice, lay the stick onto the aiming line.
2. Step forward and bend down into your shooting position.
3. Verify that the stick is on the aiming line.
4. Do the practice strokes while imagining the correct speed.
5. Stroke the shot with follow-through.
6. Observe the results and compare the reality to your intentions. Vow to make the necessary adjustments in future similar shots.

Eventually, over thousands of shots, this routine becomes, well, routine. You make the shot decisions and the next time you notice anything, you are either considering the next shot or heading to your chair. And this is the way it should be.

However, when your game is not following the expected routine and you become aware that something is slightly off, you have to go back to your fundamentals. The pre-shot routine is generally the first to be re-examined. Follow the above process, step by step, with full attention to your movements.

Try to identify what you unconsciously changed. It could be that you stopped putting the stick onto the aiming line, or you shuffle your feet into position instead of stepping forward into position. You could even have eliminated the imaging of your stroke before committing yourself to the shot. Whatever it was, firmly put it back into your routine. This will get your game back on track.

Do you perform a post-shot routine?

If you regularly watch the same players compete week after week, you can easily identify the players who will soon be winning more games. Those are the ones that always stop after a shot and appear to be staring at the table. What they are really doing is going over their shot, comparing the new table layout with what they were attempting to achieve. These are the players that learn from their mistakes.

A post-shot routine is actually a post-action analysis of the shot. It is similar to a military after-action debriefing that compares preliminary plans with actual action to determine what worked – and didn't. The results of this process justify changes in policy, process, and procedure. In the same way that the military uses this, you can apply the same attentive process on a shot by shot basis.

This requires a certain amount of self-discipline in order to get into the habit of post-analysis. But once you start doing this, it doesn't take long to become a habit. When properly utilized, it becomes as much a part of your playing style as your pre-shot routine.

To someone observing your post-shot routine, all they would see is the cue stick stroking the cue ball, followed by several seconds of holding still. What they can't notice is the furious activity of your brain, identifying what worked, what didn't, and what minor adjustment is necessary for the next time. (Whew – that's a lot of brain action.)

Having a consistent routine like this supports your playing rhythm. The pre-shot and post-shot activities help develop a stable flow and game focus.

The analysis process is pretty basic. When you first start doing this, ask yourself: What went right? What went wrong?

Ask these questions about the cue ball path, speed, and activity. Then, consider the object ball movement. Finally, consider the results of any peripheral balls. If any of these could have been played better, make a personal note of the necessary adjustment. Only then do you begin your table analysis for the next shot.

If all went right, your self-conversation is short and sweet. If totally disastrous, you may need to stand up while considering the entirety of the consequences.

Additional analysis can include consideration of your assumptions. Was the shot choice correct or could it have been better? Was the initial table analysis considered all the way through to the final stop of all balls? Was the cue ball speed what it should have been?

There is usually several reasons for a failed effort. This can range from the mental process to a physical movement. Don't attempt to correct more than one fault at a time. Fix one identifiable error first and then work on another.

Never, ever throw away the experience of a bad shot. You drastically slow down your learning curve if shooting or playing mistakes are discarded without thought. When you routinely perform post-shot analysis, the process will soon move you to the next level.

How can your game go wrong?

When your game goes off-line and your shooting results begin to deviate from your intentions, something gets out of kilter – usually your fundamentals. The problem is – how long does it take before you notice that something is wrong and take corrective action? Generally, by the time you do wake up, the game count is tough. You might recover – but the struggle to win becomes a low probability proposition.

This article identifies some of the most common situations that create a handicap you could do without. If you can train yourself to recognize when one of these situations occurs, you can more quickly take corrective action. Here are the common problems.

Suddenly Stupid

You make an intelligent shooting decision and get down on the shot. Suddenly, with no conscious intention, the cue ball is moving. Shocked, you watch the table layout change – usually for the worse. Probably, your hind brain took over, or your evil twin surfaced and used this opportunity to mess you up.

At the wrong moment in time, your intelligence and sanity jointly agree to go on holiday. This can be costly in a money competition. Of course, your opponent could be so surprised that he couldn't take advantage of the momentary disintegration of your focus.

When it does happen, all you can do is shake your head in disbelief as your opponent takes over the table. This generally happens because your brain was multi-tasking while shooting. In other words, you weren't focusing on the game in general and the shot in specific. Don't obsess about it (which can further distract you). You can recover if you can immediately go back to your pre-shot routine and start manually performing each step.

Casual Laziness

You begin the competition with all necessary awareness and intentions. Your first few dozen shots are all perfect examples of focus and attention. Your very success and the pride you feel in making the cue ball do what you want becomes your downfall. You relax your intentions (or drink one too many beers). The initial success goes to your head and you (incorrectly) assume you are at the top of your game. After all, recent history has proven your unstoppable skills. Arrogant trust in your competence becomes your new attitude.

For an observant opponent, the next few missed shots demonstrate a weakness in your game. He starts saying things like, "So close" and "You almost had that". You go along with the idea and agree that the misses are simple bad billiard god luck. He snaps up several quick wins.

Bumbling Imagination

This is another way to help your opponent win. All that is needed is an uncontrollable imagination. It occurs most often when you are doing your doing practice strokes. An alternative option bursts upon your consciousness. Instead of stomping on the idea or getting up to reconsider playing options, you change your bridge height and position and go for the new shot. You look at the table results and aren't even ashamed of yourself. Your opponent loves you and considers congratulating you on your decreased skills.

Body Distractions

Another reason to justify reduced attention on the game is bodily interference. There is a close correlation between the operational condition of the body and the ability of the brain to function. Your body has many ways to interrupt your attention. Among these are hunger pangs, headaches, an injury, or excessive flatulence.

Your body can also run out of energy. This physical weakness causes the brain to stop functioning properly. This can result from poor nutrition, weak muscle tone, or even limited stamina. Any of these reduce your ability to play well.

Competitive Distractions

This is a self-inflicted problem. For some reason, your mind doesn't want to concentrate on the game. Any kind of influence in the area demands attention. This can be environmental – music, conversation, an attractive person of the opposite (or same) sex, and others. Even sounds that previously never affected you – affect you, such as clinking ice cubes in a glass. Itemizing these are too many to list here. Basically, your brain will seize upon anything to justify your lack of focus and screw up your game.

Outside Distractions

There are times when personal problems aggressively intrude into your game. Instead of being able to use the Green Game to take a break from your worries, you carry them right along with you. They keep you company as you attempt to be competitive. If your opponent notices this, he can ensure victory by simply slowing down his routine – extending the time that you are waiting (and worrying). Either put your head into the game or go home.

Can you achieve "perfect" position?

As you improve your skills and learn more about how to apply your stick, you will reach a point in the development process where the goal of every shot is to achieve "perfect" position. You want to always get the cue ball to float gently into the intended position for the next object ball. The experience can then be extended as you pocket that ball and the cue ball gently stops for the next shot. You seek the perfection of heaven on earth. You want to be as precise as if you picked up the cue ball and placed on the table exactly where ever you want it. And (to extend this fantasy to the ultimate), do this shot after shot.

You strive for this precision shot after shot, chasing the chimera of superiority. This is a lofty goal. The occasions when even near-perfect position results help keep your hopes alive. It is the result of perfect planning, perfect execution, and perfect cue ball control. To do so more than once a week places you on par with the angels.

Perfection is achievable, once in a while. You can train, educate, and develop yourself to get nearer and nearer. It requires putting more attention on the shot than you have ever applied. Each shot is carefully analyzed and the next opportunity strives for finer and finer control. Each effort is compared to the intended result and past efforts. Improvements are gratefully acknowledged.

You begin to develop cue ball speeds and spins that can be repeated with some consistency. As these become more common, they also become more trustworthy. For example, set up a medium long shot and practice it until it will go in 80% of the time. Then work on using cue ball spin and speed to make the cue ball travel to a designated location. When done intentionally as part of your practicing efforts, improvements will sort of happen.

The process is to master one type of shot until you own it. Set up and practice one shot at a time. When you are good at it, slightly change the distance or angle of the shot and practice getting position. Proceed to another, and another, and another. There are hundreds of different shot types.

Eventually, the skills mastered to get position for one type of shot can be used for another. Keep at it. There is sufficient complexity in the Green Game to keep you busy for your entire lifetime.

When do you play a safety?

Many times while playing, you face a table layout without simple options to pocket shots. There are only bad, very bad and "%?&*@#^" choices. All of us have watched as various bar bangers seize upon this opportunity to demonstrate the width and breadth of their imagination. Actually these guys provide you with an amazing educational instance of stupidity. Some sort of silly shot will be called, often detailing three or more rails. Why do they do this? It's seems to be a bit insane to attempt something that can help lose the game. When playing idiots of this caliber, take 'em for every dollar you can get. (Who knows? They might smarten up later and actually start thinking before shooting.)

While it's fun to watch a bar banger address a poor table layout, you need to be the Intelligent Player and think before you shoot. When faced with a situation beyond your ability to shoot out of it, the best response is to make life difficult for your opponent. And the best way to do this is to be a defensive shot.

Instead of considering some low percentage shot, how about figuring out how to make life difficult for your opponent? If you can see the object ball, you are the person in charge of the table. You can decide what kind of table layout you want to hand over to your poor unsuspecting victim.

Since all aggressive options are dependent upon billiard god luck, think of this as an opportunity to tease your opponent. With an intentional defensive shot, you don't give away the game by giving your opponent an easy way to win. (It's never a good idea to let the billiard gods control your luck.) Your playing philosophy must be, "Nothing for me? Nothing for you!"

When faced with the impossibility of running out, do some proper tactical thinking. When looking at a table layout with the intention to shoot defensively, several possible shots will be immediately available. More can be identified with another 15 seconds of thought. Tailor the selection to your personal ability and the capability of your opponent. If he has a problem with banks, set one up for him. If he can't make a long shot, move the cue ball far, far away.

The lower the skill level of your opponent, the simpler it is to give him a near-impossible shot. Even a sharp cut on an object ball close to a pocket will give some trouble. When your opponent is a better player, safety shots have to be a little more sophisticated. Select a shot that will provide more of a challenge.

Keep in mind – slow speed shots are easier to control and simple is best. If the ending object ball position is important, put your hand on the location and work out the cue ball/object ball angle and speed. If the final cue ball position is critical, put your hand on the location and work out the details.

The learning curve is very easy and quick. On the practice table, a few dozen shots quickly teach you that simple solutions at slower speeds get excellent results. When you do mis-shoot, think through the shot and figure out how you should have done it.

What are the different types of safety shots?

When you face the need to shoot a safety, there are several choices. The one selected depends on the table layout, your ball control skills, and the level of respect you have for your opponent's abilities.

For this effort, there are four easy types that can be combined in different ways. All of these can be combined to add to the difficulty factor and lower the percentages of a successful shot.

These can be easily accomplished with just a little attention to your stroke speed:

- **Bad angle** - you can set up this easy shot so your opponent's target ball is either a very difficult cut or a tough bank, both with a low percentage success rate for him.
- **Distance** - another easy shot to make your opponent shoot the cue ball to a target ball far, far away, or shoot a closer target ball to a far, far away pocket. He may make it, but he will have to sweat the shot out.
- **Frozen cushion** - What is more fun than to leave your opponent looking at the cue ball resting right on the cushion. And you just happen to know he hates this type of shot more than going to the dentist.
- **Hidden ball** - Every once in a while, you will get a made-to-order setup for a shot that hides your opponent's target ball behind one or more balls. Do not resist temptation these opportunities. It is a freebie gift from the billiard gods.

There are others, but these are all that is needed for 98% of the time. Simply select the shot that you can do and that will leave your opponent a situation that he finds frustrating. (If this is a fascinating subject to you, get the only book that is entirely devoted to the entire concept of defensive play – the *Safety Toolbox*.)

What is the purpose of safety/defensive play?

When playing against a determined opponent, especially one whose skills you respect, you do NOT want to offer him an easy way to beat you. Except for the pros (and others who have no life outside of pool), you will have many shooting situations with little or no chances of shooting your way out. You are on the last shot and have to let your opponent come to the table.

Before you bend down over the shot, have a plan in mind. If you don't, the billiard gods are a very fickle group to depend on. Half the time, they kind of help, and the rest of the time they really, really hate you.

Upon deciding to shoot a defensive shot, wonderful opportunities arise. The choice you make should consider only one purpose - leave your opponent in such a bad spot that he only gets one shot. In other words, the purpose of any safety or defensive shot is to be mean to your opponent.

If you are willing, you can assume responsibility for how nice you want to be. If you want to be known as a pleasant fellow who never complains about losing – play that way. If you want to win more games, show a little vicious streak to your opponent.

If you don't assume this adversarial attitude during the game, you are gifting too many games to your opponent. You can go with the school playground doctrine, giving every opponent as many opportunities as possible to beat you, or you can take the survival-based me-win, you-lose selfish approach.

Feel free to see if your opponent subscribes to the fairness doctrine. If he does, you can win a lot more games.

What happens when applying English to the cue ball?

English is side spin that the cue tip applies to the cue ball on contact. It can occur only if you hit the cue ball on the left or right side of the vertical center line. The amount of the reaction (and any unknown results) varies depending on the distance out from center that the tip contacts the cue ball. The miscue is the ultimate unintended consequence. The resulting side spin is very obvious when using a measles cue ball or an object ball.

All pool players should do their absolute best to avoid putting any side spin on the cue ball. When trying to establish a consistent aiming technique, adding English to the cue ball introduces uncontrollable consequences that will throw the shot off.

Stroke speed affects the cue ball English. A slower speed allows more interaction with the cloth and cushions, a faster speed forces the ball to travel further on the deflected angle and less reaction off the cushions. All of these add further unpredictability to careful control of the cue ball.

Here are some cue ball reactions to the contact of the cue tip to the ball off the vertical center line:

- **Squirt** - this is the side shift of the cue ball when contacted with the tip. The further out to the side, the greater the shift. The speed will also exaggerate the shift. The movement is simultaneous with the start of forward momentum.
- **Swerve** - when side spin of the cue ball can interact with the cloth, the cue ball will curve in the direction of the spin. At slow speed, the curves are greater.
- **Cushion angle** - when the cue ball contacts the cushion with side spin, the ball will rebound in the direction of the spin. With high side spin, rebounding ball will try to dig into the cloth (losing a little energy) and slightly increase the angle out. With low side spin, the rebounding ball will actually speed up on the out angle.

Through extensive practice, advanced players automatically adjust their aim, stroke, and speed in order to achieve a successful shot. This requires tens of thousands of shots. Until you are willing to devote significant effort to mastering English spin, use center ball on your shots.

What is this "killer instinct"?

Most of the time when you play casual matches; they are, at best, played as a matter of friendly competition or something to pass the time of day. In either case, there is rarely anything of importance or of value at stake. Game wins and losses mean little to the players.

There are games with more meaning to the participants. For example, you are in a competition against an opponent which whom you have a personal long-running vendetta or a chance to win (or lose) a few bucks. There may be some friendly by-play, jokes, and teasing early in the match, but that fades quickly away as the results of each game become more and more important. This is the bare edge of the "killer instinct". It's not at the "battle to the death" strength, but the teeth and a feral attitude are beginning to show.

In tournaments, the killer instinct is more obvious. There is money at stake, along with prestige. To an observer, the players' focus and attention is much more intense. The opponents may be friendly outside of personal competition, but their attitudes are much different when they are trying to find out who is the best.

For most people, this is as far as it goes. Some individuals feel somewhat uncomfortable with even the smallest bit of exposure to the primeval animal. As players, these individuals stay pretty much at the same skill year after year.

Then there are those few who have the strength of desire and a focused drive to do whatever it takes to compete at the higher levels. These individuals must possess the full-fledged killer instinct. During the match no prisoners are taken. Each duel is to the (figurative) death, and no mercy or kindness is offered or intended.

In competitions, the desires of these individuals are obvious to any observer. There are no conversations, jokes, or comments during the match as they draw deep within themselves to bring their competitive spirit to the forefront.

The question is - how much of the animal do you want to experience? How much competitive spirit do you have (or want to have)? When playing in a friendly group, intensive competitive attitudes are a bit uncomfortable for your opponents. It may get to the point where you need to find another group with which to compete. You will have outgrown your old friends.

Some players experience an epiphany of competitive understanding while their friends do not. That is when you have to hunt down tougher opponents. If this happens, you can still have friendly competitions with your friends, but you have to give spots (handicaps) to keep the game interesting. The problem with developing a killer instinct is that you have to keep it fed.

Regardless of where you are now in the grand competitive scheme of your pool career and where you will be in the future, enjoy yourself. The game is the game at whatever levels of "killer instinct" you want to develop.

What is an A, B, and C level shooter?

This scale is a general guide to assessing skill levels when setting up matches between players. There are higher ratings used by other tournament organizations that go to double A (AA) and triple A (AAA). For our purposes, the descriptions here are limited to the levels most commonly found in the majority of pool halls across the world.

Positioning yourself within this skill grid will be somewhat fluid. Some days you will fit one level, and other days another. Overall, you will tend to stay around one level for a long time before your skills mature enough to move up.

- **A level players** are at the top of the local amateur players. They finish near the top of almost all local non-handicapped tournaments. They have strong general skills.
- **B level players** are the top regulars who place well in league competitions. They are reasonably competent shooters, usually with less than 10 years of playing experience. They are decent competitors who love the game and its competitive, yet friendly, environment.
- **C level players** are acceptable shooters. They are starting to learn some of the ins and outs of the game. If a better shooter offers suggestions and recommendations, they often pay close attention. They are just learning their stance and stroke. If lucky, they will be in the company of more skillful friends who can help them through their initial learning curve.

Sometimes this scale is extended into three sub-levels. In this case, you get C-, C, C+, B-, B, B+, and A-, A, A+. These are usually done to allocate handicaps for local tournaments and leagues.

How do energy cycles affect my game?

The underlying natural operations of the human body go through a series of up and down cycles that looks very similar to the patterns of a sine wave (see example). While you can (with some training and self-discipline) modify the heights and depths, and even shorten the frequency, you can no more avoid this than you can stop from getting older.

This is a natural flow that affects your life and how you feel at every moment of your life. In pool, you are subject to the same flow which can be directly observed in the effectiveness of your playing ability.

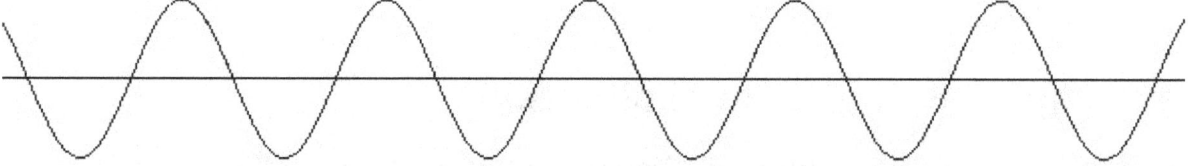

When you are operating on your up cycle, you are more accurate, and shot are easier to make. Even luck seems to go your way - as evidenced in the ways that you seem to get better ball rolls. Game wins occur with wonderful regularity and everyone is admiring you and your skills. It can get thrilling. In some aspects, this is dangerous. Because things seem so effortless, you begin to assume that this is way pool should be all the time.

On your down cycle, you experience difficulties and problems with the simplest situations. Shots are harder, routine patterns are tougher, and you seem to be exposed to bad luck rolls for no obvious reason. It can get downright unfair. Frustration becomes your primary emotion as you beat yourself up over how poorly your skills are being demonstrated. Everything is on the bottom looking down. When comparing such difficulties to better times, it just seems to unfair.

No one is exempt from these experiences. The key to surviving down cycles is to identify when the edges of your skills begin to fray and unravel. This is usually evident when you miss a couple of shots that should be within your comfort zone. With this as an advance warning, you can survive better if you immediately reduce your expectations of success. Re-size your expectations by half. For example, if you are pretty good with 4 foot shots, change your expectations of success down to 2 foot shots.

The down cycle will last however long it is going to last. It will seem to be longer than it really is. You'll be able to feel the change from down cycle to up cycle when you notice a slight rise in your confidence level because a shot that you did not expect to work - did. This is the point where you can improve your confidence and start returning to your normal game patterns and expectations.

What are some good excuses for missing?

Everyone misses shots, even easy ones. When you need excuses, it is a good idea to have a selection of available excuses ready to use.

Here is your standard excuse list:
- You were sharking me.
- The music is too loud. How can anyone think with this noise?
- I don't want my opponent to see my real skill.
- That good looking girl (or guy) distracted me.
- I not really interested in winning anyway.
- I'm trying to keep my handicap.
- There's a roll-off on the table.
- Whoops. Forgot to chalk.
- I've got to hit the can.
- A piece of chalk threw the ball off line.
- I shouldn't have had that last beer.
- I shouldn't be talking when I'm shooting.
- The ball skidded and went off line.
- The ball doesn't roll right. I want a replacement.
- I had a brain fart.
- There are only so many bad shots in me today. That was one of them.
- I like to help my friends win once in a while.
- The balls don't roll straight.
- Oops. I'm using the wrong cue.
- Can't seem to get anything right today.

For old geezers:

- I just had hip surgery and can't get down on the shot.
- Anybody know where I put my glasses?
- I forgot what I was trying to do.
- I'd rather be lucky than good.
- I should have made that. Can't figure out why.
- I can't see that far.

Add to this list anything else you need. You get extra social points when you have a humorous excuse. There is no shame in stealing someone else's line, as long as you don't use it the night you first heard it.

Can a guy mix family life with pool?

A lot is going to depend on the expectations of your spouse. If there is not an active and outright hatred of your playing pool, there is plenty of room for negotiation. Basically, this is a situation requiring careful negotiation. How well you can do this is usually related to the number of years you have been married. This can require good bargaining skills.

Initially, there will be a significant amount of horse trading. You offer a certain quantity or quality of favors in exchange for pool playing opportunities. The more sacrifices you are willing to make, the more chances you have of playing pool and for longer periods of time. For example, a good trade is offering to go shopping together Saturday mornings for a chance to get to the pool hall one evening during the week. Or, you can offer to pick up the kids on Thursday and Friday for the chance to play Sunday afternoon.

Keep the trades well balanced. Try this as a guideline - so many of your hours doing the favors to be traded for an equivalent number of hours around the table. Whatever you do, do not get into a situation where you are offering more home hours for fewer table hours. Let that happen one time and you will never get things back in balance until you enter your retirement years.

If there is some resistance to your playing evenings, you will have to be a harder negotiator. It never hurts to throw in a measured dose of whining and begging. Not too much of the kowtowing, but enough to at least tickle the fair play button. Where possible, offer an equivalency trade. You go out one or two nights a week, your spouse goes out the same number of times.

If possible, you can get a 7 footer installed in an appropriate room is your home, even if some shots will be a little cramped. You can use it to keep in stroke and for the occasional party entertainment. When not in use, it can become a clothes folding table, short-term storage area. The space under the table can become longer-term storage. With practice you can clear the table for play in minutes, and when done, restore it to its previous condition.

As the kids get a little older (usually 9+), you can take them to a family-friendly pool hall (one that serves pizza is good). Before eating, rent a table and get them started. The first few times you will need to work with them on acceptable stroke or stance. Play games where they can position the cue ball for each shot and make it easier for them to make balls. Once they have the basics down, you can leave them unattended while you go off to a grudge match on a nearby table. Assuming they stay relatively well-behaved, you might find yourself training up a budding junior state champion.

If there is outright antagonism against your playing, you are in trouble. What chances you get to play are going to have to be on the sly. And, when you do go out to play, you will have to be very careful to remove all evidences of chalk on hands and clothes. You may have to hide your sticks at a friend's house too. And, you'll put more effort in sneaking out than if you were cheating. When you get caught (and you will), grovel appropriately. Learn how to become a pretty good actor. Over time, use gentle persuasion and courteous proposals, and you will eventually gain sufficient freedom to play on a regular and ongoing basis.

If worse comes to worse and you find yourself having to give up playing, remind yourself that the Green Game will always be there, ready when you are. Your youngsters will grow up faster than you can believe. Eventually, you will retire and the many senior centers all have one or more pool tables.

How does age affect skills?

When you love the Green Game as a young shooter full of vim and vigor, it will be almost impossible to get enough playing time. As you enter maturity, a few other things (such as family, kids, making a living, etc.) intrude on your pool playing time. These intrusions might even interfere enough to cause you to give up playing for a decade or two.

Then comes the big 5-O (or 6-O or retirement) and life outside the pool hall settles down. That is a good time to renew your love of the game and its intricacies. After all, you now have the time to make pool a major part of your life again. With new maturity, you are more capable of seeing pool more of a thinking man's game with actions and consequences to be properly considered.

But that maturity in thinking also includes the consequences of aging. Your body doesn't quite work as smoothly and easily as it used to do in your memories. You might be overweight or out of shape. Pool does require some physical fitness. As such, there are only so many shots that you can shoot in any one time. Once that limit is exceeded, your game goes downhill.

One effect of realizing you are on the second half of your life expectancy is the understanding that you will not become the professional player of your youthful dreams. But you can settle down to become one of the top shooting old geezers at your local pool room. You have the time to regularly work on your game. Practice times are more productive as you focus on fine-tuning your skills.

Another benefit of being a regular is that you are now looked up to by the younger crowd - at least the ones that have any brains. These are the ones that show some respect for your age and wisdom. A few of them even ask for advice. With proper presentation, you can become the go-to guy when a shot has to be watched for legality or there is a question about the rules.

There are always a few youngsters who think they can beat up on you. They think that it will improve the rep – or they are just desperate to find someone to play. You should be able to make life difficult for such individuals. Generally, if you have half their pocketing skill, they should be easy meat. (Age & wisdom beats youth and energy.)

Basically, you get comfortable with your abilities, competence, and skills. You may not be able to play more than a few hours at a time, but your place in the hierarchy of the pool room and within those of your age group are assured. It's a good life.

There will be some loss of physical capability over the years affecting your game. Longer shots may be more difficult to consistently make, sharper cuts are harder to see. That can be offset by applying the tricks and traps learned over the years. There is always something you can do to gum up your opponent's opportunities.

There will also be plenty of players to compete against. In additional to other regulars in your home pool hall, other pool rooms will have their own collection of geezer shooters to compete against. The pool rooms of senior centers across the world contain plenty of competition. Plus, there are always those young shooters who need a lesson in respect for senior citizens.

You are addicted to pool if

How do you know when your passion for pool as taken over your life? Here are a few indicators:

- The wife said, "Pool or me." You miss her once in a while.
- There are only two times a week when you think about pool. Weekdays and weekends.
- You tear down the garage and build a bigger one to hold the pool table.
- At work, you spend more than an hour a day looking at forums and drooling over equipment.

- You have a pool table at home, and get upset because your wife wants to use it to fold clothes.
- When traveling, you pick hotels/motels next to a pool hall.
- You arrange your get-togethers with relatives only when there are tournaments in the area.
- You schedule family nights out with the kids when you don't have league nights.
- If your wife makes you baby sit, you pack the kids up and take them to a pool hall.
- When you started playing pool, your wife made you promise you will play only one night a week. You solemnly promised with fingers crossed.
- You convince the wife that a second floor is needed on the house for a pool room so that you won't interfere with her TV watching schedule.
- The only time you don't play five nights a week is when you are sicker than a dog, and your friends won't let you into the pool hall.
- You make friends with the only three people in town with home tables, so that you can go play with them two times a week - each.
- You play all night, three times a week.
- Your life can be summed up as - All pool, all the time.
- You deny being addicted to pool.
- Your only friends play pool.
- You are relieved that the medical field does not believe that pool is addictive - which you bring up constantly to prove you aren't addicted.

What is the real secret to winning?

People with all sorts of table billiards experience from everywhere in the world believes that they have the real secrets of winning in pool. Those that actually do know tend to hold this knowledge closely; and would not share, even under torture. Every generation has a few holders of the secret who let the secret out of the bag. They reveal this information to favored students. A few more require cash as an incentive to cough up the details.

Consider this question - every time you start a game, whether it is 8 Ball, 9 Ball, 1 Pocket, or another other game, what is the purpose of that game? Answers vary from the simple - "To win. Duh." to "Make balls, lots of balls." These are good answers.

Those answers tend be results. When you consider the question a little more, you realize that being successful at pool requires a very specific skill. It is not in aiming – anybody can learn to aim. All it takes is some dedicated practice. In fact, you can easily get quite good at pocketing balls from almost anywhere on the table.

The next level of realization is getting the cue ball into position for the next shot after you have made a successful shot. The pros make it seem simple. Most people can also learn this when the next target ball is not too difficult.

A simple way to say the secret is:

CONTROL THE CUE BALL, CONTROL THE GAME

Getting the cue ball to dance to your program requires a different kind of practicing. It is related to the precision in which you can consistently contact the ball with the cue tip.

When you begin to learn the game, you are happy when you can make the cue ball go in the general direction you intended. When you get a little better, you gain a little control with the speed that you make the cue ball travel.

Next, you learn to make the cue ball do little dances – draw it back a bit or follow. Soon you are applying (in controlled circumstances) a little side spin to the cue ball. Essentially, you are learning to make some of your shots more predictable.

But you truly are able to touch the lowest level of billiard god-hood when you realize that the game is based on a very simple skill. To master the entirety of the game is dependent on hitting the cue ball at a precise point at a perfectly controlled speed. The result is consistent and predictable results. That's it. Of course, to get there can take a long time. This bit of knowledge will shape how you practice for the rest of your life. By all means, develop your aiming skills, but focus on what you can do with the cue ball.

Why do you love pool?

There are such a wide variety of aspects and elements of this game that they almost defy description and definition. There is such a variety of complexity, and difficulty to a seemingly simple playing field. Yet, people's lives have become entangled in the problems of mastery.

The appeal of table billiards extends around the world. You can travel to anywhere and find pool tables in one form or another. The table quality may be of various levels and materials, but it will exist. In every locale in the world, you will find kindred souls that will share the same passion and enthusiasm of cue sports.

Once you develop even the slightest interest in the sport, you will find others with skills similar to yours. They will also have the same interest in banging candy-colored balls around a rectangular table, with the sole purpose of making them disappear off of the table into any one of six holes.

You can find mentors that will be happy to have someone listen to their advice. But the ones you really want to see you improve are those senior shooters. They have the time to help out learning players willing to listen and pay attention. Their example means that you too will be able to enjoy the Green Game into your old age.

If you like puzzles, there is no better one then figuring out how to push a bunch of balls into pockets. And, each new rack provides a brand new puzzle. The complexities are so vast that you will have an endless and lifetime supply of creative confusion.

If you are a very precise individual who lives for careful control and predictability in their life, you will find pool to be a constant challenge to bring order out of chaos. The challenge of learning how to control small movements can consume a lifetime.

There is the pleasure of watching and enjoying the artistry of the best professional shooters who constantly compete at locations across the planet. Every game and match they play are examples of what is humanly possible.

How do you know when you are good?

The level of "good" as you define it is bounded by the type of players you compete with. For example, if your competitors are neighbors meeting once a week around a home table, a little extra effort will make you the big frog. In a pool hall, the regulars are of higher caliber. It will take some time and effort become you can become competitive and even more to rise to the top of that group.

There are three things that are used to determine "good".

- Breadth of knowledge
- Pocketing skills
- Positioning skills

Knowledge is gained from experience – assuming you are paying attention. You learn the most from losing, and the least from winning. When you experience a loss, you figure out what and make adjustments to improve your chances of success. Whether we like it or not, failure is what sharpens the mind. Keep in mind that nothing can be learned from success, except that you become a little too arrogant.

You can also learn by watching other players' successes and mistakes. Recognize the playing errors of others, and you can more clearly see your own. The various instruction books, videos, and internet resources can provide a quick way to gather knowledge. The best way to improve is with an instructor.

Pocketing skills are necessary. When you first start playing, making balls fall into the holes is your absolute first priority. There are such a variety of ways to make the balls go in, that this effort will take some considerable time.

Positioning skills is the last general area that needs to be learned. This means working out the mysteries of controlled cue ball speed and spin. As you work your way through the various ways to do this, your skills will improve. It becomes a lot easier to make a target ball if you move the cue ball to a position that makes it an easy shot.

Your definition of "good" will change dramatically once you expand your knowledge of what it really takes in skill and abilities. As you improve yourself, you will move up in the pool hall hierarchy. Your lesser skilled friends will be unable to accompany you. Basically, your skill level will determine the size of the pond in which you try to become one of the bigger frogs.

What is the "Zen" of the Green Game?

Few players attain the attitude and mindset that is detailed here. Most don't even know that it exists. Yet it is experienced by many players and is most often discovered by accident rather than by intention.

The development (or growth) of your game is not simply a matter of improving skills and gaining experience. There is also a necessary mental expansion that occurs which improves your appreciation and enjoyment of the game. This is what makes playing pool worthwhile throughout a lifetime.

The process is an uneven pathway. What was important a year ago is not so today. Even your favorite game will change over time. It might start out as 8 Ball, move to 9 Ball, transition to straight pool, and then explore the possibilities of 1 Pocket. You may even enjoy multiple player games such as Golf for a decade or two. Snooker and 3-cushion Billiards can have a fascinating attraction.

Regardless of these transitory fads, each of these offers up the "thrill of victory" and the "agony of defeat". What does happen over the years is a gradual realization that the importance of the game does not revolve around the winning (however enjoyable) and losing (however painful).

Eventually, your purpose and satisfaction is not going to come from the winning of games, but from moving closer and closer to perfect control. There are many examples of how this can be achieved. In straight pool, one level will be when you can play through two racks. Then it will be when you achieve your first century (100 balls). In other games, you can set up various goals. As you achieve them, you set higher goals.

It can be transitory, such as a perfect shot with the cue ball stopping on the intended square inch of the table. Or it could be successfully running the rack. The satisfaction of either achievement can justify an entire evening at the pool hall.

Once this mindset is adopted, in many ways the game becomes more complex. You have to consider dozens, even hundreds of things when selecting a shot. You include in your evaluation the various pathways of different cue ball spins applied with different speeds. Winning becomes a mere chalk mark. Much more important will be how close you got to perfection.

What are some bad habits to avoid?

The vast majority of pool players, both casual and regular, have one or more of their fundamentals out of wack to some degree. The problem mostly arises because the player never took the time to check with someone who could show him/her how and why to do things correctly. The closest most people come to correct fundamentals is a flawed imitation of the friend who introduced them to playing pool.

If you are serious about becoming a decent player, here is a list of bad habits that can slow down your learning curve:

- Grab the cue stick as close to the butt as possible.
- Shoot with the stick hand gripping at or near the butt of the cue with your elbow as high as you can make it go.
- On the back stroke, swing your arm near your body, then on the forward stroke swing your hand to the side in a short curve.
- Shove your stick elbow as far out as possible to make it look like a chicken wing.
- When putting your bridge hand on the table, crouch forward so that you can bend the elbow as much as possible.
- On the forward stroke, pretend the cue is a corkscrew.
- Grip the stick very hard so that it will not escape and fly across the room.
- Have a long, long bridge - at least 18 inches from your bridge hand to the cue ball.
- Lift the cue stick with your stick arm as high as possible.
- Move your stick elbow in a pumping motion.
- Move as many parts of your body as possible when making a shot.
- Hit the cue ball with the butt as high in the air as you can get it - no matter how uncomfortable.
- Lift your head as far away from the cue as possible when you shoot.
- Tilt your head to one side so that you look quizzical.
- Shoot the cue ball so low that you can lift it high into the air.
- Always hit the cue ball too hard.
- Never hit the cue ball on the center vertical line.
- Always forget to chalk.
- Never consider where the cue ball will end up.
- Try to make every shot, no matter how difficult or impossible.

- Never use the same excuse more than once per night.
- Avoid anybody's advice as if they were trying to make you lose.

If you can identify one or more of these habits as part of your stroke, find someone who has a good reputation as an instructor and get help.

You are obsessive about pool when...

- The number of friends who don't play pool can be counted on one hand.
- You monthly budget includes table time, league match fees, and tournament entry frees.
- You know who played on the last five Mosconi Open teams, but can't identify the five largest continents of the planet.
- When planning family vacations, they just happen to coincide with a major tournament in the area.
- Your bridge hand is permanently stained with chalk.
- You can describe every detail about your cue, but have to think to remember the make and color of your car.
- You leave early from work to play pool at least three times a week.
- You have spent more money on your cues than your car is worth.
- Your wife stops asking, "Where are you going?" as you leave the house.
- On holidays celebrated at home, you're in the pool hall an hour after dinner.
- You know more people at the pool room than at the family reunion.
- Your pool hall knows your home and cell phone.
- Your computer at work has an online pool game available at the click of a mouse.
- Your browser at work has a couple of tabs tuned to billiard forums.
- The five major events of your life in order of importance are:
  - Your first break and run.
  - The first tournament you took first place.
  - The worst session of pool ever
  - When you finally beat the best player in the pool hall
  - Your wedding

Why is luck (good & bad) such a big part of pool?

Sometimes you hear a player say something similar to, "If it wasn't for bad luck, I wouldn't have any luck at all." This kind of statement usually occurs after a bad roll, a scratch, a missed shot, or just plain less than expected ball behavior.

Yet, you do not hear people exclaim about their good luck when it "rolls" their way. Just watch an average shooter when he somehow gets perfect position. The cue ball travels far and lands perfect for an easy shot for the win. You KNOW he doesn't have the skills, but what can you do? If he has any shame, he should look embarrassed. If he acts like he intended the shot, he is a bare-faced liar.

Regardless, good and bad results are part of the normal cycle of action that everyone experiences. Some days you can shoot the lights out, other days you couldn't pick up an object ball and drop it in the pocket.

As your skills improve, luck has lesser and lesser impact. But there is still a large role for luck. You see this in lucky kicks and banks. There may have been a bit of thought in aiming, but the results are good or bad luck.

On the occasional bit of demonstrated good luck, feel free to ask your opponent this question, "Was that luck or skill?" If he doesn't properly credit good luck, offer a bet of some appropriate amount of money that he can't repeat it. If he refuses the bet, you confidently state that it was a lucky shot, not skill. This will advance you a couple of personal points.

It helps to maintain a more steady state of mind. When you do see a couple of sequential good luck, just as gravity exists, later in the game he will have twice as many hard luck situations. When he does suffer, push hard to win.

Do not confuse luck with risk. Every shot you make has a risk factor, whether you recognize it or not. The shot itself might be a low risk, but the position play might be a high risk attempt. To the degree that you make proper allowances for risk, you can improve your chances of winning the game.

How do people get hooked on pool?

Some individuals are introduced to the Green Game when very young, either by receiving a toy table or somehow gaining access to someone's home table via the family or a neighborhood buddy. Others start as teenagers, banging balls around with friends, usually as a casual pastime. Some young players start out with a strong fascination and even learn to be a decent shooter, and then give it up for other pursuits such as school and girls. Later they come back and get more consistently involved.

Some individuals, looking for a new hobby, are introduced to the Green Game via a friend who convinces you to join the local league team. The game strikes some chord inside that develops into a fascination.

When you walk into many pool halls in the early afternoons, you find many retired individuals who come in to pass the time of day and chisel each other for a few bucks. Take your time to talk with some of these fellows. They are often outstanding resources of knowledge and local history.

In the beginning, many people become fascinated be the action of using a white ball to push other colorful balls around the table. Some of the balls occasionally go into pockets - sometimes on purpose, most often by accident. Plus all those bright colors moving randomly on a beautiful background are mesmerizing. What's not to like?

The chance to compete on an equal or near equal basis among peers, friends, and leagues is a good reason to enjoy the game. This is a sport that depends not on superior strength, but on intelligent attention. The idea of being able to play against men and women of all ages, with no stigma attached, can be attractive.

For those included to control and perfection, there could not be a more perfect pastime. Where else can you go to find a game where you use a tool to touch one ball and make it interact with other balls – that requires such careful skill.

The advantages of loving the Green Game are many. There are almost no physical medical restrictions - there are many excellent wheelchair players. There are no age limitations. There are good players as young as 8 and 9 all the way up to those in their 90s.

One shining example is an individual (87) with Parkinson's. He would shake violently on the setup and practice strokes, but when the shot was committed, you could not find a more beautiful follow-through. And even when it did interfere with a shot, he was so pleasant and self-forgiving about it. And, he played for two-three hours every day.

To play regularly, all that is really required is the ability to get to the table and take a shot. There is a legend that while an occasional player collapses while playing, no one is actually been identified as dying while playing pool.

Society exists in this microcosm universe. Here you can observe many of the human interactions - battles, skirmishes, wars, and fights for supremacy. There occurs respect, insults, snubs, and other subtle actions that indicate arrogance or desperation. There are constantly challenges for status and occasionally money. Long standing resentments and feuds can develop; fear and rage (subdued in most cases) can bloom into existence. Revenge and the desire for comeuppance can festered for years between individuals. What more drama could you want?

Where can you play pool?

It matters what the circumstances are that instilled the love of pool in your heart and mind. You may have just picked up a stick a couple of weeks ago, have a few years behind you, have played off and on for decades, or still fiercely battle your buddies at 80+.

When you want to find a place to play, there are many locations. Some of the places might not be a location where you can take children and others require membership to access their tables. Here are some places where you can stroke your stick.

Pool halls

To qualify as a pool hall, all that is needed is several tables and someone to manage the cash register. Add-ons include beverages and food. There are pool halls in almost every possible place in the world. There are places where competitions occur in an open field with outdoor tables that are folded down and stored when not in use. There are places with only three or four tables and others with 60 and more. There are halls that cater to the poor, to the rich, and to every strata of human society. Go into a new location where an unknown language is spoken. Go up to any three people and make the motions of a pool stroke. At least two of them will point you to a pool hall.

Pool halls charge money for use of their tables and equipment. The final bill will vary depending on the rules of that pool hall. Costs can based on combinations of time using the table, the number of players, time of the day, day of the week, even whether women are part of the group. To avoid surprises about the final bill, ask the counter person before getting the balls.

Homes

Home tables have always been popular throughout history. When the game was considered the sport of royalty, huge rooms were set aside to hold a couple of tables.

Throughout the history of billiard/pool tables, the well-to-do were always expected to have a "billiard" room in their home for entertainment purposes. This carries forward into modern times. You can't find any mansion that doesn't at least have one table in a separate room, whether it is used or not.

Many modern homes usually have room for a table in the 4x8 or 3-1/2x 7 size. Usually it is designated as a recreation room or TV room. Many times, an enclosed patio is added to the back yard and becomes a pool room. A lot of tables end up in the garage, usually after spring cleaning and a lot of stored junk is disposed of and the new space beckons to be used for a pool table.

Bars

Just about every bar in business in the entire world has a pool table. Usually it is the smallest common size of 3-1/2 feet by 7 feet. The entire unit is designed to be moved as a single piece of furniture as needed for parties and dances. Space is at a premium, so the larger tables cannot be placed in most of these locations, but a bar table will fit fine.

These are coin operated, meaning that money must be inserted to access the balls. The cue ball is different from the other balls so that it can be returned to the shooter after scratching. Once a ball is down, it is no longer playable because it is locked in the ball storage underneath.

The pockets are often enlarged so that even badly aimed balls have a good chance of being made. The condition of the table deteriorates quickly due to rough hands, careless strokes, cigarette burns, liquor/beer stains. It gets unlevel because the table is moved so often to make room for more or less drinking tables depending on the time of week, and is rarely carefully re=leveled.

Institutions & Associations

In any place where services are provided to groups of people based on certain conditions, there is usually a room set aside to play pool for members.

Places where pool tables are common include fraternal organizations (in the US: Elks, Moose, Oddfellows, etc.). The bar area is the first place to look for a table, but other tables may be available in a pool room. All private clubs will have at least one table. The richer their members, the more swank the tables and room.

Other places might be government-sponsored, such as senior centers and youth centers which will always have at least two tables. Some private associations will also have tables available, such as the YMCA and YWCA. Boarding schools will all have tables available for their young charges.

Other places

Condominiums and upscale apartments usually have a common area that contains many amenities such a party/meeting room, bathrooms/showers, exercise room, an adjoining swimming pool and a pool room with one or two tables. Regular players will want to select an apartment complex based on the quality of the pool table.

Outside of the US, many upper class hotels have pool rooms set aside for guests. If you plan to travel abroad, when making hotel reservations, ask if they have tables. If they don't, it may be worthwhile to send an email to several of the hotels asking about the proximity and quality of nearby pool halls.

Summary

You will never really lack for access to pool tables. There are so many tables in so many places all around the world. As you find yourself in these locations, you will observe huge variances of table, ball, and cue quality. On a good table, enjoy the truth of the rolling balls - they do so at your direct effort. On bad tables, enjoy the challenge. You can become very inventive with some shot solutions. This is one of those rare situations where a "level playing field" does not require a level table.

Got any pool jokes?

Two players play a 4 ahead race. The first player wins the toss, breaks and runs four games in a row. The second player says he needs a spot. The first player says, "Can't do that. I haven't seen you play."

What does a pool player have in common with a small pizza? Neither will feed a family of four.

How do you get a pool player to leave the front door of your home? Pay for your pizza.

Two guys get ready to play a match. The first guy asks, "Do you make good money playing pool? The second player responds, "I'm working on my second million." The first guy asks, "Really?" The other guy says, "Yup, I gave up trying to get my first million."

What do you call a pool player without a girlfriend? Homeless.

The new bride is carried across the threshold of their honeymoon suite. She sees his cue case leaning against the wall. As she looks at him with fire in her eyes, he says, "This won't take all night, will it?"

What do you call a dozen pool players in the basement? A whine cellar.

What do pool players use for birth control? Their personalities.

What's the difference between a pool player and a puppy dog? The dog eventually stops whining.

Why do pool players find themselves forced to get jobs? They have this horrible addiction to eating.

Pool is a simple game. You just have to practice and play for years and decades before you realize that.

I would love to win all of the time. It's too bad so many people want to disappoint me.

On a bar-banger being asked, "Why won't you learn how to play better? Is it ignorance or apathy?" The player thinks for a minute, then says, "I don't know and I don't care."

Joe and George loved to play pool and wondered if pool was played in heaven. They agreed that whoever went first would communicate back. Joe died. Three nights later, George dreamed he was talking to Joe. Joe said, "I have good news and bad news. What do you want first?" George said, "Good news first." Joe said, "OK. Yes, they do play pool in heaven. The bad news is – you're scheduled to play tomorrow night."

What's wrong with pool player jokes? Pool players don't think they are funny and everyone else doesn't think they are jokes.

Gambling FAQs

What about gambling?

Gambling money on your table skills can sometimes be an opportunity to learn how you play under pressure, or simply be a way to pass some time for pocket change. Your reaction to risking the available cash in your possession depends on your experiences and the amounts being risked. Here are a few suggestions and recommendations.

- **Long races.** This allows skill to shine and decrease the opportunities for luck to impact the results. For example, a race to 11 would be whoever wins 11 games first. A "5 ahead" race would be to whoever wins 5 games ahead of the other person, whether it be 7 to 2 or 13 to 8.
- **Multiple barrels.** This means you have enough reserves to suffer several losses and still be able to continue playing. Each barrel can be $5, $10, $50 or more. The requirement to enter the group might be the availability of a minimum number of barrels (5, 10, etc.).
- **Have an absolute limit.** Do not go beyond this pre-set limit. Basically, only play what you can afford to lose, and if that goes – go home. If winning, stay as long as you can play.

There are a few minimal rules you should keep in mind. If you exceed these common sense guides, you will know better the next time.

- Know the skills of your opponent.
- When comparing skills, use the lower end of your regular speed.
- Play the games you are comfortable with.
- Keep your bets comfortable.
- Be careful about drinking.
- Agree before starting on who pays table time.

These are just rough ideas, suggestions, and recommendation – all meant to be a guiding light to your explorations into the world of pocket billiard gambling. Good luck and don't take any bets with no reality to back up a loss.

Should you gamble?

There are a considerations built into this question. When something of value is at risk, the pressure to play well goes up. It gets worse if the amount lost impacts your lifestyle (the rent money, etc.). Basically, the decision to bet (and how much) on your skill depends on how the loss would affect you.

If you don't get all hyperactive (fast breathing, high heart rate, copious perspiration) when you place a bet on your competence, you need not worry about the outcome, positive or negative. A comfortable amount, wagered on your abilities against a similarly skilled opponent would be OK. The thrills and chills of a competition make the Green Game more interesting.

Some people can only play their best under this kind of pressure. Others, when exposed to this type of challenge, literally see their game fall apart. They just crash and burn.

If you find the thrill fascinating and can afford to lose, try it out. Just keep the bets within reason. And, be aware that there are predators out there that will make sure you lose AND lose more than you can afford. Among buddies, some friendly bets can be used as an ongoing scorecard.

Weekly tournaments are probably the most common form of gambling. You pay your entry fee (usually a small amount) and are assigned opponents that test you in ways that does not occur in day-to-day pool hall games.

Tournaments are an excellent way to identify weaknesses in your game against individuals of similar skill levels. From those experiences, you can develop practicing programs to strengthen those areas. Over time these contests are your gauge on how well your game is improving.

If you do decide to gamble, here are some general rules:
- Don't carry into the pool hall more than can afford to lose.
- Learn how to match up against your opponent so that it will be a fair challenge - i.e., ask for or give an appropriate handicap (number of balls, number of games, etc.)
- Don't put down a large bet against someone you've never played before.
- You will not get rich gambling, so don't expect that winning or losing will change your life.
- If you lose, consider it entertainment. If you win, buy a good dinner.

What are some gambling handicaps?

When gambling with individuals who regularly put money on their skills, they have ways to define some of the parameters (weight) given to a shooter. Here are the terms with short descriptions. The descriptions below assume you are getting the spot (advantage).

Warning: Do NOT place bets in any situation where localized bar rules are used. You will guarantee an argument or fight over how the rules and spots are applied.

General spots

- (Number of games) - In a race to 7, if your opponent spots you 3 games, you need to win only 4 games against your opponent's 7 games to win the race.
- "Break" - you break for each game. This is good when skill levels are close.
- "Last pocket" - In 8 Ball, your opponent must make the 8 ball in the same pocket as he made the last ball in his group. In 9 Ball, your opponent must make the 9 ball in the same pocket he made last highest ball.
- "Bank in the money ball" - To win, your opponent must bank the winning ball (8 ball or 9 ball).
- Spot combinations - these spots can be applied one at a time, as multiple requirements to win, or if this spot is satisfied that the spot applies (or vice versa). It is important that the exact details be understood by both parties.
- Random spots - spots can be invented to reduce your opponent's skills to a level that is relatively even. For example, your opponent shoots with the opposite hand, or one handed, whatever can be agreed upon.

9 Ball spots

- "Give the X ball" (usually the 5, or 6, or 7, or 8) or "spot the X ball" - when running the table, a legal pocketing of the X ball or the 9 ball wins the game for you. If the X ball was pocketed by your opponent, you have to go to the 9 to win. If the X ball is illegally pocketed by your opponent, it is usually spotted.
- "Spot the X ball and out" - If you legally pocket the X ball (or higher) ball, you win.
- "Straight Xv" - The X ball must be made in turn and not in a combination or carom.
- "Wild X ball" - If you pocket the 9 or X ball legally, you win. If "wild after the break", the X ball is only available if pocketed after the break.
- "Call X ball" - You must call your spotted ball in a specific pocket, and no slop. This can also be a combo/carom shot as long as it is called.
- "Last 2" - The last two balls on the table are both money balls for you (no combination or carom shots on the second highest ball until only two balls remain on the table.

8 Ball spots

- "Extra money ball" - your last ball of your group on the table can also be the money ball. Make it and you win.

- "Spot X number of balls" - (usually 1 to 3 balls) when the balls are removed is negotiated (after the break, later in the game by your choice or your opponent's choice, etc.).

1 Pocket spots

- "Break" - If you have given the break, this can be a big advantage when well played.
- "Ball on your break" - You get a ball (1 point) advantage when your opponent breaks. When you break, it's an even game.
- "Hand span" - This is an interesting handicap spot. You get the move the cue ball in any direction within the width of your hand with fingers spread. (That's a huge move.)
- "Scratches do not count" - If you scratch, you do not get penalized with a loss of point, except for loss of turn and ball in hand in the kitchen.

What is a comfortable way to handle gambling?

CRITICAL & IMPORTANT - never bet more than you can afford to lose. Trite - yup and I'm pretty sure you've heard it before. A few points are assumed here:

- You are not addicted to gambling.
- You don't make your living gambling.
- You aren't a hustler or a wannabe.
- You have no family members that can get upset if you lose.
- You don't get greedy.
- You don't let any wins make you stupid.
- You don't go crazy about making up losses.
- You are an ordinary nice person.
- You love pool more than gambling.
- Play only people you know.
- From the beginning, agree to the rules that apply to your playing session.
- Sets stay the same (race to 5, etc. or per game, etc.)
- Bets cannot increase (but can decrease on agreement).
- Payoffs are after each set or game.
- Anyone can quit any time.
- Limit the time or number of sets. That and no more, win or lose, everyone goes home.

Things that are suspicious

- You win one or two sets and your opponent wants to raise the bet. This is the trigger to take your winnings and go home, regardless.
- They change the game or the rules. Refuse emphatically.

- Your opponent doesn't immediately pay off, or put up the required money for the game or session. Solution - quit.
- Your opponent wants to quit, but suggests you play someone else. Go home immediately.

Key points

- Any winnings are "your" money, not his. It belongs to you. Treat it as your personal hard-earned money.
- Any losses should not make you "desperate". Keep your cool. If you do lose, lose under your control.
- If you are ahead, you are under no obligation to give anyone any chances to win it back.

Mainly, you want to enjoy the experience, even if you lose some. There are always lessons to be learned from your adventures. At the very least, you want the costs of learning to be cheap enough to afford and the rewards to be larger than the costs.

Playing Situations and Circumstances FAQs

How do you respond to a beaten opponent?

There is a certain amount of courtesy expected when playing competitions in various circumstances, such as matches and tournaments. On starting a match, you cannot go wrong with a handshake and generic good wishes such as "Good luck." If there is a history between the two of you, add a personal statement relating to a past good competition.

After completing a match and you are the winner, it is simple courtesy to thank your opponent for the competition. There are a number of responses you can use, depending on the circumstances.

If this is early in the tournament and your opponent is going over to the loser side, extend your good wishes on his next match. If you do knock him out of the tournament, how you respond depends on your match. If he did well, complement him for the good effort. If he was not on his game or played terribly, extend your good wishes at a future competition.

Occasionally, you will win against an opponent who hates your guts. In the interests of good sportsmanship, extend your hand with a "Thanks for the match". You don't need to say more, since there is already some dysfunction between you both. If you are jilted, shrug your shoulders and get ready for the next competition. If anyone is going to be unsportsmanlike, it should not be you. Besides, if he wants to hold a grudge, it usually hurts his game.

During a match, do not show outward pleasure at your opponent's mistakes. It is OK to complement an extraordinary shot. Accept any balls in hand with quiet courtesy. Offer any balls in hand without complaint. It is good courtesy to be quiet while he shoots.

Keep in mind, it is not your responsibility to teach someone good sportsmanship. If they have not already learned proper behavior when young, nothing you do will teach him. Accept this and leave him to his self-infliction.

If you lose the competition, never present a sour grapes attitude. Always give a firm handshake and congratulations. Keep in mind that the loss revealed some of your weaknesses, whether in skills, strategic approach, and shot choices. Address these problems at the next practice table. You will become a stronger and more competitive player.

Can a losing match be turned around?

There are two circumstances when your game-playing skills seem to abandon you. One occurs on starting the match. You start slow and your opponent gets an early lead. The other occurs when you start well, then someplace in the middle of the match, your game goes downhill.

In both circumstances, you are not at your best. The problems begin looking bigger and more difficult. You can enhance this downward spiral by focusing all of your attention and emotions into a strong effort to go into a deep depression.

It is psychological maturity that can take you out of a bad patch of poor shooting. One of the ways to gain this type of assurance is to suffer through a few too many times when you slide into tournament obscurity. It begins when finally say to yourself, "There has to be a better way to handle this."

All players go through up and down cycles where there are times when you do well and other times when you do not so well. With experience, you can take steps to shorten the down side and extend the high side of these cycles.

When you are under the bad influences, here are some workable recommendations:

- Do not "tense" up. Tightening your muscles in an exaggerated attempt to over-control yourself will not work.
- Do not go into a "can't afford to lose this game" mode. This excessive personal pressure almost always causes you to lose.
- Do not compare the shots made on the up side to what you suppose your ability to be when on the down side.

- When you set up on a shot, slow down your rhythm. Do a couple of extra practice strokes. Pre-play the shot before the stroke to verify the speed.
- Shoot softer. Worry less about "perfect" position, and focus on getting a shot on the next ball.
- Lower your expectations on difficult shots. Pick opportunities to play defensively.
- Focus on the goal of winning and not on "not losing".
- If anyone tries conversing, limit your response to grunts.
- Keep emotions under wraps. Keep your mind busy. Constantly evaluate table layouts, even when it is not your turn.
- Don't get emotional over bad rolls for you or good rolls for your opponent. It will even out. Cultivate a placid expectation that the tide will turn.

When your game goes off, make adjustments to your expectations.

How can you warm up for a competition?

The warm up process is designed to take you from an off-the-street condition to your ready-to-play condition. The process is a series of shots used to help find your groove, center, platform, etc. These shots dial in your feet positioning, weight distribution, arm/hand positions, bridge hand, head position; everything you need to set up for a shot.

In conjunction with getting comfortable bent over the table, start shooting balls into pockets, beginning with mid table straight in shots, and then incrementally working back. As you get comfortable with the standard shots, throw in a few shots that you know need some work.

Sometimes you come to the warm-up table, and discover unusual accuracy and control. When this happens, mentally examine your body positioning and stroking. That is what makes it work. If you don't, your game can go bad and you won't have a clue on how to recover. The examination helps you memorize what works.

Other times, you start off with near-total clumsiness. This tells you that your fundamentals are bad. Instead of trying to shoot your way through the problem, focus on placing your feet and work upwards from there.

You could simply start shooting, and depend on muscle memory to finally fall into place. Another technique is to run a conscientious checklist that starts with feet placement and angle, knees, butt angle, etc. Once complete, strokes and the results validate correct positioning.

At a minimum, use 10 minutes to determine if you are on top of your accuracy. If you are about average, 15-25 minutes are good for the warm-up. If you are really off your game, you will need about an hour. Get in the most shots in the shortest time frame that focus specifically on dialing in basics. Use the warm-up to settle down. You want a calm mind that can play logically.

To be systematic, set up and shoot a series of common shots. Here are several different types that can help you warm up:

- Straight in medium distance stun shots at different speeds.
- Angle shots with the cue ball going to designated locations.
- Use exaggerated practice strokes (as far back as possible, as far forward as possible).
- Basic draw and follow shots.
- Spot shots with the cue ball at various places in the kitchen.
- Throw out and practice three and four ball runs.

Whatever you do, do not depend on playing practice games with friends.

How can you get used to another pool table?

When you come into a pool room you've never been in, you need a way to quickly figure out how the table rolls and whether the rails are in decent shape. You also need to know any roll offs and the slowest speed that will overcome the problem.

A lot depends on how much time you get to spend with stick in hand. You don't want to be at a disadvantage against an opponent who knows the table and its problems. It's irritating to try something that works on your regular table but comes up short on the new table.

Here are a standard set of actions on coming to an unknown table. Lag the cue ball to the foot rail and back until you can get it to stop on (or close to) the head string. This also tells you if the table rolls off in one direction or another. The lag can be considered to be your standard shot. From that test, you can adjust all of your other shooting speeds accordingly.

At each corner, place the cue ball about an inch out from the cushion and shoot it down parallel to the rail. This tells you if there are any grooves in the cloth that suck balls against the rail.

Shoot the cue ball slowly diagonally corner to corner. Repeat this from each of the four corners.

Set the cue ball in the side pocket and slow roll it to each of the two opposite corners. Repeat the process at the other side pocket. Then shoot the cue ball from each corner to the side pocket.

Walk around the table, pushing each rubber cushion down. You don't need a lot of pressure, just look for any softness. Check all six cushions at about three or four locations each. Any soft areas will be dead spots to avoid banking for any banking.

You may not have enough time to identify every table faults. You may not be offered any time. If so, spend the first few innings playing safeties to get a feel for the table. Do some slow rolls over various distances. Try out some cue ball spins and watch the results. Then, you can make necessary adjustments and get on with the business of playing your best.

What can you expect in a handicapped league?

A handicapped league is a group of teams each with several players that compete on a regular basis (usually weekly). Each team will have players with different skill levels. Each player is assigned a certain skill level. When individuals with different levels compete, the adjustments are made to their scoring requirements. A new player will start at an initial skill level. As matches are played, the skill level is adjusted as appropriate.

These handicap systems are not perfect and there will always be some conversations about whether someone should be a higher or lower number. Usually those comments arise when an opposing team member complains – most commonly when they lose.

There is always talk about individuals who sandbag their skills - appearing to be lesser skilled than they really are. Then, when there is some actual money to be won, they open their bag of tricks and reveal their true speed. To watch out for this, a number of observers/referees watch everyone. There have been teams who were disqualified from wins because they were caught trying to be a smaller number than they really are.

There are advantages for an individual to participate in these team competitions. A lesser player can get a lot of support from the better shooters on the team. Over time, this assistance helps keep up interest.

For a better player, there are a couple disadvantages. There is usually a cap on the handicap numbers for the entire team that shoots that night. A higher skilled shooter may often find that he is unable to play. That limitation can be somewhat difficult to handle for someone who likes to compete.

Being on a league team and playing regularly among different players also maintains a standard of sportsmanship and etiquette. For new players, league play provides an example of expected behavior. Of course, there are always a few assholes who make it their lifelong purpose to spread irritation. At least their existence teaches the young and impressionable players why good sportsmanship is necessary.

The social benefits are useful for many players. They get an evening out with similar minded individuals, enjoying a pleasant activity that is relatively inexpensive. There is more emphasis on having fun then on winning at all costs - although some experience personal pain for a loss they weren't expecting.

Can I do a restroom break during a match?

Short answer - yes, long answer - you betcha. No one is going to restrict our access to the restrooms regardless of the current table conditions.

Usually the restroom break occurs between racks. In some circumstances, a restroom break may be absolutely necessary in the middle of an inning. Make sure you and your opponent work out any arrangement before you make a mad dash. No one is going to cancel a match or competition. If an extended restroom break is necessary (bowl problems), make sure the opponent knows it up front.

If playing money matches, it is always good practice to have a friend keep an eye on the opponent and his buddies. Never hurts to maintain common courtesies, but there is nothing wrong with careful caution. The rule is pretty much this: take a break as needed, but don't make it look like you could be trying to shark your opponent using this to delay the game.

What can be eaten while competing?

Most tournaments are done in a day or two. Some last longer. You are going to have to consume some food. Don't eat foods that will bloat you, slow you down, or otherwise interfere with your concentration.

Avoid these:
- Sugar-based drinks - sodas, pop, fountain drinks, etc.
- Candy - bars, boxed, bagged, etc.
- Bagged snacks - corn chips, potato chips, cheese puffs, etc.
- Starchy foods - potatoes, breads, corn, rice, etc.
- Anything deep-fried - French fries, onion rings, etc.
- Over-eating anything.

Recommended snacks (in moderation):
- Cheese - sticks, slices.
- Meat snacks - jerky, meat sticks.
- Home-made items - hard-boiled eggs, sliced veggies (carrots, broccoli, celery, radishes, etc.) with a ranch dip.
- Nuts - peanuts, cashews, mixed.
- Fruit - fresh (or canned in juice or light syrup), oranges, applies, pears, bananas.

Recommended meals:
- Breakfast - two to three eggs any style, sausage, bacon, toast, with milk and coffee or tea (no potatoes or rice).

- Lunch - 1/4 or 1/3 lb. beef sandwich (hamburger or steak) or a mini steak with a side of veggies, with milk and coffee or tea (no potatoes or rice).
- Supper - make this a light dinner, 1/3 pound of meat with vegetables only (no potatoes or rice or dessert). If you don't have time for this meal, stick with meat and cheese snacks.

Only use the snacks when you have a slight edge of hunger. Basically, you want to keep your stomach from distracting you.

What are the different tournament formats?

A single elimination tournament is straight forward - you lose, you go home. You win, you keep going. The TD (tournament director) assigns matches with the loser becoming a spectator. The winner advances to a new battle against the winner of another competition.

A double elimination is a little more complicated to track. Generally, if you lose the first match, you go to the loser's side ladder instead of staying in the winner's side ladder. (The two ladders only meet at the top level final match for first and second place money.) If you lose on the loser's ladder, you have two failures to advance - and you go home.

Many double elimination setups only guarantee you will play two matches. This means that if you win the first match and then lose the second match, you are eliminated. Sometimes, depending on the number of entries, you win the first and lose the second; you can still go to the loser's ladder.

The bookkeeping and tracking for single eliminations is straight forward. Yet, few people like to compete in this type of tournament - especially the lesser skilled players. They got out of bed and dressed for the public, drive over to the pool hall, show up on time, and paid their entry fees. The idea of playing a single match and getting knocked out is hard to accept.

If you are involved in setting up or recommending a tournament format, here are a couple of ideas. For weekly small tournaments, run them as single elimination. If you get too many complains, you can do a secondary tournament where the first round losers can buy-in at half price.

The cost of a weekly tournament will depend on the social scale of the players. A middle-class area will have $10-15 entry fees. A higher-class pool hall can charge $20-25 for a weekly tournament. For regional and national qualifiers, fees can range from $50 and up. The pool hall may toss a few more bucks into the pot to entice more players to compete for a bigger cash prize.

How can you stop missing cut shots?

Most of the time when you are cutting a shot into a pocket and miss, the cue ball almost always hits the object ball too full. The examples below shows what usually happens.

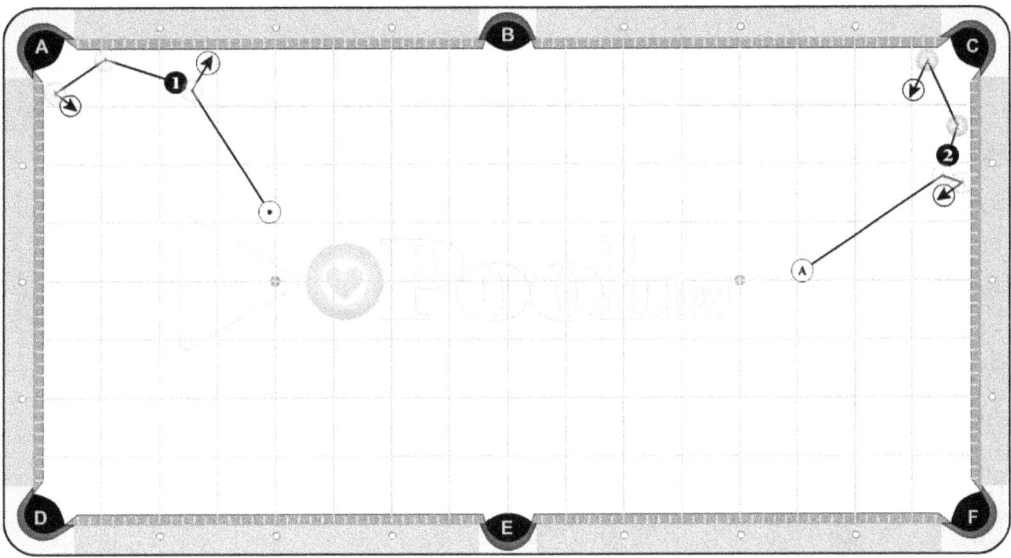

When you notice yourself consistently hitting the object ball a little too full, you can increase the chances of success by making a simple modification to your aiming technique.

When you set up on the next similar cut shot, go through your normal pre-shot routine and aim where you think you should. Once you are settled down, shift the butt of your stick over to one side about an inch (2.5 cm). To your mind, it will appear that you will be over cutting the shot. This is how you intentionally adjust for an aim that feels right, but plays wrong.

This adjustment can only be made if you are paying attention to similar shots and the results. If not tracking your misses and why, you are going to be condemned to consistently experience failure. That can cost you games you could have won.

Why do you play badly against a lesser skilled opponent?

As you are participating in the enjoyment of your passion for pocket billiards, you will find yourself playing opponents who are further back on the road to pool mastery than you are. You have long ago traveled past the point where his game is now.

Playing players far below your skill level is mainly a matter of having anyone to play with. In other words, anyone is better than no one. As the games begin, your opponent bangs away at his best speed, and you start out playing at your regular speed.

Then, something subtle happens to your game. For some reason, your results are less than you are used to. You miss easy shots, simple patterns become near impossible, and you find yourself less than satisfied. Even if you are winning most of the games, you are struggling to do so.

Part of what is happening is your sense of fair play kicks in. You (consciously or unconsciously) crank back your abilities to keep the game somewhat competitive. There is no big challenge involved and nothing to speed up your heartbeat. You relax your standards. Before you know it, you are struggling to keep up and even losing a few games.

Even if you realized what is happening and attempt to restore your standard skills, there is no incentive to maintain your focus. Your game, if possible, gets worse. You attempt to console yourself that any time on a table is far better than no time on a table. You could quit in self-disgust with only your innate sportsmanship maintaining your courtesy and good manners.

Instead of writing off the time as unworthy of wasting, change the rules. Give your opponent weight - a lot of weight. For example, if playing 9 Ball, give the 5 and up. He makes any of those balls, he wins the game. For 8 Ball, you must bank the 8 into the last pocket.

With these handicaps, if you want to him take the game seriously; offer a buck every time he beats you. All of sudden, playing every game with all of your attention becomes much more important.

There is a major difference if you are playing with someone who is your student. In this situation, the purpose is not whether there is any actual competition, but is geared towards teaching in a game environment. The net result of the games played is not a matter of who won or lost, but how much improvement was made. And, if your "student" beat you more times, that strengthens his enthusiasm for the game.

When breaking, should you inspect the rack?

In most games, the winner of the last game breaks. The loser must rack the balls for the next game. Breaking a loose rack (gaps between the balls) causes a lot of lost energy, and the balls will stay bunched up in clusters. This is not something you want to happen. It can throw off your focus and rhythm.

In most matches, you don't have to inspect every rack. But if your opponent has already put together one loose rack, he could do it again. Inspecting makes good sense.

In league competitions, inspecting every rack by your opponent is often a good way to irritate him, especially if you keep pointing out miniscule gaps as justification to try again. He can turn this against you by insisting that you do your own racking.

If you don't inspect every time, do so after he "sticks" you with a bad rack. Make it a point to closely inspect each one. And, ask for a re-rack if he gets careless. It is good manners to let him know what required the re-rack. Don't be petty.

Do not expect that you will be able to get a perfect rack on a regular basis. There is simply too many variables that can interfere with perfection. Do expect any gaps to be minimal, that most of the balls will touch. It is rare to actually get all of the balls touching.

In 8 Ball, you want the top ball to touch as least one of the two balls behind it and the lower corner balls are touching one of the adjacent balls. In 9 Ball, you want the top ball to touch one of the two balls (both is preferable).

Sometimes the other player asks if there is something wrong with the rack. In a tournament, you can respond with a smile, "I just want to make sure you are as good a racker as I am." In a league match, when you've already gotten burned, respond with, "Because", or some other answer that indicates you want a good rack.

You want to achieve tighter racks because these give you a better chance at pocketing a ball on the break, and thereby open the possibility of a run-out.

Nowadays, it is common at important tournaments for the person who breaks to rack their own balls. This prevents any bad feelings over any possible intentional or unintentional bad racks.

How do you calculate the odds on a shot?

When facing a table layout and figuring out what to do, every shot you consider falls will be within your comfort zone or in your chaos zone. A shot within your comfort zone means you can make it 7 or 8 times in 10 tries. As the chances of success get smaller, it falls into your chaos zone. Every shot has to calculate the odds.

To takes practice to apply cold numbers to a shot. In the beginning, you will overestimate your shooting ability. That opinion will soon be deflated by the results.

The better you get and as the quality of your opponents goes up, the more seriously you have to consider these numbers. Making a wishful mistake can cost you the game.

There is another important factor to be added into your odds calculator. You need to include your natural cycle of superior play and slumps. On the up side, you are shooting above average. On the down side, you miss easier shots, and failures are common. If you are not careful, you can get depressed, which only makes your slump worse.

With a trustworthy odds calculator, you can win more matches. When on the down side, simply subtract 20-30% from your regular expectations, and make your shot decisions – play offensively, play a two-way, or play defensively. On the upside, you can add 10-25% to your normal chances and make decisions accordingly.

It takes some time and practice to develop confidence in your odds calculator. But once it is working, it becomes a natural part of your analysis.

What do you need to know about one rail banking?

Almost all players have difficulty being consistent with banking. Most people (rightly so) consider banks to be low percentage. When you make an attempt, you can protect yourself by playing it as a two-way shot. If you make it, you are on the next ball. If missed, it doesn't hurt you.

Let's take all of the considerations into consideration. Speed, throw, and angles all affect the accuracy of a bank attempt. Hit it hard and you can set up less of an angle off the rail. Hit it soft and the angle opens up.

The simplest way to calculate a bank is with the ghost table. You aim the object ball at the opposite pocket of an imaginary table. This will at least get the object ball within a decent chance of success. Some practicing and you can make one cushion banks become more dependable. Ten minutes here and 15 minutes there can have a cumulative positive result.

Banking is part of the game. There are banking variations of 9 Ball and 8 Ball. There is also a popular game, Bank Pool. Some specialized resources (books and DVDs) that can be studied. Once you are competent at single rail banks, start trying two, three, and four rail banks.

What is "pocket speed"?

Pocket speed means that the object ball is moving just fast enough to make it to the intended pocket and roll over the edge. It doesn't have enough speed to hit the back of the pocket.

In several of the commonly played games, it is an extremely useful shot.

- In 8 Ball, if the aim was not correct, the object ball dies in the jaws of the pocket, leaving an easy shot for later and a pocket blocker against your opponent.
- In 1 Pocket, the slow roll puts the missed ball in the jaws, making it harder to knock out and away.
- The corner pocket could be cheated even more because the ball has a gentle forward momentum. It can kiss off the rail corner and still drop.

- When you can stroke the cue ball with careful speed, the distance it travels becomes more predictable.

Initially, it can be difficult to gauge the necessary cue ball speed to make the object ball travel at speed to its destination. You have to develop a very good feel for the table, any deviations, and a perfect aim.

It is worth the time to learn to make this shot an effective tool. There is a great satisfaction in shooting this shot, then wait and wait and wait as the ball slowly travels the length of the table to finally drop.

Why do you choke on the game ball?

When you are on the "money" ball, are you suddenly smitten with uncertainty? Do you feel like the eyes of the world are watching and waiting for you to embarrass yourself? Does a spear of fear embed itself in your guts? Do any of these situations seem a bit familiar when you finally have a shot at the ball that can win the game, match, a million dollars and the "world's greatest player" trophy?

It doesn't matter how skillfully you handled yourself before this final ball, now you are the ball that can make you the champion. This is NOT a good time to choke. And, then - of course - you choke, or feel like you are going to choke. You are experiencing pressure. The amount of pressure is directly proportional to the importance of the shot. If you make it – you are a hero. If you miss – you're a bum.

The emotional and physical reactions are an aspect of your most primitive responses to anything that you consider a danger to your well-being - the fight or flight response. When faced with danger, do you battle with all your strength, or do you run away to fight another day?

To translate this into pool terms, do you shoot to win with all of your focus and skill or do you dodge the shot and play a safety? The longer you sit on the fence between these two choices, the more painfully intense are your worries. You can't get more uncomfortable than vacillating between the choices – go for the win or play it safe?

The process that eases the pressure is experience. If you do this often enough, eventually you will accept that fact that you won't die if you fail. With regular exposure to important shots, any nervous reactions have a lesser and lesser effect on your decision.

You can also assign a value to the critical shot to help you gain experience. When you play a similarly skilled opponent, put a little money on it. If you win, he pays you $1.00. If he wins, you pay him $5.00. This obvious imbalance forces you to place a much greater value on every shot choice and decision. Make a mistake, you lose. Play intelligently, and you have a chance to win. It is also a good way to learn how to take the game more seriously.

When you can accept and can play well against such lop-sided odds, any nervousness on the money ball will have long since faded away. The constant exposure to pressure will become a routine and accepted part of your game.

How do you analyze a lost match?

Whenever you play matches, you sometimes find yourself on the losing side. When that happens you probably go through the usual post-match depression and the standard 'why me' moans and groans. You may be a person who suffers in silence or finds a sympathetic ear.

After you finish your obligatory time in purgatory, you can simply toss the loss away, scrub it from your memory, pick yourself up and rejoin the human race. That might be okay for a while. But eventually, you are might want to consider taking a different route to handling losses.

Instead of discarding the experience, try to figure out what happened. So you lost. Why? Some careful analysis might discover this and some changes can reduce the number of failures in the future.

Start with the general overview of your shooting abilities compared to your opponent. Here is a sample set of questions to ask. Modify this checklist until you have developed a standard set of self-analysis personal queries.

> **Note:** If you don't already know, I might as well tell you now. Most of the games we lose are because we gave our opponents an opportunity to beat us. Without that, we could have, no, should have won.

So let's open up your memories and get some answers.

- Was your opponent above your skill level?
- If a close match, what decisions did you make that turned helped him out?
- Did you consider the consequences of any decisions?
- When he gave you an opportunity, what did you do with it?
- What shots decisions now look stupid in hindsight?
- What was your attitude throughout the match?

Some of these answers will reveal a strategic weakness. For example, you didn't analyze what your opponent could and couldn't do. Other answers reveal a number of tactical errors. For those, you need to change the way you make shooting decisions. And you can even become aware of areas in our skills that need improvements immediately.

If you are actually serious about reducing the amount of mistakes you make, take the time to write out a plan to improve. Make yourself aware of steps you should take in the early part of the match, areas where your skills need improvement, and even more important, change your attitude on the table.

You can be close comrades with your opponent off the table, but when you face off, he is not a friend. That is the way of competition. You can learn the most from mistakes, and the least from successes.

How can you play for long periods of time?

There are times when you get yourself in a playing situation where you will be playing for hours and hours. Tournaments are a good example. Few of these are finishing in a couple hours. Unless you get knocked out early, you are going to be there for a long time, some of the time playing, some of the time waiting.

The joy of shooting amidst the competition and challenges provide something of an adrenalin rush and your competitive edge is sharp. As time passes, there comes a point when the edge starts getting dull.

This is most immediately noticeable when you realize that you are not pocketing the balls with the same careful precision, and your shape on the next ball gets worse and worse. The point is driven home most thoroughly when you miss an easy shot to win a game. That's not something you can assign to the "oops" category.

That's when you realize your game is dropping down a level, and in the frenzy of strong competition, that is the same as writing a suicide note.

There are two types of fatigue: physical and mental. You can experience them individually and together.

Physical fatigue is quite common in marathon matches. Toxins build up in your body which does not get washed out. You simply run down your reserves.

You can take some steps to restore yourself. If you need snacks or a meal, avoid sugars and carbs (potato chips, candy, corn chips, etc.). Their immediate help is offset by a mental and physical sluggishness. If you need a snack, anything protein works (meat, cheese, eggs).

You can also take short brisk stroll while doing a series of isometrics. This helps to get your blood moving a bit. You can bounce on toes a few times, do a few stretches and toe touching movements.

Mental fatigue is just as dangerous as physical fatigue. But it sneaks up on you. It's usually 30-40 minutes before you notice that your brain is not coming up with very many brilliant options. Other indicators such as missed shots and poor positioning creep into your game.

If you have the time, an effective refresher is a sitting doze. Find a chair, slump against the back, drop your chin onto your chest, and close your eyes. Simply listen to all the sounds around you while relaxing. Make a game of figuring out what actions caused what sounds. About 10 minutes later your mind is wide awake and attentive.

If you are in the middle of a match, focus your attention on your opponent. Start analyzing his actions. Pretend you are an observer, giving out blow-by-blow commentary and criticizing his playing decisions. This is a little game that can immediately refocus your mind and reawaken your intention to win.

How do you handle a bad 8 Ball break?

Many times in an 8 Ball competition, casual or serious, the person's breaking skills will leave much to be desired. It could be a bad shot, or a bad rack. Regardless, the balls don't move much, but the required number of balls that hit the rail makes it a legal break. This can be you or your opponent.

The result is that balls in the rack barely escape. Maybe one or two balls made it past the center line. The few balls that hit the rail bounce back into each other. The result is bunches of object balls clumped together in one or two loose groups. Most of the balls don't even have a clear path to a pocket. This is definitely not a run-out table.

There are a two different ways to approach this type of table layout. It can be a nightmare table, resulting in a long, drawn-out game with few opportunities to look good. It certainly provides no opportunities for a quick, decisive win.

Or, you could look at a clumped rack of balls as an opportunity to flex your skills in tactical choices and short table maneuvers. These types of layouts offer excellent opportunities to move the cue ball and object balls with careful control. All of the balls are in the lower half of the table. Once your selection is determined (stripes or solids), you can circle the clumps like a humming bird approaching a large bush of flowers.

You dart in to the mess and knock out one or two of your balls into better playing locations, while ensuring your opponent has little or no opportunity to do the same. You snatch a ball out of a three ball group, bank it into the open for later while just accidentally, push one of his balls into a cluster near a rail. Or you push a ball to block a pocket and prevent two or three balls from accessing that pocket.

What is happening is that you are dancing the balls around the table with grace and style while your opponent is clomping around with muddy rain boots. While you have a plan, he is making decisions based on faint hopes.

At a certain point, he gives you the opening you have been patiently waiting for. You utter a quiet thank you and quickly run out the game. As the eight ball drops, your opponent is left standing at the table trying figure out what just happened. There are few satisfactions in pool more enjoyable that pulling off a well-planned win from seeming disaster.

What can give you an edge?

An edge is something you have that gives you an advantage over the other player. It can be something you secretly worked on for months, just to spring when your opponent least expects it. It can be that extra refinement that pulls out a game win or slams the door on your opponent's ability to fight back.

Skill edge

Here are some examples to shots that give you an edge:

- Run an object ball down the rail from any distance.
- Consistently bank cross corner from almost anywhere.
- Sharply cut an object ball from off the rail.
- Constantly kick from anywhere on the table for a legal hit.
- Shoot an object ball so slowly it drops in at pocket speed.
- If you have a collection of instructional books or competition DVDs, look for interesting shots that you can learn to master and pull out at will to surprise your opponent.

Mental edge

The winner of many games is often determined simply by the attitude of the player. For example, if you know about the up and down energy cycles, you can patiently play tough defensive shots when he is on an up cycle. You simply wait for him to be on a down cycle and then he will be helpless to prevent you from winning.

You could convince him that you are the superior opponent, deflating his drive to win. When you make a shot attempt that miraculously succeeds, claim all of the glory and the implied skills. Depress his self-confidence and half the battle is won.

Knowledge edge

This is an advantage that is truly invisible. Often it is will be a complete surprise to your opponent who, knowing he is the better shooter, can't figure out just how he lost.

- Apply regular effective safeties. Continuously prevent him from having an easy shot.
- Constant two-way shooting that leaves you on the next shot if successful, and makes it difficult for your opponent if you miss.

- The maturity to recognize impossible shots and play defensively.
- Shot selection based on the hard realities of success/failure.
- The experience to see opportunities and consequences.

This is why old geezers rarely lose against the young guns, even when the skills are somewhat unequal. They have seen just about everything and the options in their shot library are far more extensive.

How much fair play is fair?

When you are playing pool and you see a rule violation about to be made by your opponent, how far will you go to ensure fair play? Do you do anything to win, salivating over the opportunity to get a cheap and quick advantage? Or, do you try to ensure a level playing field. Do you point out the potential error? Do you expect you opponent to be similarly concerned with an equal sense of sportsmanship?

Here are some circumstances:

- In a league match, you see your opponent getting ready to shoot the wrong ball. Do you say something before he shoots?
- The shot requires a called or marked pocket. You make the ball but don't make the call. Do you point this out to your opponent?
- You didn't make a legal hit. Your opponent fails notice and doesn't pick up his ball in hand. Do you say anything?
- You are shooting and accidentally touch the cue ball with your tip. It barely moves and your opponent doesn't notice. Do you proceed with the shot?

Self-declaring an error could lead to a game and match loss. How important is winning to you? Do you respond differently if the error occurs early in one match or on the final game? Would you act differently if he is a good friend? Does it bother you to win by such a means?

Some places have a rule that states, only the opponent can call a foul and if he doesn't, it didn't happen. Most other playing places are dependent on every player maintaining and demonstrating a sense of sportsmanship.

The problem with situational ethics is that other people notice. They may not say something, but they will spread the word that you are fully capable of being morally flexible. There are always consequences.

On the other hand, if you follow a rigid personal standard of honor regardless of playing circumstances, you don't have that pesky conscience bothering you at all hours of the day and night.

Can you get hurt playing pool?

Just watching people play pool, anyone could be forgiven if he thinks that is a safe sport. It certainly appears to be free of the personal injury dangers that plague other sports like football, basketball, rugby, even curling.

The only possible exceptions would be intentional efforts such as using cues as a club or spear or the balls being throws with vicious intentions. This is how bar fights are often depicted in bars when low-life extras are insulted by the hero. (And by the way, the hand chop that breaks a cue in half – that is entirely faked.)

But that is not the only way in which injuries can occur. Here are some examples:

- On the break, the cue ball flies off the table.
- Scratches from protrusions in pockets and from damaged table trim.
- Hitting your stick hand on the rail during a full follow-through stroke.
- Someone tossing the ball to you instead of dropping it into your hand.
- Getting jabbed in the body when passing too close to the shooter already bent over on a stroke.
- Getting tapped on the head by a stick when the player spins in place without paying attention.
- Extending yourself for a long reach shot over the table, then raising yourself up too quick to connect your head with the table lights (common problem for most tall shooters).
- When stretching too far and trying to keep one foot on the floor, and your foot slips.
- Attempts at juggling with the pool balls.

Never underestimate the ability for careless people to invent new ways to cause personal injury.

How can you play a better bar table game?

In the process of becoming a better shooter over your lifetime, you will find yourself exposed to the bar boxes. These 3-1/2 x 7 foot tables provide their own challenges unique to their size and locations.

Bar boxes are commonly found in bars (hence the name – duh). These are places where people drink adult beverages with the intention of finding clumsier ways to talk and move. In this environment, the bar table sits. It is ready to be used by any person with the requisite number of quarters to get the balls out of the box.

Walking into this type of environment means that playing conditions are a lot different than the tables you play on at home or the pool hall. If these is your choice of playing environments, here are a few tips that help you out:

- The pockets are larger, so you can be off a little and the ball will still go in. To make this work, don't slam the balls around. A consistent medium speed works.
- Hit the cue ball harder so that the object ball moves faster. Slow rolling an object ball is a sure way to discover every possible surface variation, and end up with a miss.
- When selecting your patterns, chose those that move the cue ball the shortest distance possible to get onto the next shot. Turning the cue ball loose is an excellent way to scratch.
- Find and identify the dead cushion areas in the rails. On any given table, there will be an average of at least two feet of bad cushion.
- Position play only requires being on the correct side of the next shot. With a bar table, there are no tough long shots, so you can use more of the table to set up the next shot.
- With more interference balls, you can use them to aid your position play. Those interference balls can also be used to carom your object ball into a pocket.
- A big break is more important. Check the racks and make sure at least the front balls are touching. Remember that you will never get a solid rack on a bar table.
- Only shoot to side pockets when you are near straight on.
- Shorter bridge and shorter stroke will help your cue ball control.
- Shooting off the rail is a required skill. Practice it until it is no different than other shots.
- Become very familiar with the mechanical bridge. That skill will ensure you can shoot long shots.
- Practice shooting over another ball. You will be well rewarded with more wins.
- More finesse and thinking through the shot and the next two or three is needed to thread the crowded real estate.

Using a larger table to practice for bar table games

If you planning on an evening of bar box work and your practice table is an 8 or 9 foot table, scatter the balls over half the table and work from within this spread. It will be a good approximation of bar box reality.

There is no need to practice your long table shots. Concentrate your practice efforts on various angle shots and getting shape on the next ball. Work on your positioning skills. Spend a little practice time on honing your tangent line control. On a bar table, this skill will give magic powers.

What are recommended breaking positions?

These are general guidelines. Generally, the greater the speed that you can hit the cue ball, the more the balls will spread out and increase the chances that one of the balls will fall into a pocket. This will allow the breaker to continue shooting.

Almost everyone has a favorite location to put the cue ball for breaking. They might not have a logical reason, but it is satisfactory for them. Some place the cue ball closer to the short rail so that they can bridge off the rail. Others place the cue ball closer to the head string.

Some individuals micro-manage the location an inch this way or that way. They are trying to figure out what location gives the best results. Others have general areas that they use time after time. These are three locations along the head string that are most commonly used:

- Near the rail
- About one diamond from the rail
- A few inches to the side of the head spot

Do not break from the head spot straight down into the apex ball of the rack. The energy of the cue ball spreads equally throughout the rack and the balls don't move very far.

Speed is important, but blinding speed is not the complete breaking solution. There are those who break with slower speeds and get results that are just as effective. Do a lot of experimentation. Eventually, you will find a cue ball position that gives satisfactory results. That sweet spot will vary slightly from table to table. To find it on a new table, set up a break a few racks.

How can you get over a slump?

Just like baseball players fall into slumps that last for games, you will have similar experiences in pool. Your game disintegrates and you make playing decisions that would be embarrassing for a beginner. These times can be depressing, leading to thoughts of giving up the game – a true tragedy.

When you are shooting below acceptable levels, you have to take some steps to shorten up the amount of time you spend in pool playing hell. Here are a couple of different ways to make the transition from the swamps into the light.

When you come to the practice table, rather than immediately start banging balls around, do some stretching exercises as if preparing for a physical competition, such as tennis or a track & field event. Do about 10 each of different stretches for your arms, back, neck, torso, etc. Then prepare to shoot some balls. Throw out a rack of balls on the table and just shoot them in, randomly and without thought. Keep your mind a blank. Do two or three more racks. Shooting in 40 or 50 balls while your muscles are loose, allows your back brain to take over control of your stroke.

Now is when you can set up some specific shots to work on. Maintain the loose stroke you have been using and use only stun for cue ball control. After about a dozen successful shots, use draw for a set, then use follow for a set. By this time, you should have recovered your routine skill level. You may even notice some improvements.

Another option is to simply give up the game for a week or two. Do something else that takes up your attention and time. Here are a few ideas: read a book or two, go to some movies, watch some good PBS shows, get some classic movies. When you do come back to the table, at first only work on easy shots, then slowly increase the difficulty factor. You will find that the slump has passed, and like above, may experience some improvements.

How can you learn ball speeds on different tables?

When you play regularly on the same table (or tables), you pretty much have a dialed in stick speed standard for that table. You know how far the cue ball will go on a lag shot. When you can cut a ball into a corner, you "know" what speed is necessary to pocket the ball and come off the cushion into rough position for the next shot. For you, these are part of your natural shots, and the calculations for the shot hardly require any effort.

When you come across a strange table that has a different cloth, the rolls are going to be affected. Your stick speed with all of its predictability goes out the window, along with a good portion of your confidence. If the table change is made suddenly, there is even a little bit of disorientation.

To remedy this situation, you need to figure out what the differences are when compared to your usual table. Whether the table speed differences are, it will be a consistent numerical factor. For a slower cloth, the factor will above 1. If the cloth is faster, it will be a fraction.

For example, a slow cloth will require half again the stick speed to get the same results as your regular table. That makes the factor to be 150%. A faster table might require 1/4 less effort to travel the same distance. The factor is 75%.

If you have a chance to practice a few minutes on the different table, use it for distance and speed experiments. If there was no opportunity to play around on the table, use the first half dozen shots. If you opponent is comfortable with the table, carefully watch the speed of his strokes and how long it will take the balls to stop.

With the results of these several shots combined with your observations, you can mentally dial in the stick speed adjustments. These modifications will allow you to get almost the exact same control as your original table. The control will be rough for a few times around the table, but will smooth out by the end of the second rack. You'll be knocking balls around the table like this was where you spent the last year shooting balls.

Does drinking mix with pool?

Consuming any of the many forms of alcohol is a personal preference. Almost everyone drinks responsibly, spacing their intake over time so as not to become impaired. Others do not drink at all, either through a personal preference or because they don't like the consequences. Careful drinkers usually limit themselves to two or three beers a night, spread over several hours of entertainment.

There will always be a few players who think that the consumption of hard drugs (coke or amphetamines) will give them at edge to take on other players and win more games. The pool careers of these shooters tend to be measured in a small handful of years as they burn themselves out. After their heyday, they still pop up occasionally in local bar tournaments, where they try to relive their glory days. They rarely blame themselves for losing their career.

Avoid matches where the loser buys the drinks. If you're the better shooter, those "rewards" soon screw up your abilities (not to mention the increased probability of a DUI). If you find yourself in the company of someone who insists on playing for drinks, you probably may want to wait for the winners to get a little soused and then take them on for a few bucks a game.

The penalties for getting caught by your local enforcers of the law have become significantly onerous. Even at a first offense you are looking at penalties of several thousands of dollars, loss of license for several months, and draconian educational requirements. There are a lot of people who, get caught once, totally give up alcohol in all its forms.

If you are putting on a pool party, limit the drinks to non-alcoholic beer and sodas. It eliminates your personal liability in case something goes horribly wrong. If you are playing out of your home, only bring out the real stuff if everyone is walking distance from their homes.

How can you keep score with coins?

When another scoring system is not available (moveable beads, balls, etc.), coins are placed under a cushion at each diamond to track the score of a race to a number.

The coins are placed at the zero position (head rail, center diamond) and are not touched until a winner of a game moves his coin to the next diamond to signify a win. (Usually dimes or pennies are used.) On each win, the player moves his coin either clockwise or counter-clockwise to the next diamond.

Anyone coming near the table in the middle or end of a match will know the score by locating the two coins.

If the coin was not pushed under the table far enough and any moving ball contacts the coin, there is the informal and formal solution. In informal circumstances, for fun or small stakes, the vast majority of players take it as a table hazard, such as lint or a chalk piece. Although it can be a good excuse to start an argument if so inclined.

In formal tournaments, if a coin interferes with the rolling of any balls, it is considered a foul on the player who did not properly ensure it was out of play. This is from the *Player Responsibility* rule which requires that any objects brought to the table by the player must not interfere or interact with rolling and stationary balls. The standard foul for the game is applied. (For example, if on the stroke, your knuckle hit the chalk and it flew onto the table and hit any ball, you committed a foul. If no ball was touched, no foul.)

When beads or other scoring systems are used to track points, the coins can be used to track fouls. This is necessary in games where three consecutive fouls have a serious penalty. In case of tracking fouls, the opposing player must ensure the appropriate coin is moved.

What are the different ways to keep score?

When playing in a race to a specified number of games, or a game where points need to be tracked, you will need some way to identify who gets what. Here are a number of tools used to track who gets what points, scores, marks, wins, and loses:

Point scoring beads - These are on a string and tied at each end. These are numbered up to 50 beads on each side, subdivided into groups of 5 and 10. Scores are kept by sliding beads from one side to the other. These are used to mark points in a game.

Game scoring beads - This is a double-set of larger beads that look like they are made from golfing practice balls with holes. There are 10 balls on both sides. These are used to mark games won in a match.

Table scoring wheels - These are embedded into the foot rail of the table. Usually in two sets of two wheels, each which has double digits. The numbers are changed using a thumbwheel. For scores that exceed 100, the left and right side double sets can track scores up to 9,999. (Although that will wear out more than two thumbs.)

Chalkboard - Any small chalkboard or white board hanging on a wall. The names of the opponents are listed above two columns. As points are made, marks are made below the name of the person who scored. The marks are grouped in fives. When the competition is done, the scores are erased.

Manual scoreboard - These usually have various rotating or circling number wheels. These are usually found/discovered somewhere as novelty items from a board game or another game set.

Electronic scoreboard - These are available in small sizes all the way up to the remote-controlled gymnasium scoreboards. The lighted numbers show up well in any pool room. Some of these have timers, which can be used to keep track of timed racks.

Pad & pencil - You can't get more basic than this. It always works and is cheap to use. As each sheet is used, it is simply discarded.

Whatever you use to track who wins how many games and scores so many points, it is important to have one or more of these tools available. When practicing, you can use these tools to track games won/lost against the ghost, or how many setups you've shot. Keep accurate scores and you'll never go wrong.

How does someone concede a game?

There are times when your opponent is shooting the game winning ball and the shot is well within his skills. The shot is so simple, that he couldn't miss if you blindfolded him. In such situations, you want to concede the game and get on with the next.

A game concession can be indicated in several ways, each which acknowledges that the person recognizes that the game is lost and there is no need to waste time officially finishing the game. How does someone concede? Usually, this is done before the soon to be winning player can start shooting the final ball or balls. This is how you would signal your concession:

- Reach across the table with your stick and touch or move the money ball.
- Use your stick to push or sweep the cue ball away from its position on the table.
- Get up and start pulling object balls out of the pockets and onto the table.
- Go over to the table and lay your cue on the table.
- Pull the rack out and set it on the table.
- If gambling, move the game money onto the table.
- Speak up and concede the game.
- Begin breaking your stick down. (This signifies the concession for the match, not a single game.)

It is a gesture of respect from the losing player that he knows the shooter is fully capable of completing the game to the win. The reason may be as simple as straightforward acceptance of table reality or to save table time expenses and get onto the next game. If someone concedes the game to you, a "Thank you." is good idea. Courtesy is never out of place.

In some venues, such as a pool hall where you have never played, any apparent concession that does not place balls or equipment on the table, it doesn't hurt to ask if it is a concession. Some (not many) players think it's funny to start acting as if it is a concession, but do not disturb the balls on the table. Then, when you move a ball, they claim you fouled and given them ball in hand.

Many leagues have a rule that if someone concedes the game but the other player still continues to shoot, that the concession is void. It is a slight discourtesy to do so where no rule is specified. It is also discourteous to use a stick to concede the game while the shooter is already bent down on the shot. Some consider this a minor shark attempt.

Whether you concede a game or not depends on your opponent's abilities and the table layout. If he has conceded a previous game, you are free to return the same consideration. But, you are under no obligation to do so. If, in your belief, there is the potential of a miss, you want the game to proceed just on the off-chance.

Game concessions are common when playing and practicing with friends. It saves time and keeps the interaction moving along. When playing matches or when there is some money on the game, it is an excellent rule of thumb to never offer a concession, even if your opponent does for you.

How can you handicap 9 Ball with a friend?

Assuming you are the better player, add extra opportunities for your friend to win. Here are some suggestions. Whichever one your buddy chooses, you have to follow one or more of these restrictions:

- He wins when the 6, 7, 8, or 9 ball is made on a legal shot.
- Last pocket - you win only if you sink the 9 ball in the pocket where you made the previous lower sequence ball.
- When you are on the 9 ball for the first time, your buddy picks the pocket for the 9 ball that you must put it in order to win.
- Friend picks 2 or 3 pockets on the table that you cannot sink balls in. If you do, the ball stays down, but you give up ball in hand.
- Bank the nine one or more rails to win.
- Friend gets ball in hand for every shot (or every other shot).

As the games progress, the rules can be modified to get the best equalization of skills. Using this type of handicapping (even when weighted against you), forces you to treat the game with proper attention.

Without this handicapping, you would not take the game seriously and thereby begin to play casually - not a good thing to do.

How can you handicap 8 Ball with a friend?

Here are some suggestions where the weaker player can still bang away at his best speed, and the stronger player (in this example is you) has to follow one or more of these restrictions. Playing straight up is too lopsided and the fun of playing quickly fades.

- Last pocket - you must pocket the 8 ball in the pocket where you made your last ball, he plays normally.
- Your friend picks the pocket for the 8 ball, after you sink your last ball, he plays normally.
- Your friend picks 2 or 3 pockets on the table where you cannot pocket object balls. If you do, the ball stays down, but he gets ball in hand.
- You must bank the 8 ball one or more rails to the called pocket to win, he plays it normally.
- You play where the cue ball lies, he gets ball in hand for every shot (or every other shot).
- You must shoot your balls in rotation, he can play his balls in any order.
- You must call every shot, he can play slop.

As the games progress, the two of you modify the rules until you both have some kind of agreement that equalizes your skill levels. These are also good rules to use when you are playing a girlfriend/boyfriend (so that you are able to maintain good relations).

How can you play while nervous?

Nervousness is a mental condition. It is most intense when fear is greatest. Generally, the fear is based on worries of survival – actual or imaginary. In the world of pool playing, nervousness occurs when you are doing something new. It could be entering an unknown pool hall, playing an unknown opponent; or entering a tournament for the first time.

All of these are new experiences and you will feel a certain amount of worry, simply because you are unsure of what can or might happen. When you get ready to play your first game

Regardless of the source of your worries, your stomach is tensing, your heart is racing, and your head is filled with possibilities, all with the same results – humiliating failure. So what can you do? Here are a few suggestions that can be used singly or in combination:

- Realize it's just a game. No one is going to die if you are not 100%.

- Play your own game. Your opponent can only come to the table when you let him.
- Study his playing processes. Look for weaknesses and then exploit them. The first couple of times you are successful, you will realize he has feet of clay, just like you.
- Use a series of defensive shots to confuse while gauging his state of mind. If he is also nervous, you can make him even more worried.
- Before the match take a few deep breaths and do some isometric exercises.
- Nothing takes the edge of worrying about something new then to get more experiences. Familiarity is a fine way to set your concerns at rest. (One way is to just go to the place as a spectator, looking for interesting things to watch. Watching closely can make you realize it's nothing you haven't already seen and done.
- Examine your individual concerns. Most concerns fade away when examined in the bright light of your intelligence.
- Humor to dissipate your worries.
- If nervousness follows you into the game, and you find your mind racing as you consider the hundreds of ways to fail – play a safety. A few of these and you will get into a playing rhythm.

When you get more interested in the game then in your mental condition, you will get over it.

How can you rack for 9 Ball to make it easier or harder to run out?

When you are setting up the rack for yourself, you may want to sequence the ball positions to help you out. If setting it up for your opponent, use the other setup.

The ball setup will provide a slight improvement of your chances. In the game of table billiards, even a slight advantage can add a few more wins. These configurations help you out whether the rack is tight or loose.

Easier to run out

When racking your own breaks, you want them to spread into areas where there are sequential groups. That is, you want the 1, 2, and 3 and the 6, 7, and 8 within short travel distances to each other. The racking sequence is like this:

On the break, the top three balls and the bottom three balls will group with each other within the area of a half table. This is no guarantee of course, since there is a large amount of chaos in a break. Don't forget the flip side of this configuration. If you don't make a ball on the break or get a bad leave and miss on the first few balls, you are leaving your opponent an easier table layout

Harder to run out

If you are racking for your opponent, you want a different configuration. You want to make the table layout after the break more difficult. Ideally, the ball sequences are separated by large table distances. Set up the racking sequence like this:

On the break the top three balls tend to move towards the head of the table and the bottom three balls towards the foot of the table. This will not always do so, but it does occur enough times that it is worth the consistent effort. The more distance the cue ball has to travel to get to the next shot, the harder it is to carefully manage. With this rack, a shooter will have to travel up and down at least three times. There are plenty of opportunities for a bad roll to screw up the run.

What is a well-racked set of balls?

A good rack allows all the balls to touch when pushed forward and the rack is lifted from the table. Even with a good rack, if the table cloth is uneven from dings, balls can separate. If the rack is properly made, the balls should cluster together when pushed together. A poorly designed rack will leave gaps between the balls. (The balls could also separate because of unequal diameters.)

With a good rack, even a medium speed break shot will separate the balls well. A bad rack with gaps in between balls will absorb energy and lead to clumped and clustered balls, even with a strong break.

On tables where a decent rack of balls is impossible to set up, ensure that the top three balls of the rack are touching as best as can be done. If a gap does appear, regardless of your best efforts, inform your opponent and invite him to set up the rack. (Almost all opponents are very tolerant when they realize that a faulty rack is a table condition.)

Sometimes it is loose chalk dust or simply air dust that has settled down onto the table and then mounded or clumped together because of balls traveling back and forth over the area. And don't forget that on a solid stroke with a properly chalked tip, the chalk flies off in a shotgun scatter pattern. You can partially offset this affect and get the balls to group better by brushing or slapping the cloth around the racking area. This vigorous action will, at the least, make the area more level and even. There will be less chance of the balls sitting on a small ridge and rolling away.

Several companies manufacture special tight tolerance machined racks. The cost factor will be a deciding point for you.

Do you play the opponent or play the table?

When you are in a competitive match; a few of the pros, when asked, recommend concentrating on playing the table. Their rationale is based on the fact that since you are on the table, and your opponent isn't, so just run out the balls and win the game. If you are not at that level where running the table is a common experience, then that advice is less than useful.

Leaving the rarified atmosphere of professionals, let's put some reality in the question. Yes, you do play the table when you are shooting, but you play the opponent when you have to let him play. When this occurs, knowing how skilled your opponent is helps you make cue ball placement decisions. And if you miss and your opponent has problem balls on the table, you know that another opportunity to shoot will come your way.

When competing, always take the game as far as possible. When you are stopped by a bad position, a tough shot, or tied up balls; playing a safety is a good idea. That is when you need to know what your opponent can and cannot do.

The capabilities of your opponent are a major consideration on your next shooting decision. If he is an average shooter, you can play a number of shots to leave him nothing easy to play with. If he is above average, your choices are more limited and require more care to set up and execute. Either way, you want to set up your opponent to hand back the table to you.

In essence, when the table layout favors you, take the best advantage you can. When there is no generosity from the billiard gods, play the shot that leaves your opponent with little or no opportunities.

How can you evaluate your playing skills?

There will be times when you want to determine if you are getting more skilled as a pool player. Are you advancing or standing still? Within your group of friends are you gaining or losing your place in the pecking order? Are you being greeted with greater or lesser respect when you meet last week's opponent on the street?

You might have some skill that has had a noticeable improvement, for example, finally figuring out the trick that can send a frozen object ball down the rail into the pocket. But that does not make you a more feared player than before.

or it's you are standing still in a becoming a better shooter or player. When you want to evaluate your skill level, especially to determine whether there has been any kind of recent improvement, do you pick your best day skills, your worse days skills, or somewhere in between?

To set the problem in a proper light, your rep as a player depends on only one small aspect of your game - cue ball control. You see this in the pros. They are fabulous shot makers, but more importantly, they are masters of the cue ball spin and speed.

If you want to do a comparison between your abilities now and your competencies a month ago, you are going to have to use shot setups that reveal the cruel truth. It is all in the numbers - statistics. Yup, that subject area of your youth when you had a hard time figuring out the difference between 1+1 and 1x1.

Below are very simple examples. If you enjoyed calculating the limits of pi, you can apply more complex standards. Set your evaluation shots using the paper reinforcement rings. Use a simple set of shot configurations that you can run through in five minutes.

If you are a beginner, place the cue ball and object ball closer and angled shots easy. As your skills increase, increase the distances and angles. Shoot each set with stun. Do another set with follow to a specific location. Repeat another set but with draw to a specific location. A recommended number of shots in a set is five, but shooting three of each also works.

Repeat this exercise once or twice a month. To remind yourself, mark it on the calendar. Doing this more clutters up your memory and makes it more difficult to figure out if there are any real improvements.

What is sharking?

These are techniques used by unscrupulous and unsportsmanlike opponents that distract you from playing at your normal or better level. Most individuals who are intent on sharking you are quite obvious in their actions.

Here are some of the distractions they like to use:

- Carry on a conversation with you while you are shooting.
- Drop anything that makes a loud noise just as you get set to commit.
- Move into your line of sight and make motions to grab your attention.
- Have loud conversations with friends (including distracting laughter).
- Wear loud and flashy clothing.
- Making jingling sounds with their keys and coins.
- Make jokes to get you laughing.
- Have friends do the above while you are shooting.

Some sharking efforts are more subtle and are not obvious. For example:

- Carry the table chalk back to their seat when their turn is over. Leave it there on the next turn, grab that chalk and bring back to their seat. This is a good distraction as long as you don't carry your own chalk with you.
- Anytime they fall into your line of sight, they slowly move their cue stick side to side while you are concentrating on the shot.
- Being extra complimentary when you make a tough shot.
- Being extra sympathetic when you miss a tough shot..
- Moving around within your peripheral vision.

The great majority of players do not necessarily have "evil" intentions, although that does not stop them from having "naughty" intentions. Their distractions are in the context of friendly competition with a dose of buddy-busting. They are there to have fun during an enjoyable evening. Watch for the ones who do these tricks all the time. When money is on the line, these unsportsmanlike players are very obvious.

How can you stop someone sharking?

If they are doing any sort of action before you bend down over the shot, stand still, look directly at your opponent until he notices you. When he says, "What?", you respond, "Are you done yet?" If asked, detail the action and speak loud enough for everyone around the table to hear. Once you get acquiescence, nod and continue with your inning. If he starts again later, you repeat the process, followed with a "Are you sure?"

On a third attempt, very deliberately go over to your seat, sit down, and stare him down. If asked, respond with, "I can't play with you. It is just too distracting. Do you want to forfeit this match?" At that point, embarrassment in front of their friends should stop any efforts to distract you from your game.

If he attempts sharking while you are down on the ball, deliberately stand up and repeat the above process. Be prepared to begin breaking down your stick and get ready to leave. Some games aren't worth the effort to play.

Also check out my book, "The Psychology of Losing" on the main web site. There are a few sharks you can read.

How do you handle an opponent who is a poor sport?

Sometimes you get into a match with an opponent who takes bad playing situations as a direct insult. It would be funnier, if he simply asked the table directly, "Are you dissing me?" It's the same thing. Or, he might consider every poor playing situation to be an intentional personal insult from you (as if you have any control over his poor playing and planning skills).

On every bad roll or pocket rattler, he gets overly emotional. He doesn't get what he intended and his verbal reaction is in the language of "Curse-u". He is incaution about who sees or hears him. If any friends are watching, he cries out, "Did you see that? Did you see that?"

Only one other event is even more irritating – losing. Win the game or match and he might follow the form of sportsmanship, but his attitude, voice, and tone is that of a life-long enemy.

There are several passive ways you can react:
- Get upset and play angry.
- Laugh it off.
- Pity him.
- Ignore him and get the game over quickly.

You may want to take a more sneaky reaction. For this, you adopt a strategy of denial. At any opportunity, set up some tough safeties, just for the fun of it. The only purpose is to deepen and widen his feelings of frustration. If he realizes you are doing this intentional, he may accuse you of not being serious about playing. Ignore him and continue with your plan of never giving him an easy shot.

How you handle such a person is pretty much dependent on how you feel. If you like torturing deserving brats, go for it. If you are less confrontational, use one of the passive approaches.

What if your opponent is an ass?

You do not want to do is be responsible for a physical altercation in the pool hall. That can get you kicked out or even banned from playing. In an elevated confrontation, there are always nearby buddies of your opponent ready to helpfully make their muscles available.

Upon finding yourself face to face with such a person, maintain a facade of disinterested courtesy. Hold tight onto your temper. Keep the communication down to a minimum, and do not make any comments outside the game table that could be construed as goading.

In other words, if there is going to be any accusations of poor sportsmanship or a related incident flying around, let it be very obvious that the other person was responsible. If the person does start attempting to shark you with comments, noises, distractions, etc., you can use the techniques in "How can you stop someone sharking?"

At a certain point, you may have to take additional action. In a league match, ask the team captains to do something. If the two captains cannot settle the problem, then simply refuse to continue the match. At this point, it is not your problem anymore. The next day file a formal complaint to the league operator/manager. Provide as much detail as possible and copy the information to both team captains.

In some circumstances, you could appeal to the pool hall manager. At the least do not say or do such things that could escalate the situation.

How do you handle an angry opponent?

There will be matches during your playing career when you happen to get stuck with a player who should take an anger management class (or two). This will always happen when they are behind in a match. (The same individual never acts this way when they are winning. Go figure.)

There is one very good reason to be polite to someone acting like that - you already have him beat. The only way you are going to lose is if you break both arms, one leg, and get blinded in one eye.

Regardless, you are still going to be faced with his actions throughout the match. His activities include loud negative comments as you are shooting. He will also attempt very crude sharking efforts such as banging his stick on the floor, moving into your line of sight and attempting distracting movements.

If you think those are fun, you should watch him acting up when he comes to the table. Every time he misses is immediately followed by loud complaining about the table, the stick, the temperature of the room, and any of a dozen excuses for failure.

If the person doesn't have teammates to keep him under some semblance of civilized behavior, you might also have a chance to see him start abusing his cue stick. (This is always good for some entertainment value.)

There are several ways to handle this type of person. If you are playing the match as a member of a team, you can pull his captain off to one side and ask him to caution his teammate. If a friend or friends of his are watching, ask them for some support.

You can also be more direct and ask point-blank, "Do you want to forfeit this match?" If he answers to the negative, say something like, "Please show some sportsmanship. Everybody has bad days. OK?" If you can get a grudging agreement at this point, then finish off the match with as little direct communication as possible. Properly shake his hand at the end and exit stage right.

How can you make an accurate 1 cushion kick?

The common recommended technique to kick to a rail into the target object ball is the ghost table/mirror technique. You mock up another table next to your table, joined at the cushions. You place a ghost target ball in place on the ghost table and shoot at the ghost ball. Simple enough.

Spotting of the location of the ghost ball can be accomplished easily as long as it is within a diamond of the rail. As soon as the distance goes towards the middle of the table or even the far side, guesstimating where to aim at the cushion becomes more difficult to determine.

Here is an acceptable and fairly accurate measuring tool to locate the ghost object ball:

1. Lay your cue perpendicular to the same rail you will aim into, lined up with the tip almost touching the object ball.
2. Place a finger on the stick exactly where the stick crosses the edge of the cushion.
3. Holding the finger in place on the cue, lift up the stick and move straight backwards until the tip of the cue is at the cushion.
4. Draw an imaginary line from the finger position straight at the cue ball.
5. Where that line crosses the cushion becomes the target for the cue ball.

This works very well when the object ball is closer to the kicking cushion that the cue ball. When the cue ball is closer to the kicking rail, use the cue ball to measure the ghost.

1. Lay your cue perpendicular to the same rail you will aim into, lined up with the tip almost touching the cue ball.

2. Place a finger on the stick where it crosses the cushion.
3. Holding the finger in place on the cue, lift up the stick and move straight backwards until the tip of the cue is at the cushion.
4. Draw an imaginary line from the finger position straight at the object ball.
5. Where that line crosses the cushion becomes the target for the cue ball.

The shot still has to be pure center cue ball. Any contact to the left or right side of the cue ball is going to throw all of your careful measurements into the chaos zone. Medium speed is recommended. If you are going to hit the cue ball harder than this, shift the cushion target point slightly further down the cushion. The angle out is going to be less than the angle in.

All of these calculations assume a table with good cushions. If you know a rail is dead, you should bank into it at several angles to determine what adjustments will be necessary to achieve success in game conditions.

To ensure that you can trust these measurements under match conditions, spend some time doing a variety of these kicks. If modifications are necessary (up or down adjustments of the aiming point on the cushion), this is where you work out the details. When faced with kicks, you now have a trustworthy tool ready to use.

What are the different kinds of break shots?

The break is the start of a new game. Who breaks is determined by a variety of ways, for example: lagging, coin toss, or by some other mutual agreement. On subsequent games between the same opponents, the options are: alternating breaks, loser breaks, winner breaks, or other mutual agreement.

9 Ball break - the cue ball must hit the 1 ball which is placed in the top position of the rack. The general rule is four object balls must contact the cushions or the rack must be set up again. This contact can be done at different speeds, from anywhere in the kitchen. Careful attention is paid to managing how the cue ball moves after the break is made.

8 Ball break - this break is generally made to either the apex ball or the ball in the second row. The general rule is four object balls must contact the cushions or the rack must be set up again. Like 9 Ball, the cue ball speed can vary greatly, and the angle into the rack from the kitchen can also be flexible.

1 Pocket break - this break can contact any ball from the kitchen. The break from one side of the kitchen determines that the opposite corner becomes the shooter's selected pocket. Only one object ball is required to contact a cushion. A one point penalty is assessed if this is not done, and play picks up where the balls lay.

14.1 break - this break can contact any ball from the kitchen. Two balls must contact cushions for a legal break. A penalty of two points is assessed if this is not done, and play picks up where the balls lay.

Odd break types - every once in a while, someone gets a bright idea for their own personal breaking style, just to be contrary. One example is shooting first to the long rail to drive the cue ball into the side of the rack. Another is to shoot to the short rail and come back into the rack from behind. These shots provide excellent opportunities to make the cue ball fly off the table. And, at the slower, more controlled speed, the rack will not spread open very far.

How can you improve side pocket shooting?

The obvious answer is more practice. Most players tend to avoid side pocket shots unless the object ball is directly out from the pocket. Anything with an angle makes them try a cross bank or an extreme cut to the corner. Other players will use extreme efforts (spin & speed) to avoid a cue ball position that forces an object ball shot to the side pockets.

What many people overlook is that the side pocket is the biggest pocket on the table. The angles to the side pocket where an object ball can be made is over 3/4 of the table surface. The only areas where you cannot make an object ball are shown with the diagram below. Any object ball inside the line cannot be made in the side pocket; any ball outside the line can be made.

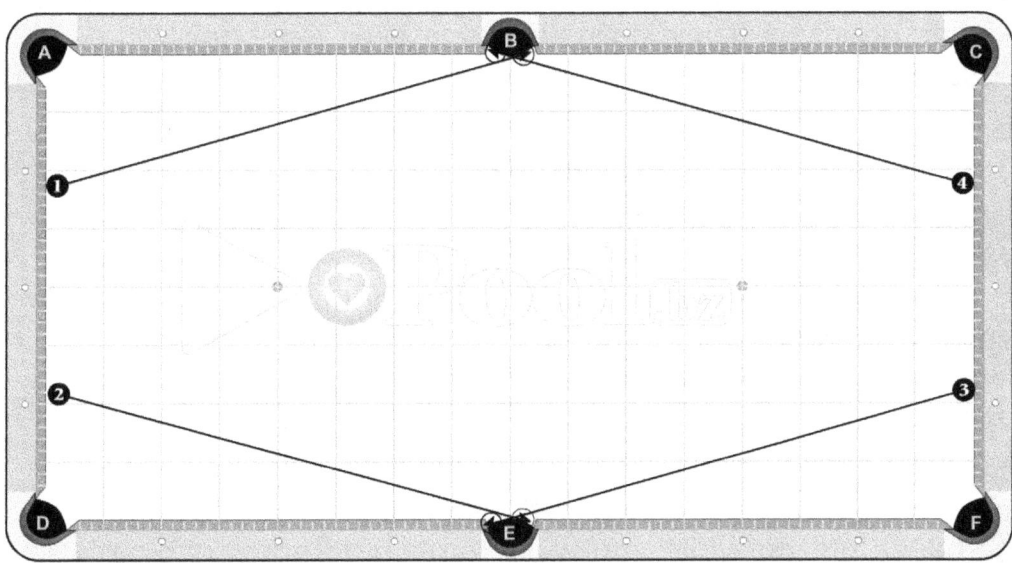

The closer to these lines, the smaller the pocket size. This is no different than running a ball down the rail for the length of the table. Both shots are targeting a very small pocket.

Your aiming point for any angled side pocket shot is just inside the far tip. When shooting into the tighter angles, use slow speeds. The more open the pocket, the higher speeds can be used.

When an object ball is on the center string, the pocket is huge. This makes cheat the pocket to get a larger or lesser angle is easier. This can be used to get a slight angle to help get position for the next shot.

Practicing FAQs

What does it take to reach the top tier of players?

If you have a secret passion to quickly reach the professional level of table billiards, you must have the drive and passion that overwhelms everything else in your life.

How much time are you willing to spend at the pool table? Can you do two hours of practice, followed six to eight hours of playing time with the toughest players you can find? And, this needs to be done 5 or 6 days every week.

If you don't have time for that kind of immediate dedication, you can still get to the top level, it will just take a longer. Regardless of which process you choose, the developmental processes (brain and muscle skills) is necessary.

Start by developing your ability to analyze table layouts and come up with a plan. If you have the necessary cue ball control skills, each shot can have dozens of options. If you don't have the necessary control, get the *Cue Ball Control Cheat Sheets* ebook. A few months working with this book will earn you very sophisticated ball control and predictability skills.

Get comfortable with all of the many different shots, such as rail shots, over ball shots, open & closed bridges, etc. Learn the many ways to get out of trouble and get your opponent in trouble.

Study the greats of the past. Video clips of many of these famous players are available on the internet. Look past the simple shooting and focus in on the speed and spin of the stroke. The cue ball action will tell you exactly what they did. Watch them and learn. Become familiar with the last two decades of top players, their records, their histories, and they contributions.

There are thousands of hours of tournament match videos. Instead of being a "spectator", look at each table layout and figure out what you would do. (If necessary hit the pause button while you work out the different choices.) Then see how the shooter played the shot. These matches provide examples of many different ways to play different types of shots. On any interesting layout, hit the pause and, on a notepad, sketch out the layout. Take those sketches to the practice table. By learning how to observe strengths and weaknesses, you know what your opponents can and can't do.

To get on this path to the top levels of the game, start locally. Take these new abilities and skills in table analysis to your local pool hall. Watch the local better players play. When you can recognize what they can and can't do, challenge them. Enter tournaments. Join local leagues and match yourself up against the best players of other teams. When you get good, attend the regional tournaments and qualifiers for national competitions.

It is not going to be the simple pocketing of balls that will require your single-minded devotion to playing pool. It is the vast number of strategic and tactical considerations that have to be evaluated before every single shot. It helps if you like to work out and solve puzzles.

And, don't forget the lessons to be learned from mistakes. Mistakes are actually your best self-indicator. They point out specific playing skills that need attention and practice.

Even with all this effort and preparation, don't plan your future only around pool. The top pros do not all make their living by pool. Many of them have jobs and businesses that are used to feed themselves so they can play the games they love so much.

When I do practice, what should I do?

Do you have a desire to improve your playing skills? When you make time for practicing do you get bored quickly? You are not alone. Nonetheless, if you have any ambition of improving, you got to do some work on your game.

The secret is to only work on one type of improvement for a few minutes. If you don't have a written plan on what to do, then use a regular routine as indicated below. These exercises or other similar workouts provide a structure that ensures that your practice time does not get wasted in a pointless waste of your time. And it doesn't take hours of daily effort. Five minutes on this exercise, 20 shots on that exercise, and any combination will work.

Shot-making exercises:

- Straight-in shots, working through various distances.
- Pocketing balls close to the rail from various angles.
- Angled shots, starting with easy cuts graduating to more difficult efforts.

Cue ball control exercises:

- Simple, short range stop shots, extending the distance as your skills progress.

- Slight angle shots with follow or draw to get to different locations on the table.
- Spot shots, shooting from the kitchen, targeting different cue ball locations (put a sheet of paper on the table and get the cue ball to roll onto the paper).

Safety practice:

- Kiss the cue ball off another ball and lay the cue ball on the first, second, third, and fourth rails. Advance only when you can repeat the shot three consecutive times.
- Repeat the same process, but the ball to control is the object ball. Get it to one rail, then two rails, followed by the third rail. Start with full hits, then 3/4, 1/2, and 1/4 ball hits.
- Practice forcing the cue ball to stay on the tangent line (and predicting the path).

Miscellaneous exercises:

- Kiss the cue ball off an object ball and run it one, two, or three rails to hit another object ball.
- Kick off rails to an object ball at different locations and angles.
- Master double-kissing the cue ball and object ball, and predicting the path and location for both balls.
- Randomly throw three balls and start with cue ball in hand. Run them in numbered sequence. When this gets easy, go to four balls.

These, and any variations that catch your fancy, should pick up your interest in practicing. Focused practice time will guarantee you will improve. Even if you can only do 10-15 minutes at a time, time spent in real practicing will have immediate results (such as more games won). When you schedule practice time - don't mess around. And more important, don't drag along a friend.

How can you get more practice time in?

Unless you have our own home table (or a relative who owns a pool hall), one of the problems you face is finding the time to practice. It takes more time to get your stuff together and drive back and forth to your local playing environment (pool hall, senior center, lodge) than actually practicing. A dedicated practice trip will take 20-30 minutes to get there for a practice time of a half hour, and then the trip back. BTW, playing with friends is NOT practicing, so get that idea out of your head. Practice is practice. Use your playing friends to demonstrate your new skills.

But all is not lost. You don't actually need a pool table to practice. You can actually fit in a multiple groups of several minutes of practice time right at home. The kitchen table works just as well. A standard kitchen table is the same height as a pool table. On the kitchen table, you can work on:

- Bridge hand setup
- Butt stick grip
- Feet placement
- Waist and knee positioning
- Head position
- Arm positioning and alignment
- Body balance

When you bend over, inspect yourself to make sure everything falls into position. You can test your balance, alignment (head, arms, and grip lined up aligned).

Work on repetitive strokes. These are related to the practice strokes before hitting the cue ball. Concentrate on making sure the stick doesn't wander side to side during the stroke. Practice this with short strokes and longer strokes. Basically, the cue tip will betray any stroke action that is not true back and forth. Make adjustments accordingly.

The stroke is the critical part of playing. It is what propels the cue ball to do wonderful things. And make sure your back elbow is over the stick and doesn't move up and down. Just let the forearm hang from your elbow and swing back and forth like a pendulum. Subdue any wavering and make the movement consistent. You will make a lot more balls more easily with this control.

You can make a practice table out of your kitchen table. And, best of all, no table charges. All you need is the following equipment:

- Kitchen table
- Blanket
- Any cheap stick from any sporting goods store
- A few old tennis balls (or small oranges)
- Small can of vegetables (16 oz or so)

Here is what to do. A good regime is two or three 10-15 minute sessions per day.

1. Drape the blanket over the table.
2. Roll-up the edges to act as a barrier to prevent the balls from falling off the table.
3. Set up a tennis ball and practice shooting it at the can of vegetables.
4. Shoot over and over and over until the tennis ball rolls straight.
5. Then set up another ball and shoot the "cue ball" into the "object ball" which must hit the can of vegetables.

Later, buy the cheapest set of balls you can find (check the internet or a local sports store). Use these to learn how to hit balls on your kitchen table. A thick blanket requires more speed; a thin blanket requires slower speeds. Because the balls are heavier than tennis balls, make the rolled up sides of the table taller. Practice with both thick and thin blankets. Learn speed control (so that you don't have to pick up fallen balls from the kitchen floor.

The best part of "practicing" at home is that you can work on something for five minutes, make yourself a snack, another five minutes, check the grass growing in the front yard, another five minutes and do this throughout the day. You only have to actually clear the table for meals.

Just a month or two of this practice routine will save you five or more years of flailing around trying to learn during matches or competitions. You will dominate your friends very quickly.

How do you move up to the next level?

Assuming that you are not already a near-pro player, here are some tips that will help.

Maintain and reinforce the mental attitude that you are able and capable of becoming better. It is the positive attitude necessary to improvement.

When in a competitive match and you are behind in the count, patiently stick with your plan. Opportunities will arise which you can take advantage. Wait for these openings. If you are ahead, continue the mindset that got you there. Do not relax at any time. If you assume you have the match in the bag, you offer your opponent an opening.

While waiting to play, watch other players. There is always something to be learned from those who are higher and lower skilled. Watch how they shoot. Follow they analysis process, how they get down on the ball, pre-shot routine, and stroke. See how that correlates with the success of each shot. If unsuccessful, figure out why. When a shot was well played, observe and identify the pluses.

You need discipline and constantly work on improving your level of self-control. And to move that improvement forward requires that you practice as much as can be done within your schedule.

Your practice has to be focused. Improve your skills based on setting up and shooting shots that need improvement. Discoveries of weaknesses during a match will provide the material for the next practice session. Don't go crazy with practice, but you do need to put in enough effort to achieve noticeable results.

Keep working on attainable improvements. Your whole pool playing lifetime will be spent finding little areas to improve. The complexity of the Green Game, it really is a wonderful way to pass your lifetime.

How can you gradually improve your game?

As you regularly play week to week, and so on into the future, it is a good idea to have some personal improvement goals. This is not the fantasy goals of becoming a professional player within two years. This is the week by week effort to become just a little better.

This doesn't require the dozens of weekly hours per week on a practice table. You have a life and are not going to sacrifice work and family over a level of skill that is probably impossible. All you want to have is a relatively painless way to get better, bit by bit.

If you have access to a practice table, that is good. If you don't, that is no bar to your plans. All you need is about 15 minutes per week to improve yourself.

Do not define your goals as some vague intention. For example, a goal of "improve my banking skills" is an unclear statement. What is your current success rate and what improvement do you want? Specify precisely..

Frame your improvements individually and as something that you can demonstrate. Specify it as, make 7 foot straight in shots, 8 times out of 10. Cut a 30 degree angle from 3 diamonds away and make it 5 out of 10 times.

When you miss a shot in a match, that is your shot to be improved. At every opportunity, five minutes of work will improve that shot. It doesn't matter whether it can be done once a week or every day.

The less time you practice, the longer it will take. You set the pace according to your schedule. If you consider the goal to be vital, put in more time. At the very least, work on the improvement on a regular schedule.

How long does it take to fix a bad habit?

You've been playing for a while and can't seem to get past a certain plateau of capability. Your lifetime progress to becoming a feared opponent is probably because of one or more bad habits.

The term "bad habits" takes in a lot of territory. It could fall into one of the body actions, i.e., feet position, butt position, head position, bridge, grip, body alignment, arm & elbow, etc. It could be a shortcoming in your stroke, such as movement, follow-through, straightness, cue ball speed and spin. Or, it might be a problem based on your mental abilities, such as layout analysis, shot selection, predictability capability. It might even be an attitude bad habit, such as one beginner that a friend was trying to help who basically said that she didn't need no stupid videos or books or instructors.

However you came about the understanding that your game needed help, you developed the awareness. Nonetheless, it can be emotionally devastating to discover that some part of your routine was, for years, actually helping you lose games.

Do realize that there can be multiple bad habits. If you attempt to fix more than one bad habit at a time, you will fail. Address the worst problem first; take the time to thoroughly fix it, before you select another bad habit to work on. You will also discover that fixing one bad habit will also cause adjustments that will either directly fix or help lessen another problem.

For an example, let's use the well-known chicken wing elbow. This happens when you get down on the shot and your stick elbow (of the hand holding the butt of the stick), angles away from your body.

The fix, of course, is simple. Simply move the elbow so that it is directly above the stick (and make the stroke a true back and forth movement). If you've been shooting for years with a chicken wing elbow, this fix is not so simple. You have made all sorts of adjustments to your stroke. Essentially, you are learning how to shot all over again. The immediate results of this correction are that your game gets worse. Eventually, with enough correct strokes in your muscle memory, you will "remember" the right way, and the wrong way will fade away into your past.

Various studies in replacing one automated physical routine with another indicate that several thousand repetitions are necessary. Fortunately, for the chicken wing fix, every correct practice stroke counts as a single occurrence. You can rack up a lot of practice strokes anytime. Ten or 20 for every shot should do it. The old habit will still pop up any time you become tired and inattentive.

If you've been using bad habits for decades, the struggle to change becomes harder. You have tens of thousands experiences buried in your muscle. Basically, changing a physical habit takes about two weeks of focused effort for each year the habit existed. Conscious physical repetition is what it takes. Being conscious during the repetition means you are mentally aware of the change's purpose AND intent.

There is one fast (well, kind of) way to overcome a single bad habit. This requires that you sit in your easy chair. With your eyes closed, mentally play the new script of the movement being mastered. Break it down into little one inch movements. In very slow motion, play the inch movements one at a time, mentally identifying each increment and preparing to perform the next increment. This is like watching a very slow motion video, frame by frame, hitting the advance button to get to the next frame. Repeat this mental process at about 10% of normal speed (about 10 times). Then move the whole action at 15%, 25%, 33% 50%, 65%, 75%, and finally, for 100 times, 100%. This one process takes about 35-45 minutes. Do this process three times a week for two weeks. That bad habit will be totally overlaid and actually be a distant memory.

It doesn't matter whether you fix the problem through physical repetition or mental repetition. It does matter that you fix the problem.

How do you plan to run a table layout?

If you've ever watched good players compete, every shot is designed to accomplish two objectives - pocket the current object ball and move the cue ball into a table location where the next object ball can be targeted. The only significant difference between the good players and the better players is their ability to do this on a routine basis.

There are plenty of excellent shooters who can pocket a ball from anywhere and don't think they need to learn anything else. They make excellent training victims for those learning how to play position. Your pocketing skills will develop as a matter of course and time. It is your positioning skills that will make you a more competitive player.

To develop your competence in positioning and have some fun doing it, start by throwing two balls out on the table. Take cue ball in hand and make one ball and get into position for the second ball, then shoot that in. Repeat until you can be successful ten times in a row.

Next, go with three balls on the table and cue ball in hand. This will take some time to master because you have to consider where the cue ball stops for the second ball. That positioning is necessary to move the cue ball into position for the third ball. Based on the experiences of several individuals, you really have to be able to make this work 10 out of 10 before you move on to four balls on the table.

The trick to get position on the third ball depends on how you start on the first ball. That first choice of speed, spin, and angle is far more important that you think. If you don't believe this, after a few hundred attempts with inconsistent results, you will believe it. If you get that figured out, moving on to patterns of 5, 6, 7 and more balls is not quite as difficult as you might initially think.

Will exercise help improve your game?

Anyone who says that pool players don't do much exercise and aren't in good shape hasn't really played much pool. If you know a scofflaw, challenge that person to 100 shots, within one hour. If they're not in good physical condition, they'll be huffing and puffing and dripping up sweat like its 120 degrees.

The better your physical conditioning, the longer you can play pool. How's that for an incentive?

If you are not a regular gym attendee, start your physical development with long walks. Carry a 24-32 oz plastic water bottle in each hand. While on your long walks, swing the stick hand (and the bottle you are holding) up to your shoulder as hard and fast as you can. This strengthens your arm for the break. As your stamina increases, stop about every 100 yards (m) and do five deep knee bends.

If you are a regular gym attendee, you want to concentrate on machines and routines that improve muscle tone and stamina. At no time do you want to physically exhaust yourself. (Pool is not an extreme sport.)

If weights are a part of your program, it's not a good idea to increase your arm dimensions. If you focus on building muscle mass, you tend to lose your ability to control the very fine movements necessary for slow rolling shots at precise distances. Games you should have won will be lost because of this loss of fine motor control. For example, a shot you could consistently roll exactly two diamonds suddenly goes four and half diamonds in distance.

Suddenly increasing stomach muscle strength changes how you hold your body in position on a shot. Yes, stronger stomach muscles does mean you can shoot more shots without getting back pains, but it also changes how far you bend over for the shot. Even a half inch different in your head height (up or down) over the stick changes how you see the lines and angles.

When you are developing a workout routine, follow these basic guidelines:

- Exercise no more than 3 times a week.

- Perform a maximum of six routines in one exercise session.

- Only make one weight increase in a single routine during the entire week.

- Only make one repetition increase in a single routine during the entire week.

- Be consistent week by week with the schedule.

- Plan on taking a long time to tone your muscles.

Follow your regular exercise routine, except when you enter an important competition. For the week before, cut back weights and reps by 10%. Stop exercise sessions two or three days before the competition.

How do you find a good instructor?

It is surprising, but the vast majority of pool players have never taken the time to take a lesson from a qualified instructor. They will spend hundreds of dollars on a cool cue stick, but not willing to part $20, $50, or $100 for lessons. They are perfectly happy to go on for years and years (and years) believing they are just too intelligent to need an instructor. If they are focused on improving, they'll watch dozens of hours of online video between pros and think that the couple of scraps of insight they can actually understand are all they need to soon become pros themselves.

Then of course, there are the "intelligent" shooters, who don't hold such superior self-opinions and will look to a qualified instructor to fix something that is holding them back. Generally, an hour or two of lessons with a bit of follow-up is all that is needed. Six months later, that player is kicking his friends' butts who previously humiliated him. (What a sweet revenge.)

The process of getting an instructor to help seems to begin with the dim awareness that something needs to be done and an instructor seems like a good idea. After percolating around in their head for two or three years, they finally decide to do something about it. This is the level where you are at.

Here are some guidelines to help select which of several instructors can help you:

- Remember, anyone can say they are an instructor. So it helps to first look for any certifications, i.e., PBIA, ACS. These groups have a code of conduct and because these are national organizations, you have some assurance of their qualifications.
- What kind of experience does the instructor have? Consider how many years playing, handicap levels in any local leagues, etc..
- How is their reputation? Talk with individuals who have past experience as students.
- Talk with each instructor one on one. What teaching tools are used, i.e., handouts, video tape, etc. Do they ask questions about what you want?
- Take an initial half hour lesson to review style and presentation.

An instructor should also ask questions about you. Here is a sampling:

- How long have you been playing?
- What is your skill level?
- What do you want to achieve, short term?
- How much time do you practice?
- Have you bought any books or had other instructors?

In order to get the best and maximum benefits from an instructor, expect to put some hard work into learning what you are taught. You have to be willing to actually practice regularly. Ask however many questions are necessary for you to actually perform what you are learning. Your instructor can teach you a lot of short cut learning tricks, but you are going to have to work on them – if for nothing else but to make sure you get value you're your money.

How do you practice with a friend?

Most of the time when you get together with a partner during a practice time, you end up just playing each other with no real goal in mind or anything accomplished. You spend a couple of hours together just to bang balls around and no one's skills were improved. That's a wasted amount of time.

Practice time is a very precious commodity. It's one of the few times when you are at the table that you can focus specifically upon improving some part of your skills and abilities. If you depend on improving when playing games, some of the shots you need to learn may only come up once or twice an hour.

If you are going to make good use of your precious practice time with two of you sharing the same table, you need to agree that self-improvement is the goal, not having a good time with a buddy. If you have a plan on things to improve, make sure your friend does to. Otherwise, while you are attempting to master an 85 degree cue with right spin, he's getting bored trying to bank the cue ball into the corner. A few minutes of that is all that he can stand and he starts engaging you in distracting conversation. You don't want to take the simple way out and inform him that his company is not required. If he doesn't have a clue what practice time means, make him follow a few of your exercises. Get him started on one and get back to your efforts. And if he attempts to make you become his babysitter and interrupts too many times, you can always use the simple solution. ;-) After that, do not every invite him along again.

Assuming you both arrive at the table with serious intentions of self-improvement, here are a few suggestions. Divide the table on the center line while you both work on short-distance shots. When long table practice shots are required, divide the table the long way. You can each work on individual strokes with an appropriate variety of stun, follow, and draw shots.

Another cooperative effort can be for each of you to take turns setting up shots that require the full table. The object ball can be positioned, and the cue ball sent down for the next shot. This cooperation means that each of you can get twice as many practice shots in a given amount of time.

When each of you have finished working on the individual shots that needed improvements, you can get play competitive games – but with a purpose to improve thinking skills. For example, one player focuses on only playing defensively and the other only plays offensively. If the defensive player can force a predetermined set of innings, he wins. If the offensive player can win the game before the number of innings is played, he wins.

These suggestions will get you started when you have to practice with a friend. When the both of you are serious about improving skills, this makes good use of a single table to benefit each of you. You can mutually support each other in setting aside dedicated practicing times.

What kinds of drills can improve your game?

Once you have learned the basics skills and developed a decent stroke and have some ability to play position - where do you go from there? There are a lot of answers. One of them is the practice of various types of drills. Drills have a specific purpose. The ball setups are constant, usually identified with paper reinforcement rings or positions identified along the diamond lines (up/down, and sideways).

Drills with two balls

The simplest drills involve only the cue ball and an object ball. With the balls in position, the shot is made and the results observed. The balls are set up again and the shot repeated. These types of drills focus on pocketing skills.

The complex drills involve the cue ball and several object balls (from two to all 15). You have to make the first ball and get into position on the second ball. If more balls are part of the drill, you have to shoot the second ball in and get shape on the third ball, and so on.

For the pocketing drills (object ball and cue ball), start with positions within your comfort zone. For distance drills, as you pocket the object ball, increase the distance in half diamond increments. Make the ball increase the distance, miss the ball decrease the distance.

When you are consistent with these up to a reasonable distance, start over but contact the cue ball with various side spins. Start with half-tip out from center beginning with 1:00, then 2:00, then 3:00 and so on around the clock. Then repeat with the tip a full width out from center and repeat. Remember, to increase the distance only when you make the ball and decrease the distance when you fail to pocket the ball.

The same process applies to angled shots. The cue ball is at an angle to the object ball that goes into the pocket. Again, start with an easy angle at a comfortable distance from the object ball. On pocketing the ball, roll the cue ball a ball width to the side and repeat. On making the object ball, increase the angle a ball width. On missing the object ball, decrease the angle a ball width.

Like the straight in distance example, when you are comfortable with pocketing the object ball consistently, start over with the half-tip out from center, round-the-clock shots. Repeat this with one-tip out.

After you have all of the above, repeat the shots with one additional level of complexity. Place a full sheet of paper any place on the table. Play the shot so that you can get the cue ball to stop on the sheet of paper. See if you can figure out more than one way to do that. Then move the paper. It can be near or far as you wish.

Drills with multiple balls

The other set of drills involve placing multiple balls on the table in various formations and positions. The purpose of these types of drills is to force you to get the cue ball into prime positions to shoot the next ball in and then be able to get into position for the next ball in the pattern.

Some of these drills, when you first try them have hidden difficulties or reveal specific weaknesses in your game. Those shortcomings can make the drills impossible to complete. For example, the rectangle drill (below) can reveal many weaknesses in speed and spin control. Get out of line for just one ball and you rapidly find it impossible to recover. This drill alone can keep an obsessive person busy for several years. If you are masochistic in nature, there are dozens of drills like this available on the internet as well as in the book, *Drills & Exercises for Pool & Billiards*.

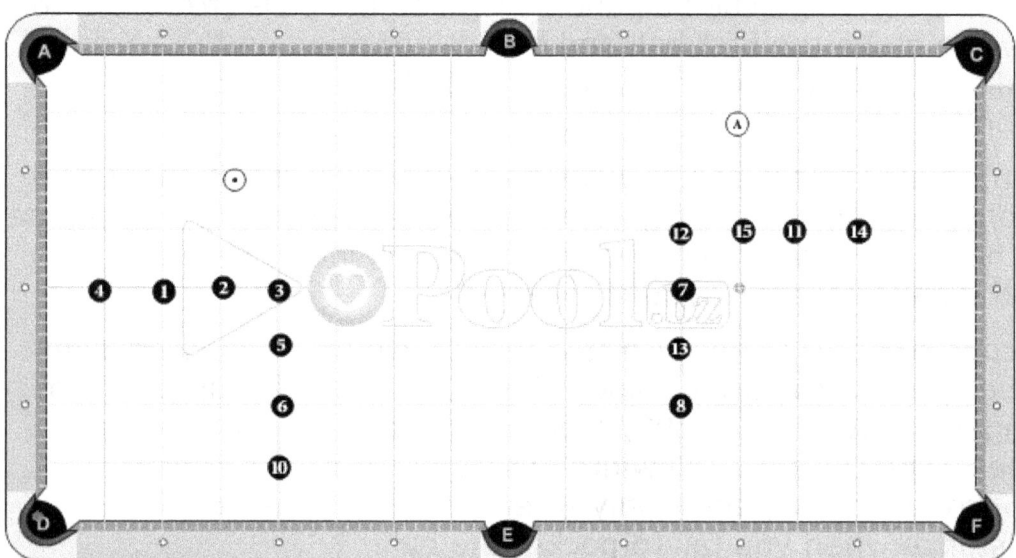

Drilling for reality

When you start off, concentrate on making small improvements of your current skills. Then set up shots to push your limits of competency and skill. Don't select drills that are too tough. You want to have some successes to encourage your willingness to practice. Concentrate on improving those skills that make you a better shooter within the group of people you currently play with and against.

Don't worry about shots beyond your current skill level. Work on drills and shots at the edge of your abilities. The advantage of using drills is that any improvements are obvious. A week or month ago, a certain shot would tough. Now it is easy – thanks to your consistent effort.

Select drills that require improvements in areas that you want to improve. When you work on those areas that interest you, it is easier to observe advancements in your abilities. Gradually you will improve your status and move up the hierarchy.

How do you use the tangent line?

Every time you hit an object ball with a cue ball, there is a minor wonder of physics that affects the cue ball, known as the tangent line. What is amazing about this little bit of table billiards activity is that you can use it to predict cue ball behavior.

Here is how it works. Regardless of the speed of the cue ball and the angle that the cue ball and object ball contact, the cue ball will travel away from the object ball and the contact point between them at right angles.

Sound a little too complicated? Let's use a couple of visual aids. In the example below, you will see a contact between the cue ball and an object ball. See the line going to the right and left of the touching point? That is the tangent line.

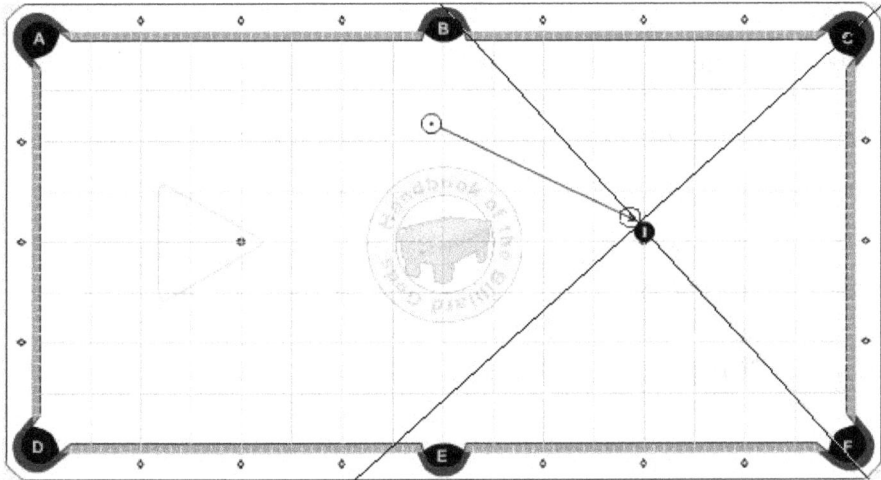

You can see from the line that the object ball will go into the corner pocket. What you also see is that the cue ball will scratch into the other corner pocket - not something you want to allow, unless there are other balls in the way.

So, what can you do? Most important - don't slam the object ball into the pocket. Use a lower speed. You have two options:

- Top spin ("follow"), combined with side spin. Use 10:00, 10:30, 11:00, 11:30, 12:00, 12:30, 1:00, 1:30, or 2:00.
- Bottom spin ("draw"), combined with side spin. Use 4:00, 4:30, 5:00, 5:30, 6:00, 6:30, 7:00, 7:30, or 8:00.

The lower speed allows the cue ball spin to interact with the cloth and force the cue ball away from the dangerous tangent line. Here is how to use that spin to get away from the dangerous tangent. With slower cue ball speeds, the follow options have the best success of missing the corner pocket.

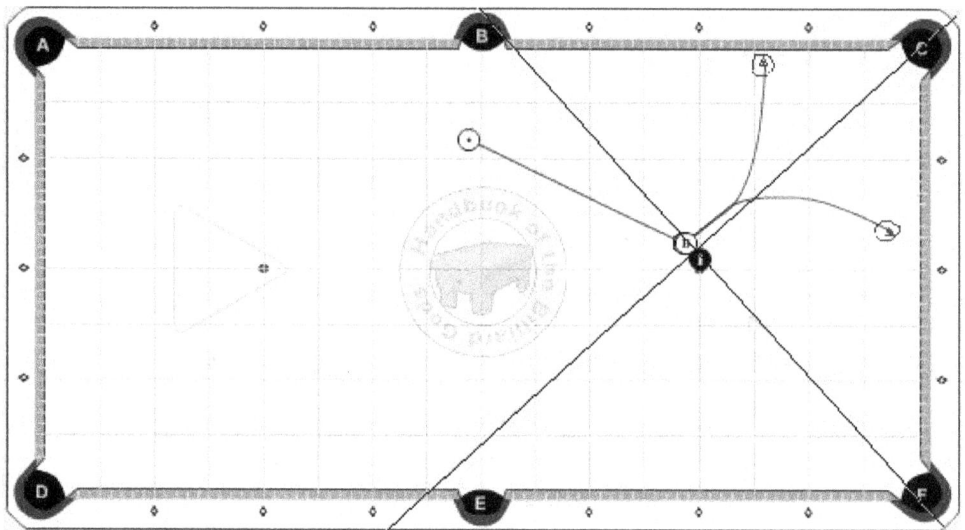

Tangent thumb technique

This technique will help you calculate the probable path of the cue ball after it contacts the object ball. This can also help determine whether that path can or should be modified with cue ball spin.

Put your hand over the object ball. Point the index finger along the line towards the pocket. Point your thumb 90 degrees out. That is the tangent line. You can check it for scratching dangers and possible contact with other balls.

Key factors

- With slower speeds, the cue ball has sufficient time to interact with the table cloth and deviate from the tangent line, either with draw or with follow.
- The more speed the cue ball is traveling on the tangent line; the more difficult it is to force any deviation from the tangent line.

Shallow angles

When the angle is very shallow coming into the object ball, it is difficult to change the cue ball path.

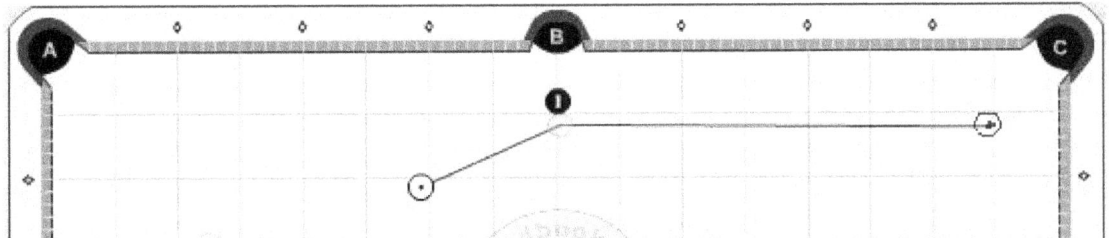

How can you shoot accurately with cue ball side spin?

When shooting the cue ball on the vertical center line, aiming at the object ball is fairly straightforward. It's easy to use any of the various aiming techniques, such as ghost ball, equal slices, line of sight, contact points, or even (after shooting enough balls), instinct.

What happens when you start contacting the cue ball to the left or right of the vertical center line? Now the physics and geometries get very confusing. You have to take into account many factors, such as squirt, deviation, curve lines, and stick speed. With side spins, the old aiming standbys no longer work as easily as they did with the vertical center line.

There is only one real and practical way to ensure some level of success when using various cue ball spins and speeds. Set up an easy shot and shoot it using a graduated series of shots that rotate through the various cue ball spins at one speed. When you can make the shot 100% of the time, repeat the process at a higher speed. When you miss, reshoot the setup until you make it three times in a row, then move on. To add just a bit more complexity - move the cue ball out 6 inches and repeat.

It will take several hundred shots under these controlled circumstances to begin automatically adjusting your aiming to allow for deviations from center ball. Do not be discouraged by misses in the beginning. It is necessary to build up a history of these shots and train your brain to make the necessary adjustments.

How do you video tape yourself?

There are times in your self-imposed intention to become a better player that you want an outside eyeball looking at you and seeing if there something that you are unable to spot. For best results, you should work with an instructor who can observe what is happening. He can tell exactly where the adjustments need to be made (usually the feet).

However, there may not be an instructor around, and you certainly don't want to depend on the opinions of friends. However well-intentioned they may be, they do not know what to look for and what needs fixing. Between both extremes is something that can work for your – videotaping yourself. If you don't have a video camera yourself, certainly one or more of your friends will. And, as soon as you finish, connect up a couple of cables and bang – there you are on TV.

Before you begin, know what you are trying to capture. It is a waste of time to simply setup a random videotaping without knowing what to look for. You aren't doing this just to prove to your relatives what a cools shooter you are. You want to have a reason for the taping. Choices for recording include:

- Stroke mechanics.
- Drill activity.
- Game routines.

This article assumes you don't have any friends who are serious enough to help you by running the camera without commentary. You do need a decent quality video camera and a camera tripod. Tripods are available in different sizes anyplace that cameras are sold. There are these cute little tripods that cost a few bucks. Set it up on a chair pointing in the right direction and you are ready to go.

Stroke mechanics

To video yourself on your stroke mechanics, you want two angles, one directly from the front and one from behind slightly to the same side as your stick arm.

TABLE: All balls on the side, ready to grab, place and stroke into the far corner pocket. Use a donut to mark the position for each ball.

CAMERA: Place the camera height about a foot above the table and about 3-4 feet away from the table. Focus the camera in at the cue ball and zoom the screen so that the top of the little view finder is about two feet above the table. Tape a couple of setup shots to ensure you have everything lined up. (Rewind the tape when done.)

ACTION: Use the same stance. As needed, empty the pocket.
1st set - 12:00 hit, soft roll.
2nd set - 12:00 hit, medium roll.
3rd set - 12:00 hit, hard roll.
Repeat as needed.

BACK ANGLE: Set the camera height at the same as for the front shot. set the tripod about eight feet behind you and four feet on the same side as your stick arm. Focus the camera in at the elbow with the top of the view finder about 1/2 foot above the elbow when in your stance. Tape a couple of setup shots to ensure you have everything lined up. (Rewind the tape when done.)

Drills

To video yourself while doing drills, you want to select a drill where you are shooting balls into the same pocket. You don't want to be continuously crossing in front of the camera to make shots.

TABLE: All balls set up for the drill. As needed, use a donut for any ball that has to be constantly replaced.

CAMERA: Place the camera height about two feet above the table and about 8-10 feet away from the table. Focus the camera in at the cue ball and zoom the screen so that the top of the little view finder is about two feet above the table. Tape a couple of setup shots to ensure you have everything lined up. (Rewind the tape when done.)

ACTION: Begin the drill, and run through it. Reset and reshoot missed shots. As needed, empty the pocket.
Record three sets.

ANOTHER ANGLE: On some drills, you may want to record a set from your stick arm side, to check the arm action.

General shooting

This is going to be a general free for all. You can record yourself shooting racks of 8 Ball and 9 Ball. You can also video yourself and a buddy shooting.

TABLE: All balls racked for the selected game.

CAMERA: Set the camera height as high as possible, and angled from one corner to get a view of the entire table. Focus the camera on the center of the table, and zoom out enough to show all pockets. (Don't worry if there is a bit too much floor space covered. It is more important to get the table in the frame. Make some test shots as needed.

ACTION: Start the tape and begin with breaking the rack. When the last ball goes in, stop the tape.

When done videotaping

After you have finished, you can hook up the camera to the TV. If you consider the details worthwhile keeping, save the details as a movie for a DVD or to play on your electronic device, such as an iPod, iPhone, Blackberry, etc.

How much practice does it take to become an "A" player?

An "A" player is someone who is able to break and run one or two racks for every ten racks. Their Balls Per Inning (BPI) average is between 4.0 and 5.0.

This is not an unattainable goal if you are willing to commit some time practicing.

You do need to be a bit obsessive about playing the game. Not so much that every waking thought is about pool, but there needs to be a passion for becoming a good player. Of course, talent can help. An ability to unconsciously calculate what it takes to get the cue ball into position is very helpful, just like a natural ability to pocket balls. But these are not necessary. A full awareness of the shot as you play it and an ability to analyze the results and figure what went wrong is more important.

When not working on specific areas of your skills, you will learn a lot by playing against the ghost. The simple rules are this: break a rack of balls, start with ball in hand, and win in that turn or you lose. The experiences of developing run out skills will show you areas where improvements are needed. Set up a drill to work on that specific skill until you own it.

If you are unable to devote that much effort, you can still fulfill your passion for learning how to play at higher levels. When you have practice time, work on drills and play the ghost. If you can't do two hours a day, try getting in 3 hours a week. All improvements are cumulative. More table time, faster improvements. Less table time, slower improvements.

As you gain more confidence in your abilities, start entering a few of the local tournaments. This gives you real-world experience. When you find yourself getting tougher handicaps, you have proof that you are making improvements.

What is "playing the ghost"?

When you practicing by yourself and have done all the drills you can handle, it is fun to rack up the balls and try to run as many as you can. When playing alone, you should always have a purpose.

The rules to "play the ghost" are to break the rack (8 Ball or 9 Ball) to start. Then pick up ball in hand to begin the run, regardless whether or not a ball is pocketed. Start pocking balls to the best of your ability. Keep in mind that your ultimate goal is to run the table, so make playing decisions with that in mind.

You are actually playing against an imaginary shooter (the ghost) who is so good, that if he could play, you lose. He never really plays, this is an assumption. Keep in mind that many of the better opponents, if given a chance to shoot do run out the table. It's a sad fact of the game that we are most often beaten because we handed the opponent the chance to play and lost.

For the purposes of this exercise, you only get one chance to run out to win the game. If you miss anywhere along the line, chalk a win up for the "ghost".

Being able to win, even once in a while is a real accomplishment. It is real demonstrable proof that you are improving. Your skills growth will be something like this: you can beat the ghost once out of 10 games. Three months later, you can beat the ghost three out of 10 games. A month later, the best you can do is two out of 10. This back and forth will go on for a while, but eventually you will see a solid numerical increase.

When first starting, if you feel the rules are initially too restrictive, you can allow yourself two balls in hand per rack. Or if you are really a beginning player, try three or even four balls in hand. Just get started and note the results over time.

How can you practice 1 Pocket alone?

When you want to practice 1 Pocket and there are no opponents available, you can be your own best challenger. Who else can give you the competitive level you deserve?

There is one drill you want to practice over and over before you start playing yourself. The break is one of the biggest possible advantages for a serious player. This is one thing to be practiced over and over until you have at least four or five possible variations. Setting up for break shots gives you a chance to experiment with different ideas. You might want to try different angles and different speeds. If you can finagle someone into setting up racks for you, you can get a lot of practice in 15-20 minutes. Take your time to consider the many options and try each one several times. Observe the results to determine if that break shot is worthy of use.

To practice the game, play Lefty against Righty. Begin the game with ultra conservative shots. Practice various single and double rail banks. Keep your speed under control. Remember where the cue ball will stop and leave as few opportunities as possible. When balls end up near the opposing pocket, work on clearing them out. Learn to recognize the attempt caroms to maneuver balls near your pocket. And, always, always, carefully think out the shot, angles, speed, and consequences.

Look for opportunities that can push two or more balls near your pocket. Get inventive and downright brilliant in the various solutions you can dream up. And whatever you do, don't lose patience and go for the quick win. Spend more time letting your brain work out the shots and speed.

Equipment FAQs

These are various FAQs about the equipment used in pocket billiards.

How do you clean your personal pool balls?

When you own your own set of balls, eventually they will need cleaning to help them maintain their shiny good looks. Pretty balls are much more fun to play with than dull dirty balls.

Here are some suggestions for cleaning and shining up balls.

- Ball manufacturer-supplied cleaners. Recommended, although expensive, they are safe to use.
- Dish washing soap and water. Soak in soapy water for one hour, use a tooth brush to clean. Rinse in clear water and towel dry.
- Rub vigorously with a clean micro towel and polish with car wax.
- Rub the balls on a white board eraser to remove marks.
- Throw in the dishwasher with liquid soap (without any rinsing add-on product). Take out after washing and buff with a micro-fiber towel.
- Clean with rubbing alcohol and use toothpaste with a toothbrush. Rinse well and towel dry.
- Clean balls with any of the above, then polish with carnauba wax.
- Take down to a pool hall with a fancy ball cleaner and pay a couple of bucks for the service.

Not recommended:

- Wax remover
- Abrasive polishes

Talk with others who have their own balls to pick up other ideas. You generally want to use something that will do the job and allow the set to last a long, long time.

Do you need cue insurance?

Once you get into owning expensive cues, you need to consider insuring them in case of any kind of loss.

Start by talking with your homeowner's insurance agent and get a verification that your cues are covered no matter where you take them. This includes places wherever you play, such as your home, car, pool halls, bars, other people's homes, tournaments, and anywhere you go for a game or match.

If you keep your sticks in a cue locker at your pool hall, check if the business provides any coverage in case of burglary, fire, etc. They will probably not have such coverage, but it doesn't hurt to ask. At the very least, it will remind the owners that they need to advise the users of cue lockers that there is no insurance coverage for cues in lockers. Keep in mind, that in the pool hall itself, the owners are not responsible for any type of loss or damage.

If you have a collection of significant value, you will want to get collection insurance. These are insurance policies that cover the value of the specific contents of a collection. The insuring company will require a certain amount of validation and verification.

Regardless of how your cues are insured, you will need to verify their value if something does happen. This means you must have receipts for purchases, pictures, or video. If you happen to pick up a valuable cue from a bet of some kind, a documented history of how you came into possession and some type of appraisal certificate would be useful.

How do you ship cue sticks?

When you need to send a shaft, butt, or the whole stick to be fixed or repaired, you need to select a trustworthy package shipping service. In the USA, many people use the US Postal Service, UPS (United Parcel Service), or Fed-Ex (Federal Express). Other services are available, but these all are well-known.

> **Note:** This can also be used as an alternative to airline baggage, especially if you are paranoid about placing your sticks into the tender care of baggage handlers.

People who ship things regularly will always use the same service until something happens. And when it does, one of the other shippers becomes their preferred provider. All of them usually provide pretty good service within the same country and to other countries. You can talk to several people who have experience to help you decide which one to use.

Each of these services can provide you a shipping container (usually a triangle box or tube into which you will place the pieces to be sent. The triangle box is recommended because it will not easily roll around. Regardless, select the container with the thickest walls.

Insure your contents. While this is optional and the decision is yours, shipping insurance is just that - a financial resolution to a what if situation. If something did happen and you didn't have something - you'll have an example for the rest of your life of what stupid is. Do not over-insure the contents. If something did happen, you will need to prove the value.

Shipping times will vary for the package to arrive, generally based on the cost. Regular shipping will be the cheapest, with 2-3 day shipping being a bit more pricy, and topped out at overnight express. Select the one that fits your requirements.

Packing the sticks requires some attention. The shipping container (triangle box or tube) does not allow excessive use of packing material. This is a recommended process.

1. Roll each piece in a newspaper sheet and hold it in place with a single piece of tape.
2. Wrap each piece in thin bubble wrap, just enough to slide easily into the container.
3. Wrap up the several pieces (if multiple) with enough additional bubble wrap to require a little effort to fit the container.
4. Add your packing slip or note for the recipient and include your address and contact information with the recipient's.
5. Bunch up a little extra bubble wrap to protect each end.
6. Seal the package.
7. Write out the address label and affix to the package.
8. Take to the shipper and send it. Use the tracking number to follow its progress on the web.
9. Send an email to the recipient to provide the tracking number and to confirm the package is in the pipeline.

Here are some don'ts:

- Do not use tape directly on the pieces. Adhesives can leave a mark.
- Do not use a rubber band or tape to keep the pieces together (even over bubble wrapping).
- Do not use Styrofoam peanuts. They have a nasty habit of shedding into small pieces which become very difficult to clean up.
- Do not over pack. You want firm packing to hold the pieces still. Over-packing can split the seams of your container.

Shipping does not have to be a pain to do. As the opportunity arises, pick up the necessary material and place in the back of any convenient closet. Then you'll be ready to ship your sticks as needed.

How should you pack cue sticks for airline baggage?

With the current airline restrictions on all things that could be considered a weapon or even a threat of a weapon, you are unable to carry your cue sticks on the airplane as carry-on baggage. For individuals who have sticks that are more than a little important to them, this restriction has made it more difficult for those who fly to tournaments and other places.

Every once in a while, an airline clerk may "approve" bringing your cue case as carry-on baggage. However, consider this with a grain of salt. TSA and the security checkers have the final word. If you are turned back, you will be stuck trying to get your check-in luggage back to place your stick within its confines.

If you have highly valuable sticks (i.e., $1,000 and up) you may not want to trust the airline baggage process. In this situation, you can have them shipped to the nearest shipping office (Fed-Ex, UPS, DHL, etc. - whichever you trust) or to your hotel to be picked up there when you arrive at your destination. Contact the local office of these shippers to get additional details about packaging, costs, etc.

Here are some suggestions based on what has worked for other people:

- Bring only the minimum number of sticks necessary for your trip.
- Place the cue case, wrapped with clothes, diagonally within a large hard suitcase.
- Purchase a special elongated hard suitcase that will hold one or two cue cases. Add bubble wrap to keep them in place.
- A hockey bag is large enough to hold clothes and your stick cases.
- However packed, place your name, address, phone, and email with the sticks or the case.
- When packed inside your suitcase, use a TSA-approved strap lock to ensure your case is not opened in transit.

What are the dangers of lending out your stick?

If you have spent good money on stick that you are using regularly, you are very careful to use it correctly and well. You take steps to ensure it is well maintained and also stored safety. If you lend the stick out for someone else to use, especially a stranger who expresses an interest, what are some of the things that could go wrong.

- On chalking the tip, the shaft is tapped against the side of the table, putting a ding in the wood.
- On an over-extension, the player slipped and broke the stick across the joint.
- Scratched and dirty ferrule.
- Excessive amounts of talc powder up and down the stick.
- Jumps up on the stroke and dings the shaft on the light fixture.
- Uses it as a break stick and flattens the tip.
- The shaft comes back all sticky.

You can prevent strangers from touching your stick by telling the person of the value of the stick (take the price paid and double it). Something like, "Excuse me, that stick is worth $900. If you want to try it, you need to buy it." This will usually cause the person to hesitate and hand the stick back with care.

As a standard procedure, do not let anyone touch your stick. If you have to leave the table for something, make sure you have a friend keep an eye on your valuables. If you don't, carry your stick with you.

If the request to use your stick comes from a good friend of proven responsibility, it might be OK. There are some people who will treat the property of others with even more care than their own. These are good friends to have.

How can you get stains out of table cloth?

Over the long life of a pool table, there will be times when liquids get spilled on table beds due to carelessness. The liquids may be soda pop, coffee, tea, water, or even (in rare circumstances) cat or dog elimination.

There are several recommended ways to clean most of these stains.

- Spray brake cleaner on a micro fiber towel and scrub the cloth. Rinse with a towel dipped into hot water. Repeat as needed. (Test on a patch of left over cloth.)
- Upholstery repair shop can steam clean the stain, followed by the whole table.
- Pour some lighter fluid on a rag and rub in. Let air dry.

For general cleaning (every 3-4 months for a home table), run a hand vacuum over the table first. Dip a towel in a large bowl of hot water and rub it over the cloth. As the towel temperature cools, re-soak in the hot water and repeat until the entire table is damp to slightly wet. Dump the dirty water down the drain. (No one has ever published the results of how dirty chalk water affects living plants.) This will also tighten up the weave as it dries, giving a faster roll. Let it dry (several hours) and the cloth will look more new.

If you are uncomfortable with cleaning stains or even general cloth cleaning, call your table mechanic. He can perform the necessary procedure while you watch and learn. After you learn once, you are good to go as long as you are responsible for the table's good condition.

How do people abuse pool equipment?

Wherever you find a pool table, you will find that someone at some time has abused the pool equipment to some degree. The vast majority of this is caused by ignorant people using the equipment for things and activities they were not designed to accomplish.

There is not much you can do about past abuse, except use the evidence to point them out to any beginners in your presence and how the damage affects the game for people using the equipment. When you do happen to observe actual abuse, raise your voice in protest (unless you happen to observe the abuse in a biker bar or other area equally dangerous to your life time.)

Cue damage:

- Tapping the shaft against the table edge to knock off excess chalk from the cue tip (that they applied by digging and grinding into the chalk cube).
- Using the sticks for sword play by kids (and child-like adults).
- Placing the stick across the shoulders behind the head and then placing full weight of the arms at each end, which warps the stick.
- Grimy and greasy from players who were eating fried food.
- Left outside in the weather.

Table damage:

- Talc powder in the form of dozens of palm and finger prints.
- Loose cushions from people sitting on the rails.
- Loose or broken side panels caused when people tried to "lift" the table to see how heavy it was.
- Inexpertly applied nails to loose pockets which tear the skin when a hand is inserted.
- Cracked slates sometimes caused by kids jumping up and down on the table. (Once known to occur when a bowling ball fell on top.)
- Cloth tears and rips.
- Tables not leveled by inattention and sometimes by kids stealing the shims.

Ball damage:

- Chips caused by bouncing the balls on cement.
- Chips caused by someone hitting it with a hammer to see if it would break.
- 20+ years of use and the table owner won't replace them.
- Balls used by kids to play catch.

If you are considering buying the table (maybe it's an antique), have a table mechanic check to see if the damage can be repaired and how much it will cost. You can use this as a bargaining point to further knock down the price.

If you know the owner, beg & plead to have at least some of the things fixed.

If the owner is an apartment manager, you will need to get a petition signed by 90% of the residents in order to either repair or replace the table. (If you take up this task, consider it a good way to get introduced to neighbors and possible new friends.) In the worst case where nothing can be done, accept the problems and get on with your games. Any table is better than no table.

Should you own your own set of pool balls?

If you are a casual player who goes down to the pool hall as a once a week league player, or you go to the senior center four times a week to play, or if you are an avid bar table player - nope, don't consider owning your set of pool balls. There is no reason to waste your money, simply because you would never have any place to use them.

On the other hand, if you frequent a pool hall several days a week, or spend more than four hours a week playing pool on decent tables, or study and practice drills from instruction books, you should have your own set of pool balls. And, you should have the best set that you can afford to buy. You want to buy a set that at least matches the quality of balls used in well-maintained pool halls around the world. For the cue ball, get the measles ball with the 6 red spots.

When you do get your own set, you can keep them in their original box as long as the box condition holds up. There are carrying cases of various qualities from the most basic box with handles to tooled leather plush cases with padded cradles.

Keep these balls in the trunk of your car. If you live in an area with below freezing conditions in the winter or above 110 degrees in the summer, it is a good idea to bring them into the house. Otherwise, you can keep them there out of sight but ready to pull out on a moment's notice.

The reasons to have your balls are many:
- Sometimes you are at a pool hall where they don't take good care of the sets. You pick up the house set and place them under the table, then use your own balls.
- Many people have home tables, but for one reason or another, got the cheap set of balls. Bring yours in and you might convince your friend to get a good set.
- Many places such as senior centers, YMCAs, kids camps, hotels, apartments, condos, etc. have tables but the balls are in terrible condition.
- Sometimes you can find a table, but no balls.

Don't forget the simple pride of ownership you get when you bring in a good set to use instead of whatever was there. And there also are the sounds of appreciation and admiration from friends. Your own set of balls in the car is proof of your dedication to playing at your best.

Why are bar table cue balls different?

There are a variety of cue balls with different sizes and weights. When you are playing on a coin-operated table, and a ball goes into the pocket, it stays down until the next set of coins is inserted. To be able to return the cue ball to a player after a scratch, it has to be different from the object balls.

Larger cue ball. When it goes through the sorting mechanism inside the table, it is shunted aside and returned via another tunnel. The same thing happens when the ball is heavier.

Heavier cue balls. The mechanism has a trap that is opened by the weight of the ball and shunts the cue ball away from the regular path. These are very difficult to apply reverse spin (draw). The effort often leads to miscues. Follow sends the cue ball much further than you would expect. After contacting an object ball, the tangent line is difficult to calculate.

Magnetic cue balls. These are usually similar in weight to the object balls. The quality level can vary. Some balls have problems with balance and will slow roll with a slight wobble. Usually, the balls have steel grains mixed with the ball material.

In an attempt to solve these problems, the latest tables do not adulterate the cue ball to return it to the shooter. Several cue balls are provided with the balls. If a cue ball scratches, the incoming shooter grabs one of the extra cue balls and the game continues. If, through horseplay, all the cue balls are scratched away into the pockets, the game gets called on account of "no balls".

When you are in a location with coin operated tables, ask one of the regulars what type of cue ball is used. Always watch a few games before playing yourself. This is not only to understand the local rules, but also to see how the regular shooters adjust their shooting to the cue ball.

What do you consider in a used pool table?

The reasons for buying a table are many. If you are buying it for personal use the room size limits the table size. You might be interested in getting a table (purchase or donation) for a non-profit location (local lodge/legion hall, neighborhood youth center, etc.). You may have found out about it through your personal network (friends, business associates, etc.), a newspaper ad, or just a call received out of the blue. Regardless of your reason for looking at used tables, you are looking at a pool table.

STEP ONE: Taking a look:
- A good rule of thumb on used tables is to consider only name brands, such as Diamond, Olhauser, Brunswick, and other companies known to build high quality tables. Don't buy no-name used tables.
- While considering it, see if you can find out more about the background history of this table. What is its age? Who owned it and where was it set up? How much of the information can be confirmed?

- ALWAYS have a friend along who has decades of playing experience. During his evaluation of the table, pay attention. He can show you and explain what is important about a table.
- If the table is set up, test the ball roll and cushions action. Use the same procedure as you would when competing on a different table.
- If the table is disassembled, come back with a table mechanic to inspect it.

If the table meets all other requirements, provisionally accept the table. Let the owner know that if the table mechanic determines there is more damage than can reasonably be accepted, you will back out.

STEP TWO: Preparing for the move:

- Work out a schedule when the owner, the mechanic, and you can move the table.
- Prepare the room where the table will be setup. This includes picking the specific spot where the table will be placed. If the floor is wood or tile, vacuum and wash the floor. If carpet, vacuum and clean the carpet on the entire room. If setting on a rug, clean it thoroughly.
- Regardless of what type of floor, get some of those furniture floor coasters for the table legs to set on. This helps spread the weight of the table to not damage the floor covering.
- Ensure there is a clear pathway to move the table parts from the mechanic's truck to the room where the table will be set up.

STEP THREE: The actual move:

- Arrive a little early with the agreed upon acquisition cost (payment, barter, tax deductible receipt, etc.).
- When the mechanic begins the disassembly, do not "assist" unless directly asked.
- Once the rails and slate is revealed, the mechanic should check them over, and evaluate their condition and quality. He can then give you a go/no go. (If it's a go, hand over the agreed arrangements.)
- Stay out of the mechanic's way, but do ask questions during the process.
- Watch everything closely so that you will gain the best knowledge.
- At the new location, help only if directly asked by the mechanic.
- Watch closely as the table is assembled so that you can gain an understanding of the process. (If needed, this is when new cloth and rubber would be installed.)
- On completion of the setup, bring your balls out, play for a few minutes, concentrating on slow roll shots so you can verify the levelness.
- Thank the mechanic and make your final payment arrangements.

After the immediate setup, the table will tend to settle a little bit over the next several weeks. The mechanic should be available to make minor readjustments. Two checks are recommended - the first should be in three months. Another check should be made six to eight months after installation. Some mechanics will provide this follow-up service at no charge; others will charge a small fee. Regardless, have it done just for peace of mind.

What are dead cushions?

A cushion is considered dead when the reaction of a ball off the rubber is less than perfect. The speed off the rail is noticeably slower and at a more direct angle out then when the ball went in. A dead rail absorbs ball energy like a sponge. Sometimes you also hear an extra rapping sound because the rubber slaps against the wood part of the rail. A cushion only works well when the rubber is forced tightly up against the wood support.

Causes for dead rails can be:

- The cushion has separated from the wood support (usually only in small areas of a few inches wide). The small strip of wood that forces the rubber against the cushion could have disintegrated.
- The rubber has hardened or softened - usually from age or because it was cheaply made.

Generally, if the affect is minor, you just play around the dead areas and continue your game. However, if the affect is widespread across a rail, it should be fixed. Playing on a table with dead cushions can make your pool playing experience less than enjoyable.

How do you take care of a pool table?

When you assume or take responsibility for maintaining a pool table, there are a number of upkeep jobs that need to be done on a regular basis. If you don't do these, the quality of play on the table will slowly deteriorate until it becomes uncomfortable to play on it.

Several things affect the cloth of the table. One is the spray of chalk that flies off the tip of the cue every time someone strokes the cue ball. Another thing is the constant contact of hands on the cloth which leaves small residues of oils. Another minor factor is dust that settles onto the table after floating around in the air.

Some individuals use a hand held vacuum cleaner to suck up any loose material that has settled into the cloth. Make sure it is on vacuum only and does not use a beater brush which can damage the cloth.

Others like to use the table brush. This is best done after each session that the table is used. Brush from one end of the table to the other, with all strokes in the same direction. Sweep any particles and debris into the pockets. You will need to brush under the cushions. Following that, use a damp rag to pick up loose dust particles.

For the rails, wipe them down to remove fingerprints and skin oils. For plastic cover rails, clean with a cloth sprayed with a counter cleaner. If wood, use a good lemon-based wood cleaner.

NEVERS

- NEVER let anyone near the table with any kind of drink in their hand.
- NEVER let anyone near the table with a lit cigarette or cigar.
- NEVER let anyone play who is eating any kind of chips, snacks, or other finger food. In fact, eating does NOT mix with pool playing. Do not allow people to play in between bites of food.

ALSOs (regularly)

- Wash and clean the set of balls used on the table.
- Clean the inside of the rack.
- Brush down the table at least once a week.

What are the different pool table sizes?

Pocket billiard tables are rectangular in shape, twice as long as wide. Table sizes are usually measured by the playing space inside the cushions. Most table sizes are:

- 3 x 6 - hard to find at a professional quality level (can be custom ordered). Usually made of cheap material for use by younger children (6 to 12). Occasionally, they pop up as antiques. This size was never popular.
- 3.5 x 7 (38" x 76") - the common "bar room" table, because this size is mostly found in bars as coin operated tables. Because space is generally limited, these tables can usually replace a couple of tables and chairs. In bars, these provide a relatively good gross sales per square foot. They can also be found in homes with smaller square foot rooms or in single car garage spaces.
- 4 x 8 home (44" x 88") - this size sells the most of all the sizes. It fits in almost all homes that have a recreation room or a basement.
- 4 x 8 pro (46" x 92") - this size is an excellent compromise between the home size and professional size.
- 4.5 x 9 (50" x 100") - used in professional tournament and pool halls, a long-time serious player who finally gets a home table will only settle for this size.

- 5 x 10 - also known as "monster" tables, this size is hard to find and usually only found as an antique, although they can be custom-ordered new. Learning how to make long shots on this size, makes a 9 footer feel like an 8, and an 8 like a 7. This size is most commonly available as a billiards table (no pockets).

There are also pool tables made in novelty forms, such as circular, square, and hexagonal, even a zig-zag table. Another common table is the bumper pool table, usually found as part of a "combination" table the offers a playing surface for poker, bumper pool, and chess/checkers.

Why should you own your own table?

Note: only a table with a real slate bed and good supporting cross-beams should be considered by any player, regardless of skill.

Advantages:

More practice time. Just step into the pool room, grab a stick and a piece of chalk, throw some balls on the table and away you go.

Cheaper per hour of use. You don't need to pay pool hall rates while using your own table. You can take breaks (take out the garbage, check the mail, etc.), come back a half hour later and pick up where you left off.

All night pool parties with friends. (spouse permitting) Get your buddies together, charge them a case of beer to get into the room, and party hearty.

Disadvantages:

Room use limitations. Once converted to a pool room, there usually isn't much room left for other activities such as foosball, ping pong, even table games (Monopoly, Risk, etc.).

Environmental and table condition differences between home and competitive locations. Unless you purchase a pool hall quality, name brand table (Brunswick, Diamond, Connelly, etc.), your table won't play the same as the pool hall. You can develop awesome banking skills on your table which will not translate to the pool hall. There will be some differences is table roll also.

Less competition available. Unless you have three or four immediate neighbors who are just as dedicated to the Green Game, it will not be easy to locate and schedule gaming times. Not everyone in the world lives to your schedule.

Table burnout. Over time, the table might get less and less use and finally end up being a laundry folding table. When that happens it won't be very long before your spouse will be demanding that you get rid of that silly space hog.

What should you consider when buying a cue?

You can get a decent cue stick in the range of $150 to $400. On looking for your first cue stick, it's always a good idea to talk it over with a friend who has previous experience and has purchased several. Here is the short list of considerations:

Cue butts - these are all about the same. Your only consideration is appearances:

- With/without points
- Wraps (linen, leather, etc.)
- No wrap (wooden handle only)

Joints – there are several options available. Select the one that feels good for you:

- Wood to wood
- Plastic to plastic
- Metal to metal (steel/brass)
- Connectors (different threads)

Shafts – you have a lot of options. It is rare to find a warped stick. Consider the use for the shaft – shooting or breaking. If for breaking, purchase one from a known manufacture. If for shooting, you have many options, such as:

- Maple (straight grain, curly, birds eye)
- Exotic woods (custom cue maker)
- High tech (laminated, composite, etc.)

Other factors are:

- Weight (16-22 oz)
- Shaft thickness (9-14mm)
- Tip (soft, medium, hard)

You want a combination that feels good in your hands as you make contact with the cue ball with both slow and fast stick speeds. Generally, you will know within three or four strokes if a stick is not right for you. Narrow down acceptable sticks to two or three, then compare those one after the other.

Try out as many sticks as are available (at least 6). Test each twice. From this, select two or three that feels good. Go back and forth between these final cut sticks, shooting at various speeds. Eventually, you will select one that fits you. This works for your first personal stick.

Over time, try out sticks owned by friends and buddies. Talk with them to see what they like about their sticks. This helps improve your ability to judge and evaluate stick choices and options. Experience is your best teacher.

Should you buy a custom cue?

The biggest advantage to getting a custom cue is that it is built to your specifications. Here is a list of custom elements that will make a stick unique:

- Balance and weight - the balance can be shifted forward or back as needed. Weights can be embedded into the joint or into the butt of the stick.
- Shape - you can have the butt shaped with turnings per your custom design and pattern.
- Butt wood and shaft wood - you can select from a huge variety of exotic woods, including ebony, tulipwood, cocobolo, birds eye maple, zebrawood, and dozens of others.
- Inlays & rings - these can be made in hundreds of designs in a variety of woods, mother of pearl, turquoise, even silver and gold.
- Points - you can have multiple points of multiple patterns with unique sequences of exotic woods.
- Length - the length can be customized to your height, and the joint placed for a longer or shorter shaft.
- Type and placement of wrap - this can be Irish linen, regular or exotic leather, other material, or no wrap.
- Ferrules - the materials used can be ivory or special fibers in various lengths.
- Tips - there are hundreds of tips of various hardness levels and types (layered or one piece) made from a wide variety of materials.
- Joints - select from any of the several common joints, made from different materials or even a wood-to-wood joint.

With this level of customizable complexity, production cue makers are unable to offer much variety. They can provide a selection of different lines of cues with options, such as different weights, points, and a few selections of lengths. With a custom cue maker, you can get as picky as you want.

To locate a cue maker, talk to several individuals who have custom cues and ask why they selected their maker. Talk about the costs, the flexibility, and turnaround times. If you decide to check out a couple, send them email and ask your questions. It doesn't hurt to ask to see any completed cues they may have. You might find something you like. If you are satisfied with the quality work, the next question is to check out the turnaround time. The really good cue makers are usually booked for a couple of years.

You can look for someone who is local (within 50 miles). Even if cue-making is a hobby or part-time, he will take pride in his work. Much of his business will probably be cue repair and tip replacement. But he will have the equipment for manufacturing a custom job for you. Talk with him.

A local maker will be available to fix any problems that come up, or handle routine maintenance. He will also be able to take a look at your playing styles and make suggestions on specifications.

Mainly, you want a stick you are proud to take out of your case and have others crowding around drooling over various elements of your prize. With a great stick, you can believe that your game will improve dramatically.

Whoever becomes your cue maker will have an almost fanatic desire to make sticks that reflect their personal sense of craftsmanship. Workmanship and multiple levels of quality control are hallmarks of his work. They will stand behind their work and are always available to fix anything that goes wrong.

You might decide to become a cue collector. You can collect cues based on styles, inlays, exotic woods, cue maker, or any parameters you find acceptable. Depending on your requirements, this can become expensive. But the love of conversing with other collectors and the process of hunting down a specific cue, combined with the bargaining can be exciting.

Do you need a jump cue?

A jump cue is designed to make it easier to bounce the cue ball over an object ball and hit the target ball. It is shorter and light weight when compared to a regular cue. And it does make a jump easier and more controllable.

When a shooter decides to jump a ball (some pool halls forbid this and masse shots), the stick must be significantly elevated and precise force applied to drive the cue ball into the table and force a bounce (the height and distance are dependent on controlled speed and cue ball contact). If the venue that you play in allows jump shots, you may want to invest in a good jump cue.

Keep in mind that you must still learn how to control the jump, in height and distance and speed. If you are willing to spend a few months working on jump balls for about 20 minutes a day or so, then you should get one. If you are good at kicking to rails to make contact with the required object ball, or you don't want to invest the time at this point in your shooting career, put the money into a spare shaft.

Several cue manufacturers make a combination break and jump cue. You will need to try these and see if they meet your requirements.

Do you need a break cue?

For the majority of pool players, whether you need a break cue is more of a matter of do you want one? Being able to get a great spread with the greatest changes of pocketing a ball will require some separate practice time. This means racking and re-racking the balls as you experiment around with various stances, body positions, and follow-through.

This development time can be spent with any house cue until you have started to gain some capabilities and control. That is when you should get a break stick. Until you are willing to setup and break about 200-300 racks to work on your breaks, there is no need to spend the money.

When/if you decide a break cue is necessary, try out a number of sticks used by other individuals. Selecting a break cue is highly dependent on personal preferences. The best way to see what you like before you commit the bucks is to see which of the many types are comfortable for you. There are several manufacturers that have a combination break and jump cue. If you get a chance, try these out to see if these can be beneficial.

Generally, these are available as production sticks, which helps keep their costs within reason. (Rarely is a break stick custom made.) It is only a matter of trying several out until you find one you like. You will also need a cue case that can hold your regular playing cue and the new break stick (and an extra shaft or two).

Do you need a shooting glove?

A shooting glove covers the bridge hand. It is used to ensure that the cue shaft will slide easily back and forth until the stroke is made. A glove helps reduce the effects of humidity, sweaty hands, and the build-up of dirt on the shaft. Any of these cause can cause skips and jerks on your stroke. And, anything that grabs your attention and takes your mind off the flow of the stroke will decrease the chances of success.

Using a glove also reduces or removes the need to use talc powder to have a smooth cue shaft. This also helps ensure you are constantly playing on a clean table, rather than a cloth covered with hand patterns and powder sprinkles.

Some individuals do not use the glove because they feel it interferes with the slick smoothness of the wood shaft. Their counter to the dirty shaft is more attention to keeping their hands clean and keeping the shaft smooth. Others will not use a glove because they think it is somewhat counter-gender. In some places, that might be the case, and the use of a glove would cause some commentary from the unwashed masses. Some who use the glove in the same circumstances care primarily for the comfort and couldn't care less about the opinions of others.

Occasionally, you will see someone wearing two gloves. Their reason usually is because they can be right and left handed and don't want the trouble of switching the glove from one hand to another hand.

There are a lot of choices in glove colors. Many people will use a glove that matches their favorite color. The more serious players will usually use black. It hides chalk color picked up from the table cloth, and has a low distraction affect.

Gloves will usually wear out on a finger or at the heel of the palm, just from the interaction with the table cloth. Chalk can also act as an abrasive to break down the threads. A well-used glove has a life expectancy of a few weeks.

What about using those screw-on cue tips?

Only the very cheapest cues will have screw-on tips. If you are getting a cue for the very first time and you really don't know what you want, these cheap cues can at least provide you with an experience on what to avoid in the future. Two main problems are:

- The tips are very soft and quickly mushroom.
- After several cue ball hits, the screw tends to loosen. Miscuing is easy to do.

This type of stick could only be found attractive by first-time cue buyers who do not have any one available to mentor them. A decent inexpensive cue will be at least 10 times the cost of the cheapie screw-on tip stick.

There is only one circumstance under which it might be useful to have such a cheap cue. When you are first getting started, you need to build up hundreds and hundreds of strokes. You can do this at home with this type of stick, and some tennis balls on a table covered with a blanket.

With these tools, you can begin to get comfortable with a bridge and moving the stick back and forth in a straight line. With the tennis balls, you can shoot them to a backstop at the other end of the table, shoot one ball into another and try to get the second ball to hit a target on the backstop. With this, at no cost, a newbie can stabilize the basic fundamentals.

If you are tall, can you get a longer cue stick?

The standard cue stick is 57" to 58". This is the common standard for sticks around the world. For 85-90% of the people this is no problem. But if you are "overly" tall, you end up holding the butt of the stick a lot closer to the butt then your shorter competitors. If you had a longer stick, the balance would feel better. And of course, when you have to stretch a bit, the longer stick allows you an even greater reach.

How much of an extension you want, depends partially on your height. One person is 6 feet, five inches and has a stick that is 67 inches long. Watching him shoot from a distance, you don't realize his stick is extended. Only when the sticks are compared side to side do you realize the difference.

There are several ways to make a stick longer. Among them is a slide-down stick extender, designed to make your stick 8 to 12 inches longer. Another option is to have a local cue maker craft a short extension (2" to 8") to be attached to the end of the cue butt. It would use a standard joint. When you assemble your stick, you put together three pieces instead of two.

You will need to give the cue butt to the cue maker and a joint can be created to accomplish this. It may or may not closely match colors, but it ensures you have a stick that will fit your height.

A longer stick has a slightly different balance point. The extension adds a few ounces. The cue maker can remove some of the weight by drilling out wood from inside of the extension.

How can dings be removed from a cue shaft?

The information is provided on a provisional basis. These are designed for dings (very small indentations), not dents in wood shafts. There is no assurance these will work for your specific shaft. They have been used by others, which is why they are provided here.

- At your kitchen sink, turn on the hot water as hot as possible. Wet a wash cloth and quickly wring out (use rubber gloves if too hot). With the ding turned face up, drape an inch or so of the wash cloth over the shaft. Keep it there for 90 seconds. Slide your finger across the ding to see if the wood has come up. If not, repeat. Some wood will require 3 or 4 applications. Dry vigorously with a clean hand towel.
- On a dampened cloth, run a steam iron over until the material is hot. Immediately place the cloth over the ding and leave until the cloth cools down (2-3 minutes). Check the ding, and repeat if needed.
- Microwave a 1/2 cup of water to boiling. Fold up a small piece of tissue and drop in the water. Use tweezers to put the tissue on the ding and press into place. Check a couple of minutes later, repeat as needed.
- Set the shaft with the ding facing up. Use an eye dropper to place one drop of water on the ding. Wait two hours. Dry overnight.
- Microwave a 1/2 cup of water to boiling. Use an eye dropper to place one drop on the ding. Wait 5 minutes and check. Repeat as needed.
- Dampen a small area of a paper towel; use your thumb to vigorously rub it across the ding for about 5 minutes. Repeat as needed.

How do you clean the cue shaft?

Here are a number of options that have been used by players for a long time. Some individuals do not recommend one or more of these; others swear that their preference is the only and best cleaning solution. Do not apply any of the abrasives or pore fillers on fiberglass, graphite, or laminate cue shafts.

- Scotch Brite green scouring pad - this is a slightly abrasive pad that you wrap firmly around the cue shaft and vigorously move up and down. When done, flick the pad against a chair or table to knock out the dust. It is cheap and makes the shaft very smooth. It will eventually (10-20 years or so of daily use) reduce a shaft's width.
- Damp paper towel - this is good for a light level of dirt. Make sure to follow up with a dry paper towel to remove any moisture.
- Rub with a pad soaked in alcohol, then seal with a pad lightly soaked with lighter fluid - do this at home where you can sit down and do a proper job.
- Extra-fine 1000-grit sandpaper - cleans well without taking much wood away.
- Micro-fiber towel - best used to clean the shaft when your hands are a little sweaty. When dirty, just throw in the laundry.
- Brown paper bag - fold around the shaft and rub vigorously (seals wood pores with a waxy additive in the paper).
- Dollar bill - fold around the shaft and rub vigorously (transfers the printed oil-based inks into the wood pores).
- Pumice hand cleaner - use primarily to remove chalk that is embedded into a wooden shaft.
- Leather pad.
- Commercial products - there are a number of shaft cleaners available that have a good reputation for doing the job.

Check among other regular shooters and try whatever they are using. Some individuals have reasons not to use one or more of these.

Why is chalk necessary?

Pool chalk comes in small cubes. It is applied as a thin layer to the cue tip. When contact is made between the cue tip and the cue ball, chalk helps "grab" the cue ball and keeps the tip from slipping around the ball, causing a miscue. It is important that the layer be thin and even.

Hitting the cue ball after applying chalk also flings the chalk dust/powder in a thin spray across the table. If you were to use red chalk on a green or blue table, you can easily see just how much of the chalk falls off the cue tip after contact. If you watch serious players play competitively, you will notice that they will consistently chalk the cue tip before every shot. On the other hand, watching bar bangers play makes you think that they are unaware that chalk exists.

Don't grind the chalk onto the tip. Feather the chalk cube across the tip using multiple strokes as you slowly turn your stick. Actually look at the tip to ensure you have successfully chalked it and that the chalk is evenly applied across the whole surface of the tip. Do this before every shot. Properly chalked tips prevent miscues.

Chalk is made from a silicate compound. Different companies have different formulas. Do not purchase inexpensive chalk. You will not get consistent results. Chalk comes in many different colors from tan to red to black. The most common color used is blue. Select a color that will not stain or discolor the table cloth. For a tan cloth, use tan chalk. For red cloth, use red chalk.

Most serious players carry their own chalk in a holder of one style or another. They make a habit of reaching for their own chalk rather than any cubes that are provided by the house. Far too often, cubes have a deep pit, that when use, also applies chalk to the ferrule of your cue - a messy business.

What sizes and shapes of cue tips are available?

A cue tip is sized to fit the width of the ferrule. The ferrule (and by extension, the shaft) can be from 9mm to 14mm in diameter. Snooker cues generally use the smaller tips 9-11 and regular pool sticks use 12-15. Variations are dependent of user preference for the cue shaft width, i.e., 12.25mm, 12.50mm, 12.75mm.

Cue tip shapes are dome-shaped, in order to contact as much material as possible with the cue ball during the stroke. The size of the shape is usually calculated by the shape of a coin. The most common shapes are dime or a nickel outline. Some people like an even small curve and shape their tips to a quarter outlines.

The smaller, thinner shafts with the correspondingly smaller width (9mm to 10.5 mm) will have the tip with the dime shape. You will see such thin shafts most often used in Snooker. A few players will have thin shafts on their pool sticks because of personal preference. The majority of pool sticks use the larger diameters with the tip curved to the nicked width.

Because there are so many custom widths for shafts, the tip manufacturers make all of their sizes in millimeter increments. You can get a 13 mm or a 14 mm, but not a 13.75 mm. To make this work, a 14 mm tip is mounted on the shaft, and then shaved or abraded away until the tip matches with width of the ferrule.

Why does a new cue tip flatten after a few shots?

When you first put a new tip on your cue, there is a certain amount of "breaking in" that occurs, even with the harder tips. When hitting the cue ball at top speeds, a lot of pressure is focused in the tip material. This compresses the tip material and flattens the curve of the tip. Instead of a nickel shape, it looks like a silver dollar shape – flat and barely curved. This, of course, does not help you when applying spin to the cue ball. The flatter curve tends to make it quite easy to miscue.

Sometimes the flattening is caused because the tip material is too soft. This is quickly noticeable. After just a few strokes, the edges of the tip start spilling over the edge of the ferrule. The term for this is mushrooming. The tip must be dressed (reshaped) immediately; otherwise you increase the chances of a miscue.

Some tips will compress quickly simply because they are too cheap. Cost of tips is an excellent indicator of quality. The businesses that manufacture tips will often have several soft cue tips. There are a number of players who subscribe to the idea that the process of mushrooming and trimming the tip over a period of time results in an excellent quality tip with very good playing features.

The selection of your tip will depend on your personal preferences. There are tips that range across a variety of different hardness characteristics. There are single layer, multiple layer and of many different kinds of material. Prices can range for a few dollars to $50 each. Whichever one you select as your standard, make sure you understand ahead of time what will be required to maintain it in shooting conditions.

When should you change cue tips?

The tip on your shooting shafts gets worn away little by little. Every time you apply chalk (especially if you do so viciously), there is a gradually wearing away of the tip material. This is also the continuous tip reshaping and roughing with various tip tools. When the tip edge wears down to a narrow side band of a millimeter or so above the ferrule, the tip should be replaced. The tip can also be replaced at whim.

If you want to experiment with several tips, it's not that difficult to pop one tip off, prepare the surface of the ferrule and glue another tip on. A few serious players have tried out a dozen or more tips over a month to check out and select a tip that has the proper personal feel. If you want to do this, purchase several different tips to test. Place each one on your shaft and play with it for a week or two. Then repeat with another tip. Over a couple of months you should find one that you like. Put it on and proceed with your playing career.

After the tip is installed, shape into the nickel or dime curve that you prefer. In a couple of weeks, a softer tip will spread out over the edges of the ferrule. Trim it and do any necessary reshaping as soon as you notice it. It will take a month or two for a medium tip to show signs of spreading. A hard tip may spread slightly over the first month or two. To trim a mushroom (however small), there are several cue tip tools that can do the job.

Replacing your own tip does take some practice in order to get the tip properly centered. If the tip is oversized, it will need to be trimmed down even with the ferrule. If you change tips only once every year or so, get the mid-priced tools. If you change tips regularly to try out new models, it is worthwhile to get the more expensive tools.

At the pool hall, there is usually someone who handles all the tip replacements for the regulars. This individual is an excellent source of information on tips both good and bad. Also talk with the regulars. Their decades of experience can provide many ideas and suggestions on various tips.

What kinds of cue tips are available?

There are a lot of companies that produce a variety of tips ranging from soft to hard. Most tips are made out of pressed leather using various tanning techniques.

Layered tips have become popular in the last decade. These are multiple thin layers of leather, compressed under very high pressure. These tips have various supporters and detractors.

Another tip that has seen more exposure is the phenolic tip that is available as a tip and as a tip/ferrule one piece. This is a high-tech plastic and is commonly available on a break/jump cue.

When you decide to try out a different tip, talk with individuals who repair cues. Long-time players are another source of information on tips. They have a history of experience on what they like and don't like. These individuals can recommend something that fits your expectations. And, if you are properly respectful, they will even let you try out their sticks with the tips they are recommending. Prices for tips can range from less than a dollar to $50.

What cue accessories are useful?

When you are assembling your cue case contents, besides your sticks you will need a few accessories. These items are necessary to ensure that pool playing time is not interrupted. Most of your minor problems can be fixed by pulling out one of these accessories.

Here are a few items that are useful to have available:

- Cue tip shaper tool - A cue tip can become misshapen during normal use, which can create some real problems in getting a consistent hit. The tool will shape the tip so it is playable.
- Tip tapper/roughing tool - As you constantly hit balls; the cue tip hardens from the constant impressions. This creates a problem in holding chalk. Without a well-chalked tip, many shots risk the chance of a miscue. The tool roughs up the tip surface, making it easier to hold chalk and avoid those embarrassing cue mistakes.
- Cue glove - Many people do not use a cue glove, believing its use is somewhat girlish. The glove ensures the cue shaft will easily slide back and forth. This eliminates distractions caused by minor imperfections in the shaft. (Have an extra as a spare.)
- Scotch green scrubbing pad - Over time, the cue shaft picks up oils from your hands which attract dirt. This can make the shaft a little rough and noticeable even through a glove. The pad is the equivalent of 1000 grit sandpaper. Wrap the pad around the shaft and pull it up and down vigorously until you feel warmth through the pad. Take the pad and flick it with your finger to knock out the dust and dirt. Store it in your case for the next time.
- Microfiber towel - Use this to keep your hands dry during your games. It can also be used to give your stick a quick rub-down.
- Chalk holder – a couple extra chalk cubes in a plastic bag.
- Cue holder – only needed it you use two sticks (regular and break).
- Small notepad and pen – to write down anything that comes to mind.

There are many other tools and accessories that can be added to this basic list. Whether you include them is a personal preference.

You can add an entire suitcase of items if you are so included. Several individuals do this. In a small carry-all, they include the several training aids, books, and DVDs with a small DVD player. These are kept in the trunk. If entering a pool hall for practice time, they bring the bag in with their cue base. They get a distant table and settle down to work on what is important at the time. If they are going to pool hall to play, the carry-all is left in the car, and they walk in with only their cue case.

What is a cue extension?

There are shots when the cue ball is mid table and you must aim it towards a ball at the opposite short rail. If you are a tall person, the shot might not be difficult to stretch out and shoot. If you are a shorter individual, you can't stretch your bridge hand out far enough to get a stable bridge for your shaft. The cue just isn't long enough to hold the cue butt steady for a trustworthy stroke.

Normally, when a shot is just outside of the comfort zone for a normal stance, you have a choice of two options. You can stretch out and attempt to force the shot with a longer bridge, grasping the stick near the butt for an uncomfortable shooting position. Or, you can get the mechanical bridge out and set up a more stable stance, which may be somewhat uncomfortable because of the lack of familiarity.

Both options have drawbacks. The stretched out body for the stroke is an invitation to the billiard gods to make you do a miscue. Yet, so many players simply refuse to make the necessary adjustment to use this tool to reach the far away locations on the table.

There is a tool that helps when the cue ball is just at the uncomfortable stretching distance. The cue extension attaches to the butt end of your stick and increases your reaching distance from 6 to 24 inches. You will still have a longer bridge, but you can control the butt of your cue with a normal grip. This gives you sufficient control to treat the shot as a near-normal effort.

There are a number of cue extension devices that are available on the market. Some slip onto the cue butt. Another type slides down the cue shaft to the butt and then telescopes out to a substantial distance. Several cue companies make an extender device that is screwed into the end of their sticks. Some cue makers can create a stick extender to make a longer 3-piece cue.

Regardless of which type of extension device you use, it would be beneficial to practice shooting the shots that require its use. This provides some assurance that you can play an accurate shot with proper cue ball spin and speed.

Teaching & learning

What is the ghost ball aiming technique?

There are approximately 4 or 5 aiming techniques in common use, and another 3 or 4 more esoteric choices. The easiest to understand and the most commonly used aiming technique is also the simplest to learn - the "ghost ball" technique.

The concept is simple. If two object balls were perfectly lined up to the pocket, all you need to do is shoot straight at the first ball and the second ball will go into the pocket.

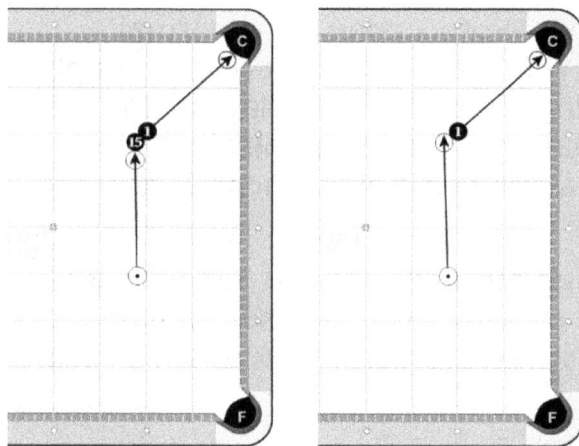

To aim at the object ball, just imagine the first ball (a ghost) is in perfect position as the example above, and shoot straight at the ghost ball to make the object ball.

That's all there is. Align your body up on the line from the object ball to the pocket. Use your imagination to drop the ghost ball into position. Walk back to your cue ball and set up for the shot. Keep your eyes on the ghost ball (so it doesn't disappear on you). When perfectly aligned, shoot straight at the ghost ball. The only reason to miss the shot would be because you imagined the ghost ball in the wrong position.

Are you right eye or left eye dominant?

Eye dominance means that (generally) one eye takes in the majority of the scene you are looking at with the other eye being used to identify depth of field (how far away things are).

When you bend down for a shot, your head aligns above the stick and you utilize your eyes to draw the imaginary aiming line. Eye dominance affects the placement of that aiming line. When the dominant eye is off to one side of vertical, the imaginary line gets skewed. This messes up the accuracy of your aiming line. The closer your dominant eye is to a vertical position over the aiming line, the more accurate your shots will be.

To help identify if one eye is dominant, hold your index finger up at arm's length. Identify an object further away and place your finger over it and focus on the finger. Close the left eye. If the finger moves to one side of the object, the left eye is dominant.

If the finger does not move, your right eye is dominant. That is the eyeball you want to place over your cue stick for best aiming results. Shift your head position to the side accordingly.

If the finger moves slightly, try it again with the right eye closed. If the finger again moves only slightly, you have no dominant eye. Place your head directly centered over the cue stick for best aiming accuracy.

How do you use a mechanical bridge?

The mechanical bridge is a cue stick with a frame that is used to allow the player to reach out for a shot that is difficult to reach. Grooves on the frame allow you to select the appropriate height necessary for the stroke.

Here is the basic procedure:

1. Place the cue stick on top of one of the slots on the bridge's frame and parallel with the stick.
2. Lift up both sticks and place the mechanical bridge down in a position close to the cue ball (and that does not touch other balls).
3. Lift up the cue stick in your dart throwing hand. With the left hand adjust the position of the mechanical bridge to about 4 to 7 inches from the cue ball.
4. Lay the mechanical bridge stick down on the table (again, not touching any other balls). Use your opposite hand to press down the bridge stick firmly onto the table.
5. Holding your cue like you would throw a dart, swing your elbow up to be parallel with the stick. Bend down as necessary to place your cue butt underneath your chin.
6. Follow the whole pre-shot routine. Watch the cue tip to make sure it does not wobble side to side on the practice strokes.
7. When ready, make your stroke a smooth effort at the pre-planned speed.

Many people will do the weirdest things to avoid using this shooting tool. This indicates a serious lack of skill. If you see them performing these gyrations, set up a number of similar shots just for the entertainment value. This weakness in their skills that be used to your advantage.

If you do not want to be the guest performer of these physical comedy routines for the audience of rail birds, practice using the mechanical bridge. About once a month, play several games of 9 Ball or 8 Ball using only the mechanical bridge.

Should you use an open or closed bridge?

There are proponents of both styles of bridges. The open bridge allows an unobstructed view of the shaft for aiming purposes. The closed bridge ensures that the stick will not deflect when hitting the cue ball out from the center.

In snooker, with the smaller balls and thinner cue shafts, the open bridge helps aiming at balls up to 12 feet away into pockets a fraction of the size of regular pool tables. All of their shots with and without spin use the same open bridge and long, down the barrel, aiming process.

In pocket billiards, professional level players use a mix of both styles. The majority use a closed bridge. In almost all of the instructional books and videos that are introduction guides to playing, the most recommended bridge is the closed bridge. Part of the reason for this is to ensure that the cue shaft goes forward in a controlled line.

For pocket billiards, it is very useful to be comfortable with both bridges. You will find that an open bridge is useful for long, far away shots. When executing a shot with higher than normal speeds, the closed bridge provides assurances that you can keep the stick continuing with a proper follow-through. For other shots that need a firm delivery, the closed bridge also helps to restrict the path of the shaft.

Which bridge you use will depend on your experience with the open and closed bridges. Even within these two options, you have individual variations that you find useful for your own needs. To get comfortable with both types of bridges, simply shoot lots of shots with both styles.

How does an instructor use a video camera to help you?

In every stroke, your stick forearm comes forward to make the cue tip contact the cue ball. The quality of a player is determined by the precision on where the cue ball is contacted by the tip and the precision of the stick speed.

If you are going to learn how to get more and more precise, request the services of a good instructor who uses a video camera. He can videotape you making various shots, and then point out areas of improvement. The video camera provides the concrete evidence that makes you more aware of your stroke movements.

The instructor will set up several shots for you to shoot. Then he sets up the camera angle. He will set the F-Stop to in a range 1/100 to 1/250. Although this darkens the picture somewhat, each individual video frame will be less blurred. When you view the video immediately after shooting, each frame can be viewed one at a time.

This is not a small project to learn about the reality of your skills. There are many shots that will need evaluation. There are several types of shots include:

- Normal speed shots (medium bridge) - center ball, follow, draw, left and right side spin.
- Normal speed shots (long bridge) - center ball, follow, draw, left and right side spin.
- Slow roll shots (short bridge) - center, follow, draw (drag shot).
- Nip shots (very short bridge) - center ball, follow, draw, left and right side spin.

- Break shots (long bridge) - center ball, follow, draw, left and right spin (use a 1/500 F-Stop with bright lighting).

Each of these shots should be closely monitored by your instructor and recorded on video. This could take several sessions. But, if you are REALLY serious about mastering speed and spin, make a listing of shots that you consider important. Prioritize them and begin the videotaping process. Record each shot 10 times (helps you get over camera shyness). Consider videotaping from a couple of different camera angles.

When you have spent an hour recording these shots, plug the camera into the TV and start with your analysis. The instructor can identify your worst fundamentals. Jointly agree on what should be practiced for the next week or two between scheduled coaching lessons.

Alternately, have your most common shots videotaped and dissect these with your instructor. Focusing on improving basics will get you the most immediate results. This process might take months, but will have the quickest and fastest payoff in skill improvements.

Break strokes could require several of these taping sessions as you experiment with the several dozen ways that breaks can be played. Following that, a video tune-up once a year will keep you sharp.

The key to mastering any cue ball stroke is to know what you want and know the stroke that gets the results you anticipate. The closer you can bring reality to your fantasy, the better player will be.

How to check your stroke for flaws?

Use either a measles ball or a striped ball for these checks on your stroke. For all these exercises, use five balls and shoot them with Set up these with five balls. Shoot five balls on the vertical center line with a 12:00 hit, one tip above center.

First set of observations (medium slow speed)

Look for a ball roll that is off to one side of vertical. If so, you are not hitting true vertical.

Set up a normal 6-8 inch bridge.

- On a 12:00 stroke, observe the roll of the ball (true vertical or not).
- On a stun stroke, observe the roll of the ball (true slide for the first part, then a true vertical roll or not).
- On a 6:00 stroke, observe the roll (true vertical spin backwards or not. After table roll takes over, true vertical or not).

Set up a longer bridge, about 12-15 inches. Repeat the ball rolling observations.

- On a 12:00 stroke, observe the roll of the ball (true vertical or not).
- On a stun stroke, observe the roll of the ball (true slide for the first part, then a true vertical roll or not).
- On a 6:00 stroke, observe the roll (true vertical spin backwards or not, after table roll takes over, true vertical or not).

If you notice a slight angle on each roll, shift your head over to one side and reshoot the balls. Generally, this will straighten out the roll and it will tell you that you need to groove in the new head position as part of your pre-shot routine.

Second set of observations (medium speed)

Look where the cue tip stops at the end of the stroke. Check for consistency in the final stopping position. Does the tip stop in the air or close to the table? If in the air, then you are dropping your elbow before you hit the cue ball. If on or close to the table, then you are holding your elbow in place after you hit the cue ball.

- Set up for a normal 6-8" bridge. After the stroke, observe where the cue tip is positioned.
- Set up a longer bridge, about 12-15 inches. Observe the cue tip position.

Is the stick pointing in line from the start of the stroke, or at an angle from the line? If in line, then your forward momentum matches the start of your stroke. If off line, then you are either turning your wrist on the forward stroke, or crossing the line from one side to the other with your lower arm.

Are you consistently stopping each stroke with the same length of cue shaft? If not, start overshooting your stroke to reach the limit of your reach. After a week of intentional over stroke, cut back to a natural stroke. The distance will have evened out.

Final exercise: This will force you to develop a true back and forth stroke.

1. Place a row of balls about 8-9 inches from the short rail cushion. Set up for the shot with the cue stick riding on the rail.
2. Use only your bridge index finger to guide the shaft. With a medium slow speed, shoot the balls into the far corners with no side roll. (Make sure you are ending the stroke with the cue tip riding the cloth.)
3. Shoot the next sets without using a finger guide until you are comfortable.
4. Shoot the next sets at a higher speed with no finger guiding. If you see the balls tilting to one side, return to slower speeds.
5. Place an object ball down the table and use the same stroke (no finger guide) to shoot the object ball into the far corner pocket.
6. Repeat this exercise once a week for six months.

7. Repeat the above two sets of observations once a month to verify good stroke fundamentals.

By following these exercises, you can verify your stroke fundamentals. Any variations are easily identified and corrections immediately applied to make you a better shooter.

What are the fundamentals of a stroke?

The definition of "fundamentals" in the dictionary reads like this:
a basic principle, rule, law, or the like, that serves as the groundwork of a system; essential part: to master the fundamentals of a trade.

In the "trade" of pocket billiards, there are a number of essential parts, each of which includes basic principles. When put together you have the groundwork of the system of playing more effectively.

Stance

You must have a shooting platform from which your battles against the world are launched. This starts with the placement of your feet. Your entire body mass must be well distributed and balanced. Without that stability, any movement elsewhere in your body will move something else, forcing you off balance.

As you bend over your stick, it needs to rest lightly upon your bridge hand. This means that your stick hand should be gripping the cue stick just in back of the balance point. The cue stick should also be as close to parallel to the table bed as possible.

As the stick moves forward and backward, propelled by your stick arm, the cue tip should be a true back and forth movement with no wobbling side to side. The shaft should not drag on the fingers of your bridge hand. Below your elbow is where the only major action of your body should take place on a stroke. Up to the contact of the tip on the ball, only the forearm moves. Any other body movement is detrimental to the stroke.

Your head and eyes must be aligned above the cue so that the aiming line can be imagined properly. There are thousands of words written about dominant eye alignment, chin height, and so on. It is enough to know that the head position is the visual input that your brain needs to determine calculate the aiming line that the cue ball will travel. If it is off to one side that skews your viewpoint which provides wrong information to the brain.

Stroke

The stroke is the physical action taken to get the cue ball moving on the table. All ball movement that occurs on the table can only occur by the single very momentary contact between the cue tip of your stick and the cue ball.

The key to successful stroking is the precise placement of the tip on the cue ball and the speed of the contact, followed by the follow-through. From that contact, the cue ball travels down the table, contacts the object ball. Whatever laws of physics that you applied will determine how the cue ball acts until it finally comes to rest. Everything else is the consequences of that action.

Brain

The brain is used in two ways. One part contains the automated activities necessary to accomplish a shot. Among these are the necessary body positions for every type of shot that have been learned from countless thousands of repetitive efforts. (This is why it is so hard to learn a new body position change - it has to constantly fight the established habits. Only when you have forced the new change over the top of those by another set of thousands of efforts can you successfully make the change.)

The second part contains the history of every shot you have ever taken along with its success or failure. This is your Shot Library. When calculating the different ways of shooting the shot, you are actually sorting through every similar shot you have ever made. Your library is trying to find the closest set of related patterns to the current situation. When you have a situation with no previous experience, you have to cut and paste other experiences into something that is worth a try. Upon execution, that shot and its results become a part of your history.

Summary

Stance, Stroke, and Brain are the three fundamental basics of your game. When these are integrated together into a functioning operation, you have the basis to become the shooter you deserve to be. To further improve your skills, focus on smaller and smaller pieces of these basics.

For example, to improve your draw, focus on a smooth stroke aimed at a precise point on the cue ball. When you can execute the shot consistently, you can have trustworthy results. With positive feedback from practices, you learn how to draw the cue ball back to pre-determined positions.

Improve any of these fundamentals by working out what needs to be changed and then practicing that improvement until you own it. Bit by bit, you can get better every day.

How do shoot one-handed?

Knowing how to do this is not a critical playing skill. It can be a useful skill that can cause your opponent to believe you are a much better player – basically scare him a little. It is a handy skill for situations where a mechanical bridge is difficult to use.

When you learn how to shoot one handed, you game will improve. This is because while you are learning, one of the benefits is the development of a smooth stroke with proper follow-through. The learning process also teach you the importance of focusing on very small movements.

Here is how to get started:

1. Bridge hand resting on the cloth (not touching the shaft).
2. Bridge hand not touching anything (some people recommend holding it behind your back).
3. Use of rails to slide the shaft (no touching the shaft)

Here is the process for shooting at a cue ball out in the table:

1. Stand behind the cue ball in the same way you do on a regular shot.
2. Hold the stick between your thumb and first two fingers just enough behind the balance point to let the tip fall downwards slightly.
3. Bend forward a little bit and line up the shot.
4. Hold the stick a couple of inches back from the cue ball where you want to contact it.
5. Focus on making sure that the stick is steady.
6. Stroke the shot using only your arm movement. (Keep the body still.)

In the process of learning to control the one handed stroke, begin with straight in shots on a half table. Work your way through angled shots. Increase the distances of the cue ball and object balls. If you get particularly comfortable shooting one handed, you can play complete games.

Make sure you also practice with the other hand. It will take extra work, but the ability to shoot one-handed with your left and right hands will devastate the morale of many opponents - not to mention making them very envious.

How do you stop from jumping up on a shot?

Jumping up during the stroke is seen almost everywhere. Just about everyone has done this, even the better shooters. To observe this in other shooter, look for this to happen. As the stroke moves forward, at the same time the head starts to move upwards, following by the upper body. At the end of the stroke, the upper body is so upright that the stick has also risen into the air.

By the time that stroke is completed, just about every part of the body has shifted around and participated in the stroke. Some people have called this a "jubilation" stroke because it appears like the shooter is already celebrating the success of the shot.

There is only one problem. The shot did not get the results originally expected. The stroke will not have followed the planned line, and the cue ball will be hit a little harder and travel further than intended.

The jump up is caused from a basic error in the stance - the body weight was distributed improperly. When more than 50% of the weight is placed on the forward foot the whole body shifts forward. This body movement is in sympathy with your forward stroke. This is almost impossible to stop except for the softest of shots.

When the weight on the back foot is about 55-60%, it is impossible to rise on the stroke. To accomplish this, shift your body weight backwards a couple of inches. The support of your weight will then shift to the back foot. Follow all of the other stance basics and the stroke should automatically become easier to execute and more accurate. Until this is an automatic part of your pre-shot routine, consciously make the effort to add this is a separate checklist item in your setup.

What is a good stroke?

There are many sources for answers to this question. For some people, the search is no further than their reach as they develop a stroke early on. The reason might be because of good coaching or mentoring, or the result of a few dollars spent on effective instruction. Others refuse to believe they have other than a perfect stroke, and they might be right if they limit their games to people who have similar beliefs. But, as soon as they step outside their group, the harsh reality is that even a mid-level league player can kick their cans without half trying.

The basis of a good stroke is a stable stance. Weight must be distributed between your front foot (40%) and back foot (55%) and bridge hand (5%).

Only two things move during a stroke - your eyes and the stick arm's forearm of your stick arm. Everything else requires a state of stillness.

Given below are the details on what a normal shot setup requires. Other types of shots, such as off the rail, stretching across the table, or shooting over a pocket require slight adjustments for the conditions.

Given that, here are aspects of a stroke that are important:

1. With the cue tip almost touching the cue ball, your bridge hand should be about 6-9 inches from the ball. At this point, the forearm drops straight down from the elbow.
2. The stick movement should be truly and perfectly back and forth – no wavering side to side.
3. The stick hand should be a gentle cradle for the stick, using the thumb and the two forefingers. This grip does not require strength, only gentleness.
4. The upper arm should be directly lined above the stick. It should not move during the practice strokes or the stroke execution.

5. Movement of the forearm is a pendulum. The elbow does not drop during the shot movements.
6. The wrist is relaxed and does not contribute to the stroke.
7. The speed forward and backward on a practice stroke should be deliberate and controlled.
8. On committing to the stroke, the speed forward is a smooth acceleration (no jerks allowed).
9. Every stroke is consistent and identical to other stroke differing only by stick speed.

The learning process can be improved by working closely with an instructor who videotapes your action. The majority of your improvement will come from thinking your way through your stroke. Keep in mind that your old stroke mechanics are the result of thousands of strokes. Any change in your shot setup habits will take weeks of careful attention to groove into your style.

How can you improve your break shot?

If you are getting inconsistent results, you have an inconsistent stroke. The key to developing a good break shot is to reduce the number of variables. Here are some tips to apply:

- Do not move the cue ball to different places each time you break. This is no way to determine which position is consistently good.
- Move your stick hand back on the butt - closer to the end.
- Spread your feet a little wider to stabilize your stance.
- Stand a little straighter (move your head a little higher).
- Line up the shot and then ONLY look at the cue ball.
- Lengthen your bridge by about 1/3.
- Do your practice strokes to come close to the cue ball dead center. When moving back, move the tip back to your bridge hand. You want to practice a fully length stroke.
- Do NOT jerk the stroke. Accelerate your stroke - quickly. Push through the ball as far forward as you can.
- Stroke at about 75% of your best speed. (This ensures you are able to maintain control of the cue ball.)

To practice the break over and over, get a young relative (niece, nephew, grandkid, etc.) to rack the balls up each time. Offer whatever bribe is necessary and you can get 50-60 breaks in a half hour.

What are the different hand bridges?

There are three basic kinds of hand bridges:

- Closed bridge - the index finger is curled over the stick and firmly touches the side of the thumb. The cue slides through the space and over the thumb.
- Open bridge - the hand is flattened on the table into a slight tent. The thumb is pressed close to the index finger knuckle. The cue slides over the groove.
- Under rail bridge – the cue rides on the rail, with the bridge hand coming underneath the stick. The thumb and index finger are on each side of the shaft, guiding the path.
- Over rail bridge – the cue rides on the rail, with the index finder laying over the top of the shaft, with the second finger guiding the path.

How the fingers are spread and arched are individual preferences. The primary purpose is to ensure that the cue shaft will slide easily back and forth and under good control without slipping to the side. When you are unable to comfortably reach the cue ball, switch to a mechanical bridge.

How can you reduce miscues?

Miscues occur when the cue tip contacts the cue ball and does not "grab". When that happens, the tip slips off of the cue ball travels in strange directions. There is a certain sound that accompanies the miscue. If there are others around, everyone will look at you. The only way to get them to look away is to pretend it wasn't you.

There are two reasons why a miscue occurs. The first (and most common) is when you didn't chalk your cue tip properly. This is why you get the constant friendly comments of "Chalk is cheap!" immediately after the miscue.

To reduce the total amount of time you spend ducking other people's stares, it is just easier to get into the habit of chalking your stick for every shot. To chalk up before your shot, use gentle strokes across the cue tip as you rotate your stick. Then inspect it closely to make sure the coating is even.

The second reason for a miscue is when you try to put excessive spin on the cue ball. The contact point is so far out from center that the cue tip, regardless of chalking quality, the tip cannot grab the ball and slips off the surface.

> **Note:** There is a way to apply extreme spin. Use a short bridge (3"-4"). Tighten your grip on the closed bridge. Use a slower speed on the stroke.

The best assurance of reducing miscues is simply paying attention to what you are doing and not shooting balls on automatic.

How do you shoot a straight stroke?

It is important to be able to have an exact center line stroke and hit on the cue ball. If any fundamental is off, you can be hitting the cue ball to the side as much as 3/4 of a cue tip off the center line. That is almost guaranteed to miss all but the simplest of shots.

How can you verify that you are hitting an exact vertical center line cue ball hit. There are two simple exercises to identify if you are and what changes are necessary:

On the foot spot, place a striped ball. Align the stripe so that it is vertical. Line up your stroke and aim it at the center diamond at the other end of the table. Hit the ball at medium speed. If you hit it perfectly, the ball will roll down the table with no wobble of the stripe. If you were off even a little bit, you will see the stripe wobble.

You can see the amount you are off line by how much the stripe wobbles. Practice this at different speeds. If you are hitting the striped ball on the side, and you swear you got the stroke right, your head and dominant eye are not directly over your cue stick. Try shifting your head to one side or the other until you get a perfect result. This is the new position for your head on all future shots.

On the long rail, line up your stance so that the stick is lined up over the line where the cushion cloth meets the rail. When you look down, your stick should cover up the line. Start stroking back and forth. Keep looking down as the stick is moving. If your stroke is correctly lined, you should not see the line while the stick is moving back and forth. If you see it momentarily during the movement, you are not truly going back and forth. If this is the case, start with slow deliberate strokes. As you gain confidence, increase the speed slightly.

Alternate your efforts between these two exercises, 20 shots with the stripped ball, then 25 slow strokes over the line. As you master one speed for both, slightly increase the speed for the next set.

How do you do a controlled draw shot?

Do you watch other players effortlessly draw the cue ball amazing distances or with carefully controlled slow rolls backwards to perfect positions? Are you filled with envy and carefully concealed jealousy over the skill? Well, be envious no longer. This will provide the necessary details that will put you on the path to achieving that control within an short amount of time.

To get started, these instructions will help you begin learning controlled draws over short distances of a half table or less. Surprisingly, the primary "secret" to managing draws is not stick speed, but the precise contact of the cue tip to the cue ball.

The setup to achieve that precise contact point must be drilled into your shot routine until you can do it without conscious thought. You look at a shot and say, "I want to draw this back one diamond." From your toolbox of trusted shots, you will know the exact bridge height and stick angle to achieve it.

Here is how to achieve a draw shot that is worthy to be added to your toolbox:

- Chalk, and then ALWAYS check to make sure that the cue tip is well covered. (This is necessary for any draw shot. It looks just plain stupid to grind the tip into a cube of chalk and then miscue.)
- Set up a straight in shot with a one diamond separation between the object ball and cue ball. (Use the paper reinforcement rings to mark the locations.)

Note: Make sure your stick is as parallel to the floor as possible. Make sure you have a firm closed bridge. Make sure you have a true back & forth stroke.

1. Shoot the shot using the same stick speed until you can dead stop the cue ball five times in a row.
2. Adjust the height of your bridge hand so that the contact point of the cue tip to the cue ball is exactly a half tip lower. Observe draw distance (about 2-3 inches) and repeat it five times in a row.
3. Drop the contact point another half tip (change the height of your bridge hand). Repeat the process with the same speed.
4. Work your way down by half tips at a time on the cue ball's 6:00 line until your bridge thumb is flat on the table with the cue shaft riding on your thumb.
5. You now have a series of trustworthy shots with predictable draw distances.

Note: You can double these distances above by stroking at twice the speed used.

Use these controlled draw shots in your regular games and you will be the envy of everyone who watches you pull off these amazing shots. Railbirds will compliment you. People will throng to watch your perfect draws. If you are still having some problems achieving good draw control, get an instructor to take a look at your stroke and fundamentals.

How do you do a half-table length draw shot?

When you are leaning how to draw, you know that the cue tip must be lowered so that the tip will contact the ball below the horizontal center line.

This explanation excludes power draws and is useful for draws of around 3 to 6 diamonds when shooting at an object ball up to 2 diamonds away.

Set up

Place the cue ball far enough out on the table so that you can do a proper bridge. Place an object ball about a diamond away. Mark both of these positions with a paper reinforcement ring. This will allow you to constantly set up the exact same shot time after time. Use several small objects (paper clips are good) to mark how far back you draw the last several shots. Use the same speed (or as close as possible).

Shooting

Use a bridge that is two inches shorter than a normal shooting bridge. Shoot the shot several times and mark the positions. Place a marker roughly where the average would be.

1. Have a friend stand to the side and watch while you bring the tip up to the ball where you think you are hitting as low as possible without miscuing. Have him push the tip down until the stick is 1/8 inch from the table.
2. Adjust the height of your bridge accordingly and do not raise the butt of your stick.
3. Memorize the position from your viewpoint, then stroke with the same speed as your test draws. Mark the results.
4. Repeat under your friend's watchful eye until you can consistently get exactly the same draw within a couple of inches apart.
5. To draw further increase your stick speed very slightly, then practice it until you can use the same speed at will.

The key to being consistent with your draw shots is consistent speed of the stick and consistently hitting the cue ball at the same spot.

Before you fool around with different speeds and different distances to the object ball, make sure you master the easy ones first. You will be surprised that with just a little practice, you can draw the cue ball into almost perfect positions. This is especially valuable when sucking the cue ball up behind another ball for a lock-tight safety.

What makes a smooth stroke?

A good stroke implies following a complete shot routine. The routine begins once a commitment to the shot selection is made. This includes:

1. Getting down on the shot and settling your body into a balanced stable platform.
2. The stick forearm hangs straight down from the elbow.
3. The grip is loose, resting on the closed fingers, not firmly grasped.

4. The only physical movement of your entire body is the forearm swinging like a pendulum back and forth, back and forth.
5. The tip contact point on the cue ball is precisely identified and the bridge hand height and placement is adjusted accordingly.
6. The practice forward and backward strokes are each exactly the same. a pendulum. The cue tip does not waver to the sides.
7. When you commit to the stroke, the movement forward starts slow and then accelerates smoothly for the chosen speed. There is no jerky start.
8. The forward stroke passes through the cue ball and continues until it can't move forward any further. When the forward movement is stopped, it does so gradually over a few inches, not with a forced jerk.

If you have a stable stick speed that you use as your standard speed, there is a simple trick you can use to slow it down for softer shots. Shorten up the distance from your hand to the cue ball. Because the distance is lessened, you will unconsciously shoot with less speed. Try it. You can shoot harder with a shorter bridge, but you will have to force yourself to do so.

How do you learn to play opposite handed?

If you are right-handed (or left), how did you learn to shoot that way? Cast back your memory to the days of yester-when. Remember when you first picked up a cue stick? Recall how awkward it felt and how awful the results were every time you tried to hit the cue ball. You probably were so bad you even missed the cue ball on a stroke. And the memories of the insults your so-called friends made when you miscued still scar your soul. (That's why you are so embarrassed when it happens today.)

These times were not very pleasant. But, you persevered. Your buddies could play (kinda), and you were determined to meet and exceed their skills. You stuck it out. Your learning curve took time, but eventually shooting the cue ball got easier. (Now if you could have just figured out more quickly how to get those pesky object balls into the pockets.)

At a certain point, shooting suddenly became natural. When it happened you couldn't guess. It just did. After that, you didn't pay any more attention to the specific muscle groups involved. There are still refinements you are working on, but those involved greater and greater control. The gross movements to shoot a ball are now automatic.

If you want to play opposite handed, you are going to experience some of that awkwardness. When you first are trying to force your muscles into the new routines, you don't need a pool table. The kitchen table works very well.

Bend over for the shot, place your bridge hand, adjust the grip on the stick (if no cue stick, use a broom), and move the stick back and forth, back and forth. This will take several sessions of 3-5 minutes. Do this for however many days it takes for the stroke to become less clumsy.

When that gets comfortable, put a small can of vegetables on the table (standing up, not on the side). Use it as the cue ball target and practice pushing it different distance. This helps you quickly get control of your speed.

When you have reached a level of skill that does not embarrass you (you decide), you are ready to take your practice time to the pool hall. There are times when no one is there but the cashier. Grab the furthest table away and get to work.

Just as the first time around, work on your easier shots. Get comfortable shooting balls in. Gradually increase the distance and angles. You decide at what skill level you want to stop.

Many players only want to be good enough to shoot simple shots that would normally require a mechanical bridge. You may want to become equally good so that you can switch hands and will. If that is the case, there is one final test – the break. When you can break equally well and with control using both hands, you are a competent dual-handed shooter.

The opposite handed learning curve will be much shorter. You have an extensive knowledge base in your head. That information does not get wiped out. There is one additional side benefit for your strong shooting side that you get from this experience. Because you spent so much time forcing yourself to be accurate on your off-hand, stroke speed control and concentration both will be noticeably improved.

How do you play a cue ball on the rail?

This is one of the more difficult locations to shoot from. Because the cue ball is so close to the rail, it is impossible to contact the ball with other than a top spin. Draws and any variations are impossible, unless you are an expert in shooting masse shots with a near-vertical stick. If you are one of those players who believe that the cue stick must be elevated to shoot a cue ball on the rail, you provide your friends with a lot of entertainment. Unless you have put a serious effort into playing masse shots, your raised stick guarantees a miss and uncontrollable cue ball behavior.

Learning how to shoot masse shots takes a lot of time and practice. When you raise your stick to stab at the ball, you are using a masse stroke. These types of shots are very sensitive. Even the smallest imperfection on the stroke will cause unpredictable results.

If you watch good players (the ones that you admire from afar), they never use a masse shot. When the ball is on the rail, they use something different – the rail follow stroke.

This stroke is controllable and provides predictable results. It uses a level stick, parallel to the floor with no more than a 2 to 4 degree angle. The shot requires a carefully chalked cue tip and slower speeds.

Let the shaft ride on the table rail. Use an open bridge from underneath or loop a finger over the shaft to guide it. Bend down on the shot just a little more than usual and perform your regular aiming process. Use a longer than usual follow through to make sure the stroke flows through the cue ball.

If the shot is straight at the object ball with the pocket close by, use a soft stroke so that the cue ball doesn't travel very far past the contact position. For all other shots, use a normal medium speed. Avoid high speed strokes – these increase your chances of miscuing and embarrassing yourself. Even if the shot leaves you with a tougher shot, accept it and take your chances on the resulting cue ball position. If the next shot is too difficult, simply play defensively.

How do you teach children?

If you are a player who also happens to be a parent or aunt/uncle to one or more kids, you have an opportunity to help those children bypass the stupid peer teaching and tons of bad habits that occur when kids learn about it on the street. Like sex education, you want to set the record straight and not allow ignorance to affect their understanding of the sport.

When is the kid old enough? A good indicator is when he is hand-rolling balls and trying to get them into pockets. This is usually around the age of 9 or 10. He will have a slightly longer attention span and still be willing to listen to an adult authority figure.

Get your hands on several good quality house sticks. Prep the tips so they are ready to use. Explain to him how important it is to chalk for every shot. (It is always good to teach good habits early.)

Teach him how to respect the table, equipment, sticks, and accessories. Make sure he understands that playing on the pool table requires careful actions and is a privilege. They can only play when they behave themselves. This encourages the eating of veggies and the completion of chores.

Start teaching him how to hold the stick approximately in the right positions, with an open bridge and decent stance. He will need a lot of repetition, so grab all the balls and set them up one by one for him to hit.

Do no more than five minutes of coaching at a time, and then let them bang away at the balls. Only make corrections for the lesson you just taught.

Don't worry if they forgot previous lessons. You will have many refresher lessons as time goes on.

Start with slow speeds and then gradually increase to a medium speed level. Do not teach him about high speeds. For one thing, he doesn't have enough control. For another, his desire to show off can have bad consequences, such as miscuing, airborne balls, and other potential disasters.

Never teach more than two things per lesson. Make sure you encourage him to practice between lessons. Keep things on a general level. Do not do any "fine tuning" until he can shoot balls into pockets with some speed control, accuracy, and minimal spinning.

As the lessons proceed, help him learn about center ball hit, speed control, stance, and stroke. Give him lots of opportunities with ball in hand under your attentive eye. Once they are happily knocking balls into pockets, they are building up the number of strokes they need to groove in their body control and physical effort necessary to shoot with some confidence.

This is also an excellent opportunity to teach them how to play opposite handed. If they grow up knowing how to play both left and right handed, you have provided them a huge advantage over their opponents.

Monitor them very closely at this stage. There is a transition point coming up here that you cannot afford to miss. Look for the point in time when he considers using ball in hand to shoot the object ball to be too easy. That is when you require that he play from where the cue ball stops.

If you have a budding star junior player, you can coach him into the greater complexities of the game - table analysis, shot selection, cue ball control, position play, and all the other intricacies.

Even if they quit playing after a short time, they have the basics. Later in life, when they pick up a stick again, they will start with good fundamentals and quickly begin to kick their friends' butts up and down the table.

How do you help a beginning player?

If you are in the situation of helping someone learn how to get starting in playing, here are some ideas that will simplify the process. If you are deeply involved in the process, plan about two to three months to get a person to an acceptable level of play. This assumes you have good reasons to help them this much, and your budding player is dedicated enough to stick to the learning process.

There are a lot of initial conditions that have to be shown and your beginner needs to learn. Here are some rules to help be stick the course:
- Be VERY patient.
- Keep the lessons short so as to not strain yourself.

- Expect to show the same thing at least 5 times.
- Start at the rough level and then work on refining.
- Experience is developed by repetition.
- Be VERY patient.

During the first couple of lessons, work on an acceptable stance and how to hold the stick.

- Identify if he is comfortable with left hand or right hand shooting. At this point, it is very easy to learn to be ambidextrous - if so inclined. Otherwise, don't force it.
- Set up the feet for balance and stability when bending over the table. Adjust the body position so that the stick can freely move back and forth.
- Teach an open bridge. Let him figure out how to make a closed bridge.
- Adjust the stick arm so that the upper arm holds still and only the forearm moves. Work with the back and forth movement for a couple of minutes, enough to ensure it stays somewhat in a back and forth line.
- Place a row of balls on the table on the foot string. Assist his lineup positioning and focus on center ball hits. Let him shoot them into the corner pockets at a moderate speed. Repeat.
- Set up a ball in front of the side pocket, and let him shoot it in. Reset it and repeat. Provide the basics on using the ghost ball. This provides the necessary positive feedback needed to keep up the interest level.

The first half of follow-up lessons goes over the previous lesson's work. Continuously encourage his self-practicing. After about the third lesson, play a couple games against him. Watch his playing and note necessary adjustments for the next lesson.

Once he has the basics, acquaint him with playing circumstances, such as using the mechanical bridge, shooting off the rail, etc. This allows you to move slowly to introducing some of the advanced concepts.

After this point, you can turn him loose. Let him know that when he needs some help, he can always ask. If he expresses interest, recommend useful books and videotapes. Turn him loose on a league team and your job is done. You will be remembered by that person for the rest of their life. It is a very good legacy.

How do you coach a new player on a team?

If you are one of the better players on a league team, eventually you will be called upon to coach a playing situation for a new player or a lower-skilled team member. Your superior knowledge and experience is needed to make sense of a confusing table layout.

The first order of business is to figure out how to shoot the shot. With your greater experience, the solution may be obvious or require some thought. Remember the abilities of your temporary student. A solution you would find simple might be beyond his abilities. Craft a recommendation accordingly.

Describe only enough information to solve the immediate problem. Do not go into a full and complete explanation as to why this is the best way to play the shot. He won't be ready to listen and he only wants to get out of the current problem, not learn the theory of physics behind the shot. Just provide the simplest instructions – set up like thus, aim here, medium speed, no spin – stuff like that.

Once you provide the necessary assistance in setting up the shot, shut up. Let him shoot it. If successful, congratulate him warmly. If not, say something supportive, i.e., "Came pretty close there." Do NOT go negative or picky or bitchy about anything he did. If he wants details about how the shot could be more successful, provide your best analysis. If he doesn't ask, do NOT force the information down his throat.

In a sense, you are helping to mold the habits and attitude of a new player. Your educational moment will give him ideas on how to handle similar shots for the rest of his pool playing lifetime. This is no small responsibility.

Quickie Tips

These are little notes that provide useful information.

Watching your betters

If you are serious about improving and anxious to learn as much of pool as possibly, the perfect teaching by example is immediately available to you at local tournaments. This is where you will find good and bad examples of stances, strokes, rhythms, tactics, strategies, and etiquette. All of this right out in front of you on every table.

This is significantly better than watching professionals play (who are under more constraints and restrictions, plus the watchful eye of referees). Their skills are far above you and their bad habits rare. Locally, you get the benefit of watching examples of the good, the bad, and the ugly. And, it's all free.

Twirling your stick

NEVER, EVER attempt to twirl the cue stick like it was a baton. It looks silly and stupid if you are playing at a pool hall. In a bar, sooner or later you will hit something and be liable for the damages, or you will hit someone and be liable for assault.

Talc powder

Avoid using talc powder or any other fine powder. It tends to get dirty and clumpy with the slightest exposure to dampness. It also gets the hands dirty, the cue shaft dirty, and the table dirty. If your hands get a bit sticky, wash them.

Standing on a pool table

Occasionally, a light fixture or electrical problem has to be fixed at a location over a pool table. Slate and the underlying table support system can handle a lot of weight. The more you can spread out your additional weight by placing a small sheet of sheet of plywood.

Throw a blank on the table and place the plywood on top. To raise yourself up onto the table top, use a step ladder to get up to the table. Step over the rail (do not put any weight on the rails). Do your business. Descend by the same process. A second person to hold the step ladder would add additional safety.

Speed kills

Stroking a shot at higher speeds magnifies stroke faults. If you can make shots at medium and soft speeds, but are missing them at higher speeds, find an instructor to help your stroke. This is one area where you need someone to observe your action and recommend solutions.

One lesson will be enough if you follow the routines and drills provided. If no competent instructor is available, set up a video camera to tape your movements. Don't ask friends to provide feedback. They don't know what to look for. Case care and attention

When you have a nice cue case, you want to keep it in places where people won't touch it with passing parts of their bodies. It can cause your heart to flutter a bit when you come back to sit down and someone has knocked it over into the path of passing players who are overweight and very, very clumsy. Lessons such as this soon teach you to keep your case out of harm's way.

When done shooting and breaking down your sticks, take a moment and clean the chalk from the tip. You can do this by laying a paper napkin on the floor and then twisting the tip to remove the chalk. This keeps the inside of your case clean. Otherwise, after months and years of use, particles of chalk dust get around inside the case and create little messes (kind of like a little puppy).

Reduce choking (failure by fear)

To reduce choking (missing) on critical shots that are not too difficult, here are a couple of suggestions:

1. Take a walk around the table, looking at the shot and remembering past times you made this one.
2. Take a couple of deep breath before bending over for the shot.
3. Complete a proper pre-shot routine.
4. Pretend you have one more shot after this to win the game.

Recommended bridge lengths

As a general guide to bridge lengths, the following is provided:

- Normal shooting - 7 to 10 inches (regular open or closed bridge)
- Draw shot - 5 to 7 inches (tight closed bridge recommended)
- Follow shot - 8-12 inches (open bridge recommended)
- On the cushion - 4 to 7 inches (stick rides the rail)
- Mechanical bridge - 4 to 7 inches

Time to practice

Few people are able to do worthwhile practice for more than 30 minutes. Set specific targets to achieve.

- Warm-up - 5 minutes in basic stun, follow and draw control shots.
- Problem fixes - 5-10 minutes on shots screwed up during the last competition.
- Designed growth program - remaining time is devoted to specific skill development.

An easy way to stop jumping up on the stroke

If you are jumping up on the stroke and are having trouble staying down, there is a flaw in your stance. You have more than 50% of your body weight distributed on your front foot and bridge hand.

To fix this problem, shift your ass backwards just a little to place slightly more than half your body weight on your back foot. When you stroke, no matter how fast you hit the cue ball, you will be unable to jump up.

MP3 player use

When you are practicing, using a music player with earphones is no problem. It is especially helpful in reducing external distraction factors such as noise from nearby tables/players, etc. You don't even actually have to have it turned it. It can also be a signal to friends coming up to the table that you are focused and don't want to be disturbed.

When you are in a league match or a tournament, wearing ear phones is a lack of etiquette. The phones make it difficult for the two opponents to communicate effectively. Attempting to communicate with someone using ear phones means they have to pop out one side every time.

Home table room sizes

The minimum recommended space you will need is 10 feet added to the table width and length. Any additional room above will feel more comfortable. For example, a 4 x 8 table will need a room size of 14 x 18.

If you add additional accessories, such as a table & chairs (maybe for poker nights), a bar (for parties), and a couple of pool chairs (to properly observe the game), the room size will need to increase a bit.

In case of very desperate shooters who absolutely MUST have something to practice on in order to develop their stroke, a table can be pushed up against a wall to leave at least two sides free. The wall blocked pockets can be filled with rolled up socks to gently eject the ball when it goes in.

High humidity problems

If you are playing pool when the humidity level is high, the extra water in the air also affects the balls and cloth. The following results occur:

- Balls get dirty very quickly, picking up chalk dust and dirt from the table bed.
- Ball rolling stops much sooner.
- More energy and speed is required to move multiple balls.
- Miscuing becomes significantly easier.
- Any cue ball spin becomes difficult to apply.
- Banks are affected and usually come up a little short.

Check for cue straightness

For a house cue, lay it on the table and roll it. If there are no warps, the roll will be smooth. If there are only a few cue sticks to use and all are wobbly on the table, use the cue with the wobble near the butt instead of up near the tip.

Cue stick lengths

Most general production cues available are 57" and 58" long. Generally, the shaft of a two piece stick is 30". Some manufacturers have longer butts available, enough for a 60" stick. These are also the general lengths used by custom cue makers. You can have a custom stick built with longer and shorter lengths.

Cue ball jumping

Few players spend time working on the third dimension (height) of the physical world. It is not easy to make the cue ball fly through the air with intentional control. This requires a lot of practice. When doing so, place an extra piece of table cloth underneath the ball to prevent damage to the table cloth. There are several videos which show how to do this.

You may want to invest in a jump stick or a jump/break stick. These make jumping easier to control and help develop accuracy. If you are considering whether to learn this, see if you can borrow a jump cue and give it a try. If you like the idea of mastering this skill, buy your own.

Clean chalk from clothing

If you get chalk on your shirts or pants, the normal laundry process will clean them up fine. If your shooting glove gets a lot of chalk, fill a bowl with water, add some dishwashing liquid and let soak for two hours. Squeeze out as much of the color as possible, then throw in the laundry with your regular wash load.

Buy your own balls

If you're a serious player interested in competing well, you should buy a high quality set. If you spend any amount of time at a pool hall, you may not want to use their regular balls. In most pool halls there are always several regulars who also play with their own balls. The pool owner won't give any price breaks. Purchase a set that does not match the regular balls.

Besides the pool hall, there may be other places you frequent with an available pool table. It might be at friends with a home table, or an institution where balls are locked up someplace. These are also places that only have poor quality balls. Being able to pop out to your vehicle and grab a set of good balls and your sticks will make you a temporary local hero. If only for personal use, a high quality set of balls will last more than 10-20 years.

Game Rules Simplified

These are rules of the many different games that can be played on a pool table. The rules have been simplified to make the games easier to understand. Details may not be an exact match to the official rules.

There are other games that have been invented, copyrighted and generally available to the playing public. Web searches will turn these up and the rules printed out for use.

14.1 Continuous

The game has been around for over a century. It was adapted from *Straight Pool*.

Object

Score 150 points for a full game. Shortened games can go to 50 or 75 points.

Opponents

Two sides (players or doubles).

Balls

Regular set of balls.

Racking

Standard random rack.

When one object ball remains on the table, the 14 pocketed balls are racked with no apex ball and game continues. If object ball is within the rack, it is included. If cue ball is within the rack it is played from the kitchen.

Breaking

Initial breaker determined by local rules (coin, lag, card draw, etc.)

Breaker can call a ball and pocket.

Legal break is cue ball contacts the rack and then a rail plus two object balls contact the rail. (Failure is a two point penalty.)

If no legal break, incoming player can request a re-rack and re-break or accept the table layout.

Regular play

Call ball and pocket.

Each ball counts as 1 point.

Additional balls pocketed on a successful call are counted.

Player's turn ends on a miss or foul.

Illegally pocketed balls are spotted with no penalty.

Cue ball is always played from its table position.

Player's score can goes negative on penalties. (Option: score goes to zero and any penalty points added to opponent's score.)

Safety/defensive play

On a safety call, if a ball is pocketed, it stays down. Inning ends. No score for that ball.

Fouls

These fouls have 1 point penalties and loss of turn. (Optional: *Three foul rule* applies.)

- No legal hit
- Object ball off the table
- Cue ball scratch (incoming player has ball in hand in the kitchen)
- Illegal ball touching (optional – moved balls can be replaced with opponent's approval and play continues with no penalty)

Straight Pool

This is the version of pool played from which 14.1 Continuous was developed. The game is not commonly played nowadays. It can still be found in some small town pool halls.

Object

Score 150 points for a full game. Shortened games can go to 50 or 75 points.

Opponents

Two sides (players or doubles).

Balls

Regular set of balls.

Racking

Standard random rack.

Breaking

Initial breaker determined by local rules (coin, lag, card draw, etc.)

Breaker can call a ball and pocket.

Legal break is cue ball contacts the rack and then a rail plus two object balls contact the rail. (Failure is a two point penalty.)

If no legal break, incoming player can request a re-rack and re-break or accept the table layout.

Regular play

Call ball and pocket.

Each ball counts as 1 point.

Additional balls pocketed on a successful call are counted.

Inning ends on a miss or foul.

Any pocketed balls are lined up from the foot spot.

If all balls pocketed, the inning continues with the balls lined up from the foot spot.

Unless scratched, cue ball is always played from its table position.

If scratch on the break and the break was otherwise legal, incoming player shoots from the kitchen.

If player's score goes negative on a penalty, player's score goes to zero and any other points added to opponent's score.

Safety/defensive play

On a safety, any pocketed ball is spotted and does not count. Inning ends.

Fouls

These fouls have 1 point penalties and loss of turn. (Optional: *Three foul rule* applies.)

- No legal hit
- Object ball off the table
- Cue ball scratch (incoming player has ball in hand in the kitchen)
- Illegal ball touching (optional – moved balls can be replaced with opponent's approval and play continues with no penalty)

Speed Pool

Tactically, the cue ball can be moved a better position by making a legal shot at a ball that is in a bad location (thereby improving it) and rolling into a better shooting position.

Object

This game requires balls to be pocketed as quickly as possible. Another person uses a stop watch to track the time and to track penalty times. The player with the shortest time wins.

Opponents

Any number of players.

Balls

Regular set of balls.

Racking

Standard random rack with 8 in the middle.

Breaking

Breaker determined by local rules (coin, lag, card draw, etc.)

The rack is broken with a standard break shot.

Regular play

As soon as the cue ball is hit for the break, the timer starts.

Cue ball must come to a complete stop before shooting.

Any ball may be pocketed, but the 8 ball must be last.

Optional: call ball and pocket.

Fouls/penalties

- Scratch on the break - 5 seconds added, cue ball played from the kitchen.
- Scratch - 10 seconds added, cue ball played from the kitchen.
- Cue ball jumped off table - 10 seconds added, cue ball played from the kitchen.
- Illegal shot - 5 seconds added, table layout as is.
- Uncalled ball pocketed, 5 seconds added, table layout as is.
- Contact 8 ball first (before it is a legal ball) - 10 seconds added, table layout as is.
- Illegal double-hit shot - 10 seconds added, table layout as is.
- No legal hit on the 8 ball (when legal) - 10 seconds added, table layout as is.
- 8 ball pocketed out of turn - 10 minutes added to current score and player's inning immediately ends.

Rotation

This is also known as **61**, when played by two opponents.

If played as a gambling game, everyone antes into the pot. Highest score wins the pot. Fouls require an additional ante to the pot. Several balls, equally separated (i.e., 3, 6, 9, 12 15 or 4, 8, 12, 15 or 5, 10, 15) can be designated as "money" balls. If the shooter pockets a money ball, other players pay the ante.

Object

Score the highest number of points by the time the last ball is pocketed.

Opponents

Two or more players.

Balls

Regular set of balls.

Racking

Balls are racked in the standard triangle in any order, with the one on the top, 2 and 3 at the other corners. The 15 ball is in the center.

Breaking

Breaker determined by local rules (coin, lag, card draw, etc.)

Breaker must break the rack by hitting the 1 ball, with four balls contacting the cushions.

Regular play

The lowest ball on the table is the target object ball.

Scoring is the addition of the value of legally pocketed balls in that inning.

Illegally pocketed balls are spotted.

Combinations are legal.

Optional: Call ball and pocket.

Fouls

Penalty is loss of turn and last ball made is spotted and score adjusted. If no score, only loss of turn.

- Ball off the table
- No ball to a cushion or pocket
- No contact on lowest numbered ball
- Illegal ball touching (optional – moved balls can be replaced with opponent's approval and play continues with no penalty)
- Scratch (cue ball is played from kitchen). Incoming player can decide to shoot or force the violator to shoot.

If shooting from the kitchen and lowest ball is also there, it is spotted.

Game variations

This game can be played with partners, or as Scotch doubles.

Strict rotation rules - only the lowest ball can be targeted and pocketed and counted. Combinations not allowed. Incidental balls are spotted.

Ball count – all balls are played in rotation (no combos). Winner pockets 8 balls. Similar to 1 Pocket, but balls count if made in any pocket.

Rotation 8 Ball – Games is played as 8 ball, but with each group (solids or stripes) played in rotation. Solids are played 1 through 7, stripes are played 9 through 15.

Pool Snooker

This game is an adaptation of American snooker rules to the pool table.

Object

Score the highest number of points.

Opponents

Two sides (individuals or teams)

Balls

3 - 8 (replaces 2-7 balls used in snooker). 10-15 are used as the red balls. Plus cue ball.

Racking

Following is the table setup for this game.

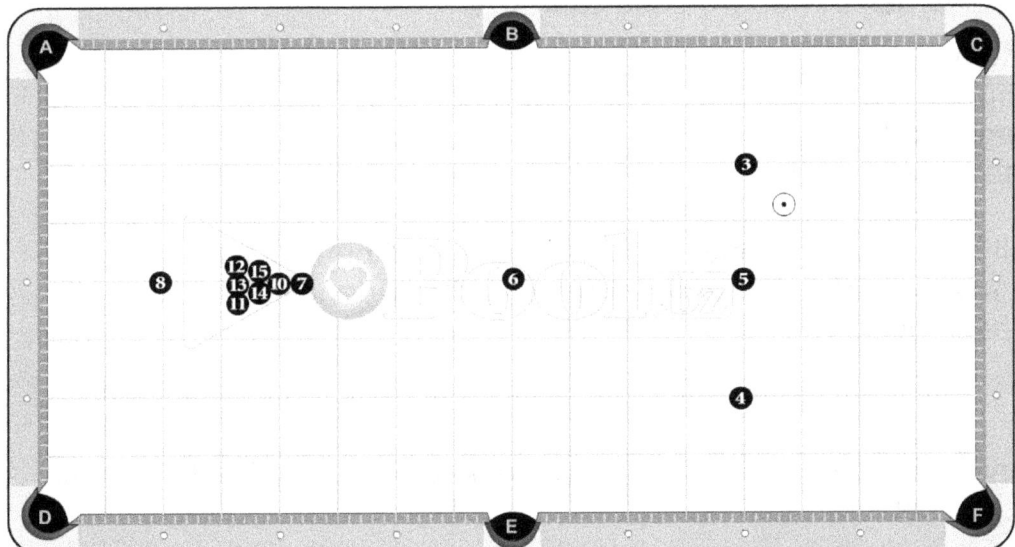

The "D" in snooker is replaced by the kitchen (behind the head string). See example setup for 3 ball, 4 ball, and 5 ball (head spot) placement.

The 6 is on the center spot, the 7 is placed above the foot spot, the 8 is placed one diamond up from the center diamond on the foot rail.

10-15 balls are racked in a triangle on the foot spot.

Break

Breaker determined by local rules (coin, lag, card draw, etc.)

Cue ball from the kitchen. A legal break must contact a striped ball. At least one striped ball must hit a cushion or a ball is pocketed.

Pocket a striped ball, any solid (3-8) is the next target ball.

Scoring

The 10-15 balls each are worth 2 points. The 3, 4, 5, 6, 7 & 8 balls score their face value.

Regular play

Combinations are legal for the stripes. No combinations with solids.

While stripes remain on table, incoming player must pocket a stripe and then a solid (immediately spotted), followed by another stripe and solid (immediately spotted), and so on until all stripes are pocketed with the related shot on a solid. Then, solids are pocketed in sequence

Optional: Call ball and pocket.

Fouls

All of these include loss of turn and 3 points added to the opponent's score. Incoming player has ball in hand on the table.

- Cue ball scratch
- No legal hit
- Pocket illegal ball
- Ball off the table
- Scratch
- Illegal ball touching (optional – moved balls can be replaced with opponent's approval and play continues with no penalty)
- Uncalled balls pocketed

One Pocket

Each side or player can only score points by pocketing object balls in their designated foot pocket.

Object

Reach 8 points by legally pocketing object balls into the designated pocket.

Opponents

Two players or (rarely) two doubles teams

Balls

Regular set of balls.

Racking

Standard random rack.

Breaking

Breaker determined by local rules (coin, lag, card draw, etc.)

A legal break is one object ball to a rail.

If illegal break, penalty is one ball.

Regular play

Pocket choice is made by the breaker. Opponent has opposite pocket.

Ball in player's pocket – 1 point.

Ball made in side or head pockets - spotted after inning ends.

Inning continues if a ball is legally pocketed.

If pocketed in opponent's pocket, score for opponent.

If incoming player shoots from kitchen and all remaining balls are behind the head string, object ball nearest the head string is spotted.

Fouls

Penalty is always loss of turn and 1 point.

- No ball to a cushion or pocket after contact of object ball
- Scratch (any balls pocketed are spotted)
- Illegal ball touching (optional – moved balls can be replaced with opponent's approval and play continues with no penalty)
- Three successive fouls by the same player is loss of game

Variations

Designated pockets are head pockets.

Designated pockets are side pockets.

Kelly (Pea) Pool

This is another one of the "old geezer" games that were very popular up through the 1980s. The version presented here is the gambling version.

Object

Balls are played in rotation, lowest to highest.

Highest score wins the pot. In case of a scoring tie, the pot is split.

Opponents

Two to 15 players (three to six is best).

Balls

Regular set of balls.

A shake bottle with 15 numbered beads.

Racking

Standard random rack, 1 on the head spot, 2 on the right corner and 3 on the left corner (viewing from foot rail).

Before the break, every player gets a bead (their secret number) from the shake bottle. If 2 to 5 players, each player gets three beads. If 6 to 7, two beads, more players get one.

Every player puts up the predetermined ante amount (i.e., quarter or $1)

Breaking

Breaker determined by local rules (coin, lag, card draw, etc.)

Legal break is cue ball to the one ball with four balls to the rail or a ball pocketed.

If not legal, incoming player can accept the table and shoot from the kitchen, or re-rack the balls and break himself.

Scratch on the break - incoming player can shoot from the kitchen or force a re-rack and break.

Regular play

Balls are pocketed in rotation, and each pocketed ball is one point.

Call ball and pocket.

If shooter pockets his secret numbered ball, he gets one point and every player pays him the amount of the ante.

If shooter pockets the secret number of another player, he gets one point, and the owner of the number pays him the amount of the ante.

If no player pocketed his secret numbered ball and all balls are pocketed, the pot is paid out. The next game doubles all values and antes.

If shooting cue ball out of the kitchen and lowest ball in the kitchen, spot it.

Incidental pocketed balls on a successful called shot count.

Fouls

If a player does not announce his secret numbered ball when pocketed, all points are lost, pays double to the shooter who made it plus pays two antes to the pot.

Normal penalties are loss of turn, and an ante to the pot. Any balls pocketed in that shot are spotted.

- No legal ball contact
- Ball off the table (spotted)

- Scratch (shoot from the kitchen)
- Illegal ball touching (optional – moved balls can be replaced with opponent's approval and play continues with no penalty)

On a foul, incoming player can accept the table as is or force the offending player to keep shooting.

Fargo

This game uses elements of straight pool along with rotation. Players of all skill levels can enjoy the challenge of this game.

Object

Play 10 innings. Each ball is 1 point. Pocket as many balls as possible of the 15 balls. Scores are added for each inning to determine final score.

Opponents

Multiple players.

Balls

Regular set of balls.

Racking

Standard random rack.

Breaking

Breaker determined by local rules (coin, lag, card draw, etc.)

Break is a free shot. No penalty for scratches, balls off the table, etc. All balls pocketed or jumped are spotted.

After breaking, start with ball in hand and begins the inning.

Regular play

Call ball and pocket.

Each inning has a "random" and "rotation" segment. A coin, placed heads up, starts of the inning as random - each ball is 1 point.

The shooter (at will) can flip the coin anytime to tails and shoot balls in rotation – each ball is 2 points. Only one switch allowed per inning.

Incidental pocketed balls count when made on a pocketed legal ball.

Inning ends on a miss or foul.

Incoming player starts with a new rack.

Fouls

Penalty is end of turn.

- No legal shot
- Ball off the table
- Scratch
- Illegal ball touching (optional – moved balls can be replaced with opponent's approval and play continues with no penalty)

Variations

This game can be played by smart phone with any group of players at their tables. Innings are started together and scores reported to the scorekeeper.

Equal Offense

Based on *14.1 Continuous*.

Object

Score a higher number of total points in a group of opponents with an agreed number of innings. Or, if playing against yourself, beat your previous best score. Generally a game is 10 innings with a 200 point maximum.

Balls

Regular set of balls.

Racking

Standard random rack.

Breaking

Standard break. Any pocketed balls are re-spotted.

Start shooting from the kitchen.

Regular play

After break, first shot is from the kitchen.

Call ball and pocket. See 14.1 rules.

Skill levels

Play at the level of your skills and abilities.

Level 1 - Beginner: After the break, start with ball in hand anywhere. Three misses or fouls to end the inning. After each miss (1st and 2nd), ball in hand anywhere. Advance to the next level when your total score reaches 120.

Level 2 - Intermediate: After the break, start with ball in hand anywhere. Two misses or fouls to end the inning. After the first miss, start with ball in hand anywhere. Advance to the next level if your total score reaches 120.

Level 3 - Advanced: After the break, start with ball in hand from kitchen. One miss or foul ends the inning. Advance to the next level if your total score reaches 120.

Level 4 - Professional: After the break, start with ball in hand in the kitchen. One miss or foul ends the inning. For each inning, the goal is to reach 20 (playing through the rack like 14.1). Reaching 170 would be considered top-level.

Fouls

Penalty is end of turn.

- No legal shot
- Ball off the table
- Scratch
- Illegal ball touching (optional – moved balls can be replaced with opponent's approval and play continues with no penalty)

Cut-throat

Just as the game suggests, this is a vicious game, full of short-term alliances and stabs in the back.

Object

Pocket all opponents' balls while keeping one or more of your balls on the table.

Opponents

Three players.

Balls

Regular set of balls.

Racking

Standard rack. Any of 1-5 ball on the top, 6-10 ball on one corner and 11-15 ball on the other corner.

One player owns the balls 1-5, another 6-10, and the third 11-15.

Breaking

Breaker determined by local rules (coin, lag, card draw, etc.)

Note: On following games, winner breaks, first player knocked out is third and racks the balls.

Four balls to the rail or ball pocketed.

If no legal break, incoming player can accept the table layout or force a re-rack and break himself.

Scratch on the break, incoming player shoots from the kitchen. Any balls made are spotted.

Regular play

Call ball and pocket.

If multiple balls are spotted, lowest is closest to the foot spot.

> **Note:** If the shooter sinks his last ball during his inning, he can still win if all other balls are pocketed in the same inning (no balls left on the table).

All illegal balls (balls not called, jumped, or made on a foul) are re-spotted. (Unless they belong to the shooter, then they stay down).

If player is down to one ball and commits a foul, he can spot one ball from each opponent instead of taking a ball off the table.

If a player was previously knocked out, and a foul restores his ball to the table, his turn is restored.

Fouls

Penalty is loss of turn and removal of personal ball from table or spotting one ball for each opponent.

- No legal shot
- Ball off the table
- Scratch (incoming player shoots from the kitchen)
- Illegal ball touching (optional – moved balls can be replaced with opponent's approval and play continues with no penalty)

Golf (simplified)

Golf pool is most often seen played on a snooker table, but is also common in pool halls on regular tables. The rules presented here are simplified. If you come across a group playing Golf on a table, make sure you understand their rules before participating.

Object

Play 6, 12, or 18 holes. Lowest score wins the pot.

Hole 1 is right-side head pocket, Hole 2 is left-side head pocket. Holes are counted clockwise to Hole 6 (right side pocket). Standard par is 2.

Track the scores on a whiteboard or piece of paper.

Opponents

Multiple players.

Balls

Cue ball plus each player selects a ball from the rack.

Racking

Each player starts his turn with object ball on the foot spot.

Regular play

Starting player determined by local rules (coin, lag, card draw, etc.)

Object ball on the foot spot, cue ball on the head spot. To start, bank object off the short rail towards Hole 1. The number of shots it takes is his Hole Score which is marked down.

Every player plays for the first hole and marks their score – always starting with the object ball on the foot spot and the cue ball where it lays.

The game continues with Hole 2 as the target pocket and so on around the table (clockwise).

Lowest score wins the pot.

Fouls

Penalty is loss of turn and 3 strokes added to score.

- No legal shot
- Ball off the table
- Scratch
- Wrong pocket
- Illegal ball touching (optional – moved balls can be replaced with opponent's approval and play continues with no penalty)

Scratches must be played from the head spot.

Cribbage

This is an interesting conversion of a popular card game to a pool game.

Object

One player (or side) pockets the most cribbage points when all balls have been pocketed. Each cribbage point is the total of two balls that equal 15. For example, pocket the 1 and 14 for one cribbage point.

Opponents

Two or three sides (opposing players or doubles teams).

Balls

Regular set of balls.

Racking

Standard random rack with 15 ball in center.

Breaking

Breaker determined by local rules (coin, lag, card draw, etc.)

Four balls to the rail or a ball pocketed.

If no legal break, incoming player can accept the table as is or make the breaker repeat the break.

Pocketed balls are spotted (unless equal to 15) with breaker continuing.

On a break with a foul, incoming player can accept the layout or shoot from the kitchen.

Regular play

Call ball and pocket.

Two balls made consecutively must equal 15 to count as a cribbage point.

Missing the second ball ends inning. Re-spot the first ball.

If an uncalled second (or third) ball is sunk when calling one ball, the inning ends and all balls spotted.

The 15 ball cannot be targeted until all other balls are pocketed.

House rules: The game could be extended by using the 15 ball as a break ball (similar to 14.1 Continuous). If the 15 is pocketed on the new rack shot the player continues. The 15 is res-potted after the inning ends. Game ends at a pre-determined number of cribbage points - i.e., 15, 20.

Fouls

Penalty is loss of one cribbage point. Balls are spotted. If score is zero, player owes. Owed cribbage points must be paid after the inning earned.

- No legal shot
- Ball off the table
- Scratch (incoming player shoots from kitchen)
- Illegal ball touching (optional – moved balls can be replaced with opponent's approval and play continues with no penalty)

Cowboy Billiards

This game is another adaptation of caroms and pocket billiards that hones your skills in both pocketing and object ball path control.

Object

Score exactly 101 points.

Opponents

Any number of players.

Balls

Object balls - 1, 3, 5 plus cue ball.

Racking

1 ball on the head spot, 3 ball on the foot spot, 5 ball on the center spot. Cue ball in the kitchen.

Breaking

Starting player determined by local rules (coin, lag, card draw, etc.)

From the kitchen, shoot the 3 ball. If no contact, next shooter can request a reshooting, or take over where the cue ball stops.

Regular play

No call shot.

Scoring the first 90 points can be done by pocketing and caroming:

- Pocketed balls: scores ball number (i.e., 3 ball counts as 3 points).
- Caroms: cue ball to two object balls - 1 point, cue ball to three object balls - 2 points.

To score points for 91 through 100, only caroms can be counted.

Point 101 counts only if cue ball caroms off the 1 ball into a called pocket (cue ball must not touch another object ball).

Any pocketed ball is spotted immediately before the next shot. If position is occupied, ball stays off table until the position opens up.

If on 100 points and the 1 ball cannot be spotted, it is moved to the next available spot.

On a scratch, incoming player shoots out of the kitchen. If all balls in the kitchen, 3 ball is moved to the foot spot.

Fouls

Loss of turn and any points made during that inning.

- No legal shot
- Balls off table
- Illegal ball touching (optional – moved balls can be replaced with opponent's approval and play continues with no penalty)
- Scratch (except on point 101)
- On scoring the 90th point, any points other than caroms
- On point 101, if the cue ball does not touch the 1 ball. Also if cue ball touches any other ball.

Chicago (rail version)

On this version, all object balls are positioned along the rails.

Object

Multiple players. In money version, all players ante up for the pot. Highest score takes the pot, ties split pot.

If money balls are designated (3, 6, 9, 12, 15 or 5, 10, 15), players pay the shooter a specified amount.

Opponents

Multiple players.

First player determined by local rules (coin, lag, card draw, etc.)

Balls

Regular set of balls.

Racking

Balls are placed on the cushions by the diamonds. The 1 ball is placed on the right diamond on the foot rail. Going counter-clockwise, balls are placed at each diamond around the table. Only the head rail has no balls at the diamonds. (Ball placement can also be clockwise.)

Regular play

Lowest target ball can be made in any pocket. Each ball pocketed counts as one point.

The starter shoots from the kitchen to pocket the 1 ball. The shooter continues shooting at the lowest ball on the table and continues as long as balls are pocketed.

Incidental balls made while pocketing the lowest ball also count for the shooter. If the lowest ball is missed, and the incidental ball is made, the extra ball is spotted in its location.

Shooter must make a legal hit on the lowest ball on the table.

Fouls

Penalties are loss of turn and ante to the pot.
- No legal shot
- Ball off the table (re-spotted)
- Illegal ball movement (optional – moved balls can be replaced with opponent's approval and play continues with no penalty)
- Scratch (incoming player shoots from kitchen) If the lowest ball is the 8, 9, 10, or 11, that ball is spotted for the incoming shooter.

Variations

Place balls in a random order on the diamonds. Shoot any ball.

Rack balls and play regular rotation with money balls.

Chicago (carom-scratch)

Object

Score points by shooting object ball off of cue ball into pocket. Each ball counts as one point.

Opponents

Two players.

First player determined by local rules (coin, lag, card draw, etc.)

Balls

Regular set of balls.

Racking

Regular random rack. Cue ball is placed on top position (apex ball).

Breaking

Object ball is played from kitchen off of cue ball. If any object ball is pocketed, play continues.

Regular play

Any object ball is selected and caromed off of the cue ball into a pocket. If successful, scores one point. Another object ball is shot off the cue ball, etc.

Incidental object balls pocketed count.

Shooter must make a legal hit off the cue ball.

Inning ends on a foul or no ball pocketed.

Fouls

Penalties are loss of turn, loss of 1 point, and an object ball re-spotted. (If at zero points, 1 point added to opponent's score.)

- No legal shot
- Ball off the table (re-spotted)
- Illegal ball movement (optional – moved balls can be replaced with opponent's approval and play continues with no penalty)
- Scratch (cue ball is pocketed) – cue ball is placed on center spot and incoming player starts

2 Cushion Pool

Opponents

Two to three players.

Balls

Object balls 1, 2, and 3 (no cue ball).

Racking

One ball on foot spot, 2 ball on head spot, 3 ball on center spot.

Breaking

First player uses 1 ball as cue ball, second player uses 2 ball, third player uses 3 ball.

Regular play

Inning ends when no point is scored.

Basic rules of 3 cushion billiards are used, except that only 2 cushions must be contacted. There are two ways to score:

- Cue ball contacts one of the other two balls, then two or more rails, and then contacts the third ball.
- Cue ball contacts two or more rails and then contacts the other two balls.

If a legal point was made and a ball is pocketed or off the table, it is spotted and playing continues.

Fouls

No general fouls.

Variations

1 cushion contact instead of 2.

3 cushion contact instead of 2.

These adjustments can also be used as handicaps.

Bowliards

This game uses the scoring system used in bowling. As a tool to test your improvements over time, it keeps a solitary player's interest. This is similar to *Equal Offense*.

Object

Score a perfect bowling score of 300 points in 10 frames (innings) in solitary play. Scoring uses bowling rules. Each pocketed ball is 1 point.

Opponents

One to four players.

Balls

Set of balls (1-10) plus cue ball.

Racking

Balls are racked in a four-row triangle.

Breaking

Free break to start inning. Balls pocketed are spotted. If scratch, no penalty. Cue ball goes to the kitchen for the first shot.

Regular play

After break, shoot from kitchen to pocket balls.

Call ball and pocket.

Two innings for each rack. First inning starts after break. On a miss, first inning ends. Second inning starts and ends on a miss.

If all balls pocketed in this frame, scores as a "spare". (10 points for frame plus points in first inning of next frame).

If all balls pocketed in the frame are made on the first inning, scores as a "strike". (10 points for frame plus points from next two innings.)

If a strike or spare in 10th frame, additional innings as necessary.

Balls on the break or jumped balls are immediately spotted.

Fouls

Foul ends inning.

Bottle Pool

This game combines carom and pocket billiards. It includes use of the shake bottle.

Object

Score 31 points.

Opponents

Two sides (opposing players or doubles teams).

Balls

Balls (1-2) plus the cue ball and the shake bottle.

Racking

Place 1 ball frozen to the foot cushion on the left diamond. Place the 2 ball frozen to the cushion on the right diamond. Place the shaker bottle upside down on the center spot.

Breaking

Starting player determined by local rules (coin, lag, card draw, etc.)

Breaker shoots from kitchen to contact an object ball.

If an illegal shot, incoming player can accept the table as is or reset the table and the breaker shoots again.

Regular play

A shooter continues the inning as long as a point is made on a stroke.

Inning ends when:

- no score is made on the stroke
- no legal shot
- contacts the bottle with an object ball
- bottle knocked off the table
- cue ball is jumped off the table
- object ball is jumped off the table
- exceed 31 points.

Points are scored for:

- Pocket a numbered ball to score 1 for 1 ball and 2 for 2 ball.
- Carom the cue ball off both numbered balls for 1 point.
- Carom the cue ball off one numbered ball and knock down the shake bottle scores 5 points.
- Carom the cue ball off one numbered ball and knock down the shake bottle so that it sits right-side up is an automatic win.

Note: You can get 9 points in a single stroke by sinking both balls while doing a carom, and then knocking the shake bottle over.

Any balls knocked off the table are re-spotted. If the cue ball is knocked off the table, play starts from the kitchen.

Any balls pocketed are spotted. If the ball's position is blocked, the center spot is used. If that is blocked, the head spot is used. For spotting both balls, the 1 ball is placed first.

If a player goes over 31 points on a shot, the score is reduced to the number over 31 and loss of turn. (For example: a score is 29 and the 2 ball is pocketed but also contacts the 1 ball, the score goes to 32 which then reverts to a score of 1 plus loss of turn.

Reposition bottle

Whenever the bottle is knocked over, it is placed upside down at the point where the mouth of the bottle is located.

If the bottle was knocked off the table, it is spotted on the center spot. If this is blocked, place the bottle on the head spot. If that is blocked, place on the foot spot. If all three are covered (extremely rare), hold the bottle off the table until the next shot is done, then spot the bottle.

Fouls

Penalty is one point. If three consecutive fouls without a legal shot, the player loses game.

- Ball off the table
- Scratch
- Upset bottle with object ball
- Cue ball contacts bottle before an object ball
- No legal shot
- Illegal ball touching (optional – moved balls can be replaced with opponent's approval and play continues with no penalty)

Stalemate

In a refereed match, if the referee feels that neither player is attempting to win, he may so declare. At that point, if, in the referee's opinion, the players do not make any attempt to win for the next three turns, the match is considered a stalemate, and the game is restarted with the same original breaker.

Bank Pool

Bank Pool is a game where legally pocketed balls must be banked into the pocket using one or more banks.

Opponents

Two sides, individuals or a team of doubles.

Balls

Regular ball set.

Object

Each ball is 1 point. To count, it must be banked 1 or more rails. 8 points to win.

Racking

Regular random rack.

Breaking

Starting player determined by local rules (coin, lag, card draw, etc.)

Legal break is two object balls to the rails with one object ball past the center line. If a ball is pocketed, breaker continues.

If no legal break, incoming player can play the table, or require a new break. No other penalties.

Any pocketed ball, not called, is spotted after shooter's inning.

Regular play

Call ball, rails and pocket. Cue ball contact must be to object ball first. (No rail-first. No double-kiss.)

House rules can permit three or more rail kick to a ball close to a pocket.

Fouls

Penalty is end of inning and one ball spotted. Balls made on foul shot do not count and are re-spotted. Balls can be owed.

- Ball off the table (spotted at end of inning)
- Scratch (shoot from kitchen)
- No legal shot
- Illegal ball touching (optional – moved balls can be replaced with opponent's approval and play continues with no penalty)

On shooting from the kitchen, if all balls inside, ball closest to the head string is spotted.

Variation

9 Ball Bank Pool – one version allows any ball, another version requires banking balls in rotation.

Any Eight

This game combines skill requirements for 9 Ball, 1 Pocket, and 14.1 Straight.

Object

One player (or side) pockets any eight balls into legal pockets.

Opponents

Two sides (opposing players or doubles teams).

Balls

Regular ball set. To count, balls must be pocketed accordingly:

- 1-5 (reds) - head pockets
- 6-10 (blacks) - side pockets
- 11-15 (yellows) - foot pockets

Racking

Standard random rack with one "color" at each corner.

Breaking

Starting player determined by local rules (coin, lag, card draw, etc.)

A legal break is 4 balls to the rails or a ball made.

If no legal break, incoming player can accept the table as is or re-rack and break himself.

If ball(s) on the break, shooter continues. Balls incorrect pockets immediately spotted.

Foul on the break - incoming player shoots from kitchen.

Regular play

Call ball and pocket.

Combinations are legal.

Ball made on a called safety are spotted.

Incidental balls not called ae spotted.

Fouls

Penalty is end of turn plus spot one ball. If no balls to pay, owes.

- No legal shot
- Ball off the table
- Scratch
- Illegal ball touching (optional – moved balls can be replaced with opponent's approval and play continues with no penalty)

(Optional: *3 foul* rule can apply.)

9 Ball (Back Pocket)

This 9 Ball game has overtones of one pocket.

Object

Make 9 ball in your designated corner pocket (at head of table).

Opponents

Two players.

Balls

Set of balls (1-9) plus the cue ball.

Racking

Regular 9 ball rack. (If 5 is also a money ball, place at bottom of rack.)

Breaking

Starting player determined by local rules (coin, lag, card draw, etc.)

A legal break is 4 balls to the rails or a ball made.

Player who does not break places a marker next to his pocket.

Regular play

Call ball and pocket.

If the 9 ball illegally pocketed, it is spotted.

Fouls

Penalty is end of turn and incoming player has ball in hand. (Option: cue ball fouls only – ball in hand)

- No legal shot
- Ball off the table
- Scratch
- Illegal ball touching (optional – moved balls can be replaced with opponent's approval and play continues with no penalty)

If 9 ball pocketed during a foul, it is re-spotted.

(Optional: *3 foul rule* can apply.)

9 Ball

These are the common set of rules used for the majority of versions of 9 Ball.

Object

Pocket the 9 ball to win. Rotation - lowest numbered ball on the table.

Opponents

Two players.

Balls

Set of balls (1-9) plus the cue ball.

Racking

Standard 9 ball rack.

Breaking

9 ball on a break wins.

Starting player determined by local rules (coin, lag, card draw, etc.)

Legal break is four balls to the rail or ball pocketed.

Ball off the table is end of turn.

Regular play

Not call ball and pocket. Slop works.

Lowest ball on table must be contacted first.

(optional) Push out allowed.

Fouls

Penalty is end of turn and incoming player has ball in hand. (Option: cue ball fouls only – ball in hand)

- No legal shot
- Ball off the table
- Scratch
- Illegal ball touching (optional – moved balls can be replaced with opponent's approval and play continues with no penalty)

If 9 ball pocketed during a foul, it is re-spotted.

8 Ball (standard)

These are common rules used for the majority of versions of 8 Ball.

Object

One player (or side) pockets all balls in their group, and then legally pockets the 8 ball.

Opponents

Two sides (players or doubles teams).

Balls

Regular set of balls.

Racking

Standard random rack with 8 ball in center, stripe on one lower corner, solid on other lower corner.

Breaking

Breaker determined by local rules (coin, lag, card draw, etc.)

Four balls to the rail or a ball pocketed.

If no legal break, incoming player can accept the table as is or make the breaker repeat the break.

In most locales, if the 8 ball is pocketed on a break – shooter wins.

In most locales, if one or more balls are pocketed on a break, that group is the breaker's group. In some places, group is selected only on a called ball and pocket (table still open).

Regular play

Call ball and pocket. (Optional – only the 8 ball must be called.)

One side's group is solids, the other stripes. If no side has a group, any solid or stripe can be targeted. Group selected when a ball has been legally pocketed.

Before the 8 ball can be played, all group balls must be pocketed. On the 8 ball, the pocket must be identified.

Incidental pocketed balls stay down. Object balls made on any foul also stay down.

Fouls

Penalty is end of turn and incoming player has ball in hand. (Option: cue ball fouls only – ball in hand)

- No legal shot
- Ball off the table
- Scratch (if on 8 ball, loss of game)
- Illegal ball touching (optional – moved balls can be replaced with opponent's approval and play continues with no penalty)

If 8 ball pocketed early – loss of game.

Variation

Last pocket - 8 ball must be pocketed in the same pocket as the last ball of your group.

8 Ball (coin-op table)

On a coin-operated table, any ball that falls into a pocket is gone from the table (except the cue ball which does return). Therefore, no balls can be re-spotted, including the 8 ball if it goes in early (loss of game by whoever made it go in). Otherwise, local 8 Ball rules apply.

8 Ball (Chinese)

Please note that the name for this style of 8 Ball is not the way that 8 Ball is played in Asia. (If you attempt explaining how to play this style of 8 Ball in Taiwan, Singapore, or China - you are going to have a hard time explaining yourself.)

After the break, object balls are caromed off the cue ball into a pocket.

Carom combinations are allowed (ball into cue ball, then combo in a ball).

All other playing rules apply.

Ball in hand allows moving one of your balls and position it for the carom to a pocket.

8 Ball (bar rule notes)

If you are a consumer of adult beverages, you have occasionally (or more) frequented bars or taverns or pubs or cocktail lounges where a bar table is in regular use. Generally it will be a coin operated 3-1/2 x 7 table with a wall rack of beat up house cues. Its purpose is to provide entertainment to the patrons while they consume quantities of alcohol.

Because every set of balls costs money, and people want to get the most entertainment possible, a set of very complicated rules has been established to extend the amount of playing time between the necessary insertion of money.

The standard bar table game is eight ball. There is some similarities to pool hall rules, in that one player or team has solids, and the other stripes. Once all balls in the group is pocketed, the eight ball is next.

Every shot must be fully called - not just ball and pocket, but every incidental action along the way. This includes every carom and cushion that occurs with the object ball until it reaches the pocket.

Cue ball is always played where it lies. Only on a scratch is the cue ball allowed to be placed and only within the kitchen.

Do not EVER be obvious with a defensive shot. In some bars, intentionally and obviously playing safe can get somewhat dangerous. The viewpoint of a bar player is somewhat medieval in nature. "Always attempt some kind of offensive effort." If you were to try and explain that that kind of effort will let them win - they'll just smile and say, "You have to try."

 If you do play defensively, disguise the shot. (Don't forget to apologize when you accidentally don't leave him a shot.) After all, you don't want to be called a dirty pool player or cheater or shark - right?

Keep in mind that people have gotten into fights of all kinds, just to settle a point whether a shot was legal according to the localized bar rules, or not.

8 Ball (1-15 side)

This is a common version of 8 Ball often played in lodges and senior centers. Decades ago, it was the most common version of 8 Ball played in the United States.

Regular 8 Ball rules apply according to the location.

The player with the solids (1-7), must make the 1 ball in the designated side pocket (usually the right side when standing at the head of the table).

The player with the stripes (9-15), must make the 15 ball in the designated side pocket (usually the left side when standing at the head of the table).

7 Ball

This is a rotation game.

Object

Legally pocket the 7 ball.

Opponents

Two players.

Balls

Set of balls (1-7) plus cue ball.

Racking

A special 7 ball rack is normally used, if available. 1 ball is at the top, with the 2 through 6 in random sequence. The 7 ball is in the middle.

A regular or 9 ball rack can be used. Place 9 ball in the apex (top) position, and the 1 ball in the left wing position. From the side of the table, position 1 ball on foot spot. Remove rack, roll the 9 ball into a pocket. The rack of balls is ready for breaking.

Breaking

7 ball on a legal break is a win.

Breaker determined by local rules (coin, lag, card draw, etc.)

Four balls to the rail or a ball pocketed.

If no legal break, incoming player can accept the table as is or make the breaker repeat the break.

7 ball on the break wins.

Regular play

Immediately after the break, and before another shot, the breaker places a marker for which long side of the table to pocket the 7 ball for the game win. Opponent must make 7 ball in opposite side to win.

Balls are pocketed in rotation, lowest first.

Fouls

Penalty is end of turn. (Option: cue ball fouls only – ball in hand)
- No legal shot
- Ball off the table
- Scratch

- Illegal ball touching (optional – moved balls can be replaced with opponent's approval and play continues with no penalty)

Loss of game

No 3-foul rule. The shooter loses the game if:

- 7 ball is pocketed out of turn.
- 7 ball is pocketed on the wrong side.
- Scratch on the 7 ball.
- 7 ball made during an illegal shot.

6 Ball

Object

Following the rules of 9 Ball, the winner legally pockets 6 ball.

Opponents

Two sides (players or doubles teams).

Balls

Regular balls (1-6) plus cue ball.

Racking

Triangle with 1 on top, 2 balls in second row, and 3 balls in third row (6 in middle).

Breaking

Breaker determined by local rules (coin, lag, card draw, etc.)

Three balls to a rail or ball pocketed.

Regular play

Regular 9 ball playing rules apply.

Fouls/misses

Penalty is end of turn. (Option: cue ball fouls only – shoot out of kitchen)

- No legal shot
- Ball off the table
- Scratch
- Illegal ball touching (optional – moved balls can be replaced with opponent's approval and play continues with no penalty)

3 Ball

This is a money game. Every player puts up an ante and takes a turn at the table. Single lowest score takes the pot.

If one tie, all tie. Another ante is added and another inning played.

If an excessive number of entries, in each round, all highest scores are eliminated from the next round. When down to four players, no further eliminations. Every round requires an ante.

Object

Break and pocket all three balls in the least number of strokes in a complete round.

Opponents

Multiple players.

Balls

Set of balls (1-3) plus the cue ball.

Racking

Ball on the foot spot, two balls in a triangle behind the head ball.

Breaking

Cue ball shot from the head spot. (Optional – from kitchen.)

Regular play

The player breaks and keeps shooting until all object balls are down.

Every stroke is counted. Total is recorded for that inning of play.

Fouls

All standard fouls count as one stroke.

Basic Pool Playing Rules (BCA/World Rules)

The Billiard Congress of America has been long known as the go-to source for the basic underlying playing rules. These rules for table billiards are generally followed throughout the world. When not otherwise affected by local traditions, these are the basic foundations of games, tournaments, and leagues.

Some of these rules may be modified by local, regional, and national playing associations and leagues - such modifications are documented within their rules.

There may be very specific additional rules - often embedded within localized practices. Such locations are usually bars with one or two tables.

The generalized pool playing rules are here:
http://home.bca-pool.com/displaycommon.cfm?an=1&subarticlenbr=54

Use these rules to resolve disagreements.

Pool Terminology

These terms are commonly used throughout the world of pool players. Some are no longer in common use, although can often be heard when discussing pool with some old geezers. Other terms are regionally used, but not everywhere known. Immediately following most of the terms is a word that indicates where in the world of pool the word is most commonly used.

A

Act of God (games) - An unforeseen action that impacts the stability of the tables and the ball layouts of any games in progress. Examples: earthquake, material collapse (building, wall, ceiling, lights, etc.), or anything else that shouldn't happen, but does. Also see *Billiard Gods*.

Action (gambling) - The amount and type of betting going on between challengers and side bettors.

Action room (gambling) - A separate room with one or two pool tables that only open when active betting on players take place.

Aim (stroke) - The process of lining up the cue stick to hit the cue ball and send it to a specific point at an object ball or to a point at the cushion on the table.

Aiming line (stroke) - Object ball - the imaginary line that runs through the object ball to a pocket or another target on the table. Cue ball - the imaginary line that runs from the cue ball to the object ball.

Alternating break (games) - A convention for some tournaments where the opposing players alternate breaking the rack for each new game in their match.

Amateur (player) - The designation of any player who has not qualified at any of several venues to be a professional player. A player can be of very high skill but still be considered an amateur.

Angle shot (balls) - See *Cut shot*.

Apex ball (balls) - The top ball of a rack of balls. The ball at the apex is racked so that it rests on the foot spot. (aka Head ball)

Around the world shot (balls) - A shot where the cue ball contacts a long rail, short rail, and the other long rail. Most often used to kick at a ball in a corner.

B

Back spin (balls) - See *Draw*.

Backer (gambling) - A person who puts up the money for a shooter. Generally winnings are split, and losses are absorbed by the backer.

Bad hit (balls) - When the cue ball hits an illegal ball. Considered a cue ball foul with the penalty of ball in hand.

Balance Point (cue) - the fulcrum point on the cue length when it will be balanced.

Ball (balls) - Any ball used in pocket billiards. It can be the cue ball or any of the numbered balls.

Ball and pocket (games) - A shortened term that means that the called ball is intended to be made for the called pocket.

Ball off (balls) - Any ball that has been knocked off the table.

Ball in hand (games) - The reward to the opponent when a cue ball foul (or other foul determined by game rules) occurs. The cue ball may be picked up and placed anyplace on the table.

Ball rack (balls) - A storage rack for balls when they are not in use. Can also refer to the rack used to set up balls for a game.

Ball return (table) - An internal channel system to bring balls from the pockets to a holding box at the foot of the table.

Bank shot (balls) - The object ball is driven to one or more cushions towards an intended pocket.

Bar Banger - Slang for a beginning level pool player who does not understand (or care to learn about) the beauty or intricacies of the Green Game. Usually is an insult when used by skilled players to reference a beginner.

Bar box (table) - The smaller sized coin-operated table used in bars because of limited floor space. Usually 3-1/2 x 7 feet table size.

Bar player - A player who generally only plays in bars on bar boxes.

Bar pool (games) - Those sets of games generally played only in bars on bar tables.

Bar rules (games) - Those sets of game rules found only in bars. Because the tables are coin operated, a wide variety of very strict rules are used to gain the maximum number of innings possible from a single rack of balls.

Bar table (table) - See *Bar box*.

Bed (table) - The area of the table within the cushions of the table.

Behind the 8 ball (slang) - In an uncomfortable shooting position usually with the target ball on the far side.

Big ball (balls) - When a target object ball is to a corner of the table and the shooter must kick to that ball. It is "big" because the incoming cue ball can hit the target object ball directly, off the long rail first, or off the short rail, or off the long and then short rail. It is a big target because of the location.

Big pockets (table) - The sizes of the table pockets are either at or larger than the outside limits of regulation pocket widths. Usually found on coin operated bar tables so that games can be finished quickly.

Billiard Gods (games) - The unseen spirits or invented invisible entities of the Green Game who crowd around every pool table. They often just observe, but are known to interfere in the rolls of the balls at their whims for and against the shooters. Mentioned, usually in jest, but sometimes with apparent serious belief (aka pool gods).

Billiard room - An old-fashioned, more upper-class term for a pool hall. A room within a private home that has a pool/billiard table.

Billiards (games) - Specifically refers to games played on a carom billiards table. In general refers to all table games using balls and various tables. Includes snooker, carom billiards, and pocket billiard tables of all sizes.

Black ball (balls) - The 8 ball. In the English version of 8 Ball, there are no stripes or solids, only yellow and red balls with 1 black ball. Rules are similar.

Blocker (balls) - An object ball that covers a pocket preventing the opponent's balls from being made.

Body English (shooter) - A series of gyrations of the shooter's body used to assist the rolling balls to take the correct directions and accomplish the shooters goal.

Bottle (games) - A leather or plastic bottle that contains 15 numbered beads (aka peas or pills) used in several games. (aka pill bottle, shake bottle.)

Bowliards (games) - A game of 10 object balls that scores using the rules of scoring for bowling

BPI average (games) - Balls per inning average. The average number of balls made by a shooter over dozens of innings. If a shooter makes 30 balls over 15 innings, the BPI is 2.0.

Bracket (tournament) - The ladder used to pair shooters as matches are completed.

Brain fart (games) - A momentary lack of intelligent thinking or proper shot execution.

Break (games) - The beginning or first shot of a game. Balls must be moved from the break rack according to game rules. (aka break shot)

Break and run (games) - The shooter breaks the rack, pockets a ball and runs the remaining balls to the win.

Break cue (cue) - The cue stick used specifically for breaking the racked balls.

Break down (cue) - To take apart a two piece cue to be placed in a cue case. The act is an indicator that the player is done playing.

Bridge (general) - The guide for the cue stick near the cue tip. (Also *Mechanical bridge*)

Bridge hand (stroke) - The hand used to guide the shaft of the cue stick for the shot.

Bridge head (equipment) - The plate at the front of the mechanical bridge onto which the shaft rests.

Brush (equipment) - Tool used to sweep the table bed and cushions to ensure a clean table without debris.

Bumper (cue) - See *Butt cap*.

Burn mark (table) - A small white mark on the cloth caused by friction when a cue ball is hit by the cue tip very quickly, usually during a break shot.

Butt (cue) - The larger and heavier part of the cue. It is the bottom part of a two-piece stick. Before the playing rules finally formalized the proper use, it was acceptable to shoot with either end of the cue stick.

Butt cap (cue) - The rubber end at the butt of the stick.

Bye (tournament) - When there is no opponent in a ladder, the player will get a bye and advance as if he had won that match.

C

Calcutta (gambling) - A way of gambling on the outcome of a tournament with the odds determined by the high bid amounts on various players. Highly regarded players have a higher bid offered. Winners are those who chose the top finishers in the tournament.

Call shot (games) - The shooter must indicate or identify the ball and pocket into which it must be made. (Some regions use call shot to indicate any intervening activity (banks, caroms, etc.), and refer to Call pocket as their designation of called ball and pocket without having to designate intervening ball activity. (See *Ball and pocket*.)

Called ball (games) - The designated ball to be pocketed.

Called pocket (games) - The pocket that the called ball will go into.

Carom (balls) - Occurs when the cue ball or object ball contacts one ball and goes into another ball or pocket, intentionally or unintentionally.

Center ball (balls) - Indicates where the cue tip should contact the cue ball. Generally refers to the exact center both on the vertical and horizontal line. Sometimes means hitting on the vertical center line.

Center pocket (balls) - When a ball enters the pocket with equal space on both sides of the ball to the pocket corners.

Center spot (table) - The center spot on the table that is midway between the two side pockets and midway on a line drawn between the center diamonds of the two short rails.

Center string (table) - The line drawn the width of the table between the centers of the side pockets.

Center table (table) - The middle area of the table bed loosely bounded by a rough circle one diamond out from the center spot.

Century (games) - In 14.1 , when a 100 balls (or more) are made by the shooter in one turn at the table.

Chalk (equipment) - (n) A cube of colored abrasive used to rub onto the tip of a cue. (v) The process of applying chalk from the chalk cube to the cue tip.

Chalk holder (equipment) - A hollow device used to hold a cube of chalk. While most pool halls have loose cubes of chalk, many players have a personal chalk holder. By carrying it around, they can easily and routinely grab their chalk and use it without having to take their attention from the table analysis process to look around the table for a loose cube.

Chalk up (cue) - The action of applying chalk to the cue tip (aka dressing the tip).

Challenge (games) – In some venues, any player can approach any other player to offer a "challenge". Generally, this takes the form of an inquiry whether the other player wants to compete. The challenge can be as common as casual series of games played together up to any level of betting based on races.

Champion (tournament) - The top winner of a tournament. The title may be fleeting (i.e., that tournament only) or claimed forever (i.e., First place, US Open 2009).

Cheap shot (games) - See *Slop shot*.

Cheat the pocket (balls) - Aiming the object ball to enter the pocket to one side or the other.

Cheating (games) - Any number of ways to change the outcome of the competition, i.e., equipment tampering, incorrect scoring, improper racking, using the body to hide intentional ball rearrangements.

Choke (stroke) - Missing a critical shot when the importance of the shot is high. Usually caused by nervousness or loss of concentration.

Clean (balls) A ball is pocketed "clean" when it enters the pocket without touching the rails or corners of a pocket on either side.

Clean bank (balls) - The object ball is banked into one cushion and into a pocket without caroms or combinations.

Clean the table (games) - On coming to the table, the process of pocketing every required ball through to a win during one inning.

Cling (balls) - When dirty balls contact each other, the dirt between the two balls grabs slightly, keeping the two balls in contact fractionally longer than normal. This contact changes the normal paths of the two balls in unpredictable ways.

Clock system (cue ball) - A way of explaining where to hit the cue ball to apply cue ball spin.

- 12:00 (above center) - follow
- 3:00 (right of center) - right English
- 6:00 (below center) - draw
- 9:00 (left of center) - left English.

Closed bridge (stroke) - A hand bridge that has the index finger looped over the shaft of the stick. This is the most common bridge used by players.

Cloth (table) - The material used to cover the bed and cushions of the table. (aka felt).

Cluster (balls) - Group of balls that are clumped together in a small area of the table.

Coach - (n) A person who assists a player to shoot better and make good table decisions. (v) Providing advice or suggestions on how to shoot. Game rules usually specify whether to allow coaching.

Coin toss (games) - A coin is tossed to determine who will begin the match with the break. The person who does not toss the coin calls "heads" or "tails".

Coin-operated table (table) - A pool table that requires that coins (or paper currency) be inserted before the object balls can be accessed for a game. When an object ball drops into a pocket it is lost for that game. When the cue ball drops, a mechanism returns it for use by the incoming player.

Combination (balls) - When the cue ball contacts one object ball which then hits another object ball (which can be pocketed or not).

Combo (balls) - See *Combination*.

Commercial table (table) - A high quality, well-constructed table designed for heavy use in pool halls. Commercial tables are used for all top level tournaments.

Concede (games) - A player can concede a game or a match. Usually this is done when it is impossible for the player to win. One action that concedes a match is the unscrewing of their cue.

Consecutive fouls (games) - When the player causes a foul on two or more consecutive turns at the table. Some game or tournament rules have a consecutive foul rule (usually three), others do not.

Contact (balls) - When one ball touches another while either or both balls are moving.

Contact point (balls) - The exact point where one ball contacts another ball. This point can be used to determine tangent lines and direction of travel.

Corner-hooked (balls) - Occurs when the cue ball stops within a pocket area without sinking. The corner or edge of the pocket blocks the cue ball from a direct shot at the target object ball. Rarely occurs.

Corner pocket (table) - Any of the four pockets on the table at each corner of the rectangle.

Corner shot (balls) - Any shot where the target object ball is aimed to a corner pocket.

Counter (equipment) - A device used to keep score.

Counting string (equipment) - A string of marking beads used to keep score. Usually 50 on each side, with markers for 10, 20, 30, 40, and 50. An alternate color bead indicates the 5's.

Cripple (balls) - See *Duck*.

Cross corner (balls) - A bank shot where the object ball is banked into a corner pocket.

Cross side (balls) - The object ball is banked into the long rail to be made in the opposite side pocket.

Crutch (equipment) - Slang for the mechanical bridge.

Cue (equipment) - The stick used to strike the cue ball. Can be one piece, two piece, and (rarely) three piece.

Cue ball (balls) - The white (or mostly white) ball that is hit by the tip of the cue to make a shot.

Cue ball control (balls) - Applying precision strokes to the cue ball that will move it to a preferred location for the next shot.

Cue ball foul (games) – Occurs when the shooter commits a foul, generally illegally touch, scratch, or off the table. Penalty is loss of turn and incoming player with ball in hand on the table. See *Ball in hand*.

Cue ball in hand (games) - see *Ball in hand*.

Cue ball in hand behind the head string (games) - The cue ball may be placed by hand anyplace behind the head string (in the kitchen).

Cue ball on a string (games) – To continuous play perfect position, moving the cue ball using draws, follows, and tangent lines to get the cue ball into position to shoot the next object ball.

Cue butt (equipment) - See *Butt*.

Cue case (equipment) - A container that holds a one or more two piece cues with a holder for any tools necessary for maintenance.

Cue extension (equipment) - An additional device added to the butt of the cue to allow the shooter to extend his reach for a shot.

Cue joint (equipment) - See *Joint*.

Cue maker - A specialist who makes cues. The cues can be made from exotic materials and woods. Cues can be of a specified weight, length, shaft, and butt.

Cue rack (equipment) - A wall mounted rack to hold house cues.

Cue tip (equipment) - The very tip of the cue stick that contacts the cue ball to make a shot. It is made of special material designed for its purpose.

Curve shot (balls) - When the tip comes down at an angle into the cue ball off to one side, the cue ball path can be curved. Sometimes the technique is used to attempt to maneuver around another ball that partially hides the target object ball. Also see *Masse*.

Cushion (table) - The rubber edge, covered with the same cloth as the bed of the table. that goes around the bed and limits the travel path of moving balls which are rebounded back into play.

Cushion first (balls) - A shot where the cue ball contacts a cushion before it hits the object ball.

Cushion nose (table) - The leading edge of the cushion that juts out onto the table surface.

Custom cue (equipment) - A cue built by a cue maker to specific requirements of the person ordering.

Cut shot (balls) - The cue ball contacts the target object ball off center (to the left or right side) in order to send the object ball in an intended direction.

Cut-throat (games) - The process of thoroughly defeating an opponent without consideration of emotions or consequences.

D

Dead ball (games) - A ball that does not count as a score and is no longer playable (cannot be re-spotted).

Dead stop (balls) - The cue ball stops perfectly still on contact with the object ball.

Dead combination (balls) - A perfectly lined up combination of two or more balls that will sink the ball closest to the pocket without aiming.

Dead rail (table) - A cushion that is loose and does not properly rebound balls.

Dead stroke (games) - Playing at a level that is above normal skills.

Dead zone (table) - An object ball which is in those areas of the table where getting an angle on the ball is limited to very small table areas. For example, a ball on the center short rail is in a dead zone and is difficult to get shape.

Defense (games) - The effort through a shot to prevent the next player from having any viable shot or opportunity to advance their game.

Deflection (balls) - The angle and path that a moving ball travels after contact with another ball.

Delay (game) - An extended period of time between shots, intentional or unintended. Game rules may specify what a delay is and the appropriate penalty.

Deliberate foul (games) - An action taken by a player to intentionally foul and lose his turn to the opponent. Most often used to create ball layout difficulties.

Dent (cue) - An indentation in the cue shaft bigger than a ding.

Diamond system (table) - Any of several ways to calculate ball travel off several cushions to an intended location.

Diamonds (table) - Marks along the rails of the table (3 between each pocket) used to calculate various banking and kicking systems.

Ding (cue) - A small indentation on the shaft of the cue.

Dirty pool (games) - An effort to cheat or shark an opponent.

Dog a shot (game) - A miss (intentional or accidental) on an easy shot.

Double bank (balls) - The object ball is banked so that it hits one rail then the opposite rail and then back again into a pocket.

Double elimination (tournament) - To be eliminated from this tournament, the player must lose two times.

Double hit (balls) - The cue tip hits the cue ball two or more times during a single stroke.

Double kiss (balls) - When a ball contacts another ball which comes off the rail and hits the first ball again.

Double round robin (tournament) - Each player plays against every other player two times.

Double-shim (table) - See *Shim*.

Doubles (games) - Any game played with two partners on each side. Play is alternating sides and alternating partners. (i.e., Player A1 shoots first, followed by B1, followed by A2, followed by B2, followed by A1, etc.

Down on the shot (stance) - The position of the body as it bends down over the cue stick in preparation for a shot.

Down table (balls) - Aiming or sending balls towards the foot end of the table. Also see *Up table*.

Drag shot (stroke) - The cue ball is hit with draw. As the ball travels towards the object ball, the cloth wears off the reverse spin which also slows the cue ball speed before it contacts the object ball.

Draw shot (balls) - When the cue ball is hit below the horizontal center line, the back spin will pull the cue ball backwards after it contacts an object ball.

Dress code (tournament) - The higher level tournaments usually have a minimum dress code for professional players.

Drift (balls) - If the table is not level, a slow rolling ball can move off line.

Drill (games) - (n) An exercise to improve one or more skills. (v) to hit the cue ball hard into the object ball which is slammed into the pocket.

Drop pockets (table) - When balls are pocketed, they stay in the pocket until manually removed.

Duck (balls) - (n) An object ball so simple to pocket that it is considered virtually impossible to miss. For example, an object ball in the jaws of a pocket. (v) To shoot a defensive shot instead of an offensive shot.

Dump (gambling) - To intentionally lose the game in order to win a secret side bet. Also used to raise the expectations of a targeted victim in a hustle.

E

Easy shot (balls) - Any simple to make shot, usually with the target object ball very close to or in the jaws of the pocket.

Eight ball (games) - One of the two most popular pocket billiards games in the world. Two sides (singles or partners), each must pocket their group (7 balls) and then must legally pocket the 8 ball to win the game.

Elevation (stance) - The height of the cue stick butt from horizontal level. Raising the butt increases the elevation.

End rail (table) - The short rail at the foot or head of the table.

English (balls) - The cue tip contacts the cue ball to the left or right side of the vertical center line, spinning the cue ball in the direction.

Equal offense (games) - A game for individuals to practice their abilities to pocket balls. See the games rules section.

Equipment - All the hardware used in playing pool. Includes tables, cues, lighting, scoring, chalk, etc.

Escape (games) - A lucky or intentional legal hit and table leave when the chances of successfully making a legal hit appeared near impossible.

Even up (gambling) - A match is played with no handicapping for either player.

Exhibition - A demonstration from a highly skilled player of various interesting and trick shots. More than one person may be demonstrating. Rules are rarely enforced in order to display shots.

Extension (cue) - A device on a cue butt that extends the reach for a shot. Can be attached to the butt or built into the butt as a telescoping extension.

F

Fancy shot (balls) - Any shot that has unusual or unexpected results. Can be a trick shot of some complexity.

Far side of pocket (table) – When an object ball comes in from an angle, the side furthest from the ball and which becomes the target area for the object ball.

Fat (games) - When shooting an object ball, hitting it with too small of an angle and missing the shot. Also see *Thin*.

Fast cloth (table) - A thin cloth installed on a table that allows balls to travel further because of less resistance.

Feather shot (balls) - The cue ball scrapes the paint of the object ball which barely moves.

Feel (stroke) - A sense of automatic aiming and adjustments that does not require conscious effort.

Felt (table) - The table cloth material. Table cloth is made from woven fibers. Felt is pressed fibers, which is not used on a table.

Ferrule (equipment) - - The material (plastic, ivory, or metal) attached at the end of the cue stick that is the base which the tip is glued to.

Finesse (stroke) - A carefully crafted and precision shot that travels exactly as intended.

Fish (gambling) - An easy victim for a money player.

Five ahead (gambling) - A match winner is determined when one player is ahead by five games.

Flagrant foul (games) - Any foul that is excessive. Generally results in a higher penalty such as loss of game or match or expulsion.

Fluke (games) - Any accidental lucky shot.

Follow (balls) - - When the cue ball is hit above the horizontal center line, the cue ball will continue forward after hitting an object ball.

Follow through (pocket billiards) - - The continuation of the cue stick stroke through the cue ball.

Foot of table (table) - The end of a table where the balls are racked for the beginning of a game.

Foot on floor (games) - A standard rule that requires the shooter to have one foot touching the floor during the stroke. Violation is a foul.

Foot rail (table) - The short rail at the end of the table where balls are racked.

Foot spot (table) - The spot at the foot of the table where balls are racked. It is located on a line drawn across from the 2nd diamond on the foot long rails, and the line through the center diamonds on the short rails.

Foot string (table) - The line drawn across the 2nd diamonds on the long rail at the foot of the table. This is an imaginary line and is not used in any games.

For the time (gambling) - Two players compete with the loser paying the table time charges.

Force draw (balls) - Cue ball is shot with additional force so that the cue ball jumps sideways slightly and then draws backwards. The tip contacts the cue ball about 1/2 to 3/4 tip below the horizontal center line.

Force follow (balls) - Cue ball is shot with additional force so that the cue ball jumps sideways slightly and then the spin grabs the cloth. The tip contacts the cue ball about 1/2 to 3/4 tip above the horizontal center line.

Forfeit (games) - When one player acknowledges the game or match loss. In a tournament, a referee can call a forfeit when a player commits a gross violation.

Foul (games) - A violation of the game rules, in which a penalty is applied to the player. In some games, incidental object ball contact only requires re-positioning the moved balls – no foul, no penalty.

Foul stroke or shot (games) - The stroke or shot which results in the foul.

Free ball (games) - See *Ball in hand*.

Free ride (games) - In 9 Ball, the opportunity to combo the 9 ball and send it on an uncontrolled path around the table, with the hope (or expectation) that the 9 ball will fall into a pocket for an easy win.

Freeze (froz) (games) – Screwing up a shot because of excessive pressure.

Frozen balls (balls) - One ball touches a second ball.

Frozen cushion (balls) - The ball touches the cushion.

Full hit (balls) - The cue ball contacts the object ball head on.

G

Gambling - Any situation where the loser must forfeit something of value (money, favors, etc.) to a winner.

Game (games) - A contest between two players that begins with a racked set of balls and ends when the required actions are completed and no further shots are required.

Game ball (pocket billiards) - The ball, that when legally pocketed, wins the game for the shooter.

Ghost (games) - A imaginary practice opponent. A rack is broken. Starting with ball in hand, the purpose is to run out the rack to a win. On any miss, the ghost wins that rack.

Ghost ball (balls) - An aiming technique that uses an invisible imaginary ball that lines the target object ball with the pocket. The player shoots the cue ball directly straight at the ghost ball which then hits the target object ball and sends it to the pocket.

Ghost table (games) - An aiming technique used in banking. An imaginary table is lined up cushion to cushion. The target object ball is then aimed towards the imaginary pocket. The shot then banks the target object ball into the rail and back to the real pocket.

Glove (equipment) - A three fingered glove that fits over the bridge hand. Helps the shaft slide smoothly back and forth on the stroke.

Good hit (games) - A legal hit. Usually a statement made by someone verifying whether a watched shot was good or not.

Green (table) - The length of table space between the cue ball and object ball.

Grip (stance) - How the stick hand grasps the butt of the cue.

Grip (cue) - The area of the cue butt grasped by the stick hand. This area may or may not have material wrapped around.

Grouping (balls) - The process of pushing balls together, usually to make it difficult for the opponent to easily win the game.

H

Half-ball (balls) - The cue ball center is aimed at the edge of the object ball.

Hand chalk (equipment) - Powder applied to a bridge hand to allow the shaft to slide freely during a stroke.

Handicap (games) - An intentional adjustment of the rules to allow players of two different skill levels to compete evenly.

Hanger (balls) - A ball that is setting on the edge of the slate within a pocket. Part of the ball overhangs the edge pocket.

Hard shot (balls) - Any setup that has a very low percentage of success for the shooter.

Head ball (balls) – See *Apex ball*.

Head of the table (table) - The top quarter part of the table where the break area is. (aka kitchen).

Head on (balls) - See *Full hit*.

Head rail (table) - The short rail on the end of the table with the head spot

Head spot (table) - The spot at the head of the table. It is located on a line drawn across from the 2nd diamond on the head long rails, and the line through the center diamonds on the short rails.

Head string (table) - The line drawn across the 2nd diamonds on the long rail at the foot of the table. This is a marked line and determines the edge of the breaking area (kitchen).

Heart (games) - The strength of the player's intention and will to win.

High run (games) - In 14.1, the largest number of consecutive balls made during one turn. In match play, the highest number of games won by one player.

Hill (games) - See *On the hill*.

Hill-hill (games) - When both players are on the hill and need only one game win to win the match.

Hold (balls) - Spin that prevents the cue ball from following a natural path by nearly stopping.

Home table (table) - Table designed for home use, usually a 4 x 8. Refers to any table installed in a personal home.

Hook (games) - A cue ball position where a legal hit cannot be directly made at a target object ball.

House cue (equipment) - A variety of one piece cues of different weights available for casual players who do not own a personal cue. Usually well abused over time.

House rules - Any playing rule generally accepted as a playing rule by the local regular players. Also, a behavioral rule enforced by management, i.e., no jump shots, no masse shots allowed.

Hug the rail (balls) - When a ball runs straight down the rail.

Hustle (gambling) - A plan used to prepare a targeted victim to lose money.

Hustler (gambling) - An individual who uses various tricks or stories to play for money against a weaker player.

I

Illegal ball touching (game) – when any ball is moved except by a properly hit cue ball and cue/object ball interaction, it is illegal. Game rules determine if there are penalties or the balls are moved back into approximate position with opponent's approval.

Illegal shot (games) - A shot that does not meet the requirements of a legal hit.

In hand (games) - See *Ball in hand*.

Incoming player (games) - The person who comes to the table to play his turn.

Inning (games) - A shooter's inning starts on coming to the table and ends on either a miss, foul, or a game win.

Inside English (games) - English is applied on the cue ball on the same side as the angle that the object ball will travel.

In the rack (games) - In 14.1, when a ball on the table interferes with re-racking the balls.

Insurance (games) - In any game, the positioning of balls so that the opposing player cannot run out the table during his inning.

Insurance ball (games) - In the game of 8 Ball, any ball placed in or near a pocket that allows the player to shoot that if position play was unsuccessful.

Intentional foul (games) - Player will purposely make an illegal shot or commit a foul. Can be done as part of a safety play or because the ball positions are in such a condition that an advantage is gained by committing the foul.

Intentional miss (games) - A shot where the purpose was not to make a ball, but to either position the object ball or cue ball in a location where the opponent will have difficulty shooting.

Interference (games) - Any action or activity which distracts the shooter. Can also be anything that disturbs the ball layout.

Ivory (equipment) - Material made from elephant tusks. Extremely restricted in legal use. Nowadays used only for custom inlays and ferrules.

J - K

Jack up (shot) - When the cue ball is next to the rail or over another ball, the cue butt is raised up and the bridge hand is extended vertically to guide the cue shaft in the downward stroke.

Jail (games) - A hidden ball starting position that is very difficult or impossible to shoot out to attempt to make a legal hit.

Jaw (table) - The space on the table within the edges of the cushions that ends on both sides of a pocket.

Jawed ball (balls) - A ball that stops inside the jaw of the pocket but is not far enough in to fall. Usually rests against one side of the pocket.

Joint (cue) - The connecting devices that join the cue butt and shaft together and allow the stick to be broken down to two pieces.

Joint protector (cue) - A cap that is inserted into the cue shaft to protect the opening, plus another cap covering the joint screw to prevent it from being damaged by other contact.

Jubilation stroke (stroke) - When the shot is executed, the process of continuing the stroke by lifting the cue stick up from the bridge and at the same time standing up. The end result is the stick pointing up into the air in a celebratory stance. (Usually the shot ends with less than satisfactory results.)

Jump ball (balls) - The ball that is jumped over the object balls

Jump cue (cue) - A special cue designed to make it easier to jump balls on the table.

Jump shot (balls) - Occurs when the cue ball is forced to rise from the table and attempts to clear another ball.

Jumped ball (balls) - The ball that was jumped over by the cue ball.

Key ball (games) - In 14.1, the last ball on the table before the balls are re-racked. In 8 Ball, the last ball of the player's group necessary to get shape on the 8 ball.

Key shot (games) - The shot that, if successful, allows an easy run to the game ball.

Kick shot (balls) - The cue ball is aimed at one or more rails in order to make contact with the target object ball, and make a legal shot.

Kill shot (games) - A shot with appropriate spin and speed that causes the cue ball to reduce the distance it would normally travel.

Kiss (balls) - When the cue ball caroms off one ball, or an object ball caroms from another object ball.

Kiss in (balls) - When the object ball caroms off another ball and then is pocketed.

Kiss shot (pocket billiards) - See Kiss, see Carom

Kitchen (table) - Common term to describe the head of the table between the head string and the head cushion.

L

Ladder (tournament) - A ranking of players to determine skill levels. Typically, a lower skilled player can only challenge someone at the rung above himself. If he wins, the two player's positions are swapped.

Lag (games) - The cue ball is driven from the kitchen to the foot rail and back towards the head cushion.

Lag for break (games) - Between two players, the lag is used to determine who will break and begin the match. The winner is the one who comes closest to the head cushion without touching the long rail cushions.

Layout (games) - The positions of all balls on the table.

League (games) - A formal group of players/teams that play using a common set of rules. Play between players/teams is prescheduled with results reported to the director or coordinator who tracks results and rankings.

Leave (pocket billiards) - After one player misses, the table layout that the incoming player must address.

Leather (equipment) - Used for making most types of cue tips. Sometimes used as a wrap on a cue butt. Some cue cases are made from leather.

Left English (balls) - Occurs when the cue ball is hit on the left side of the vertical center line. The spin can be horizontal (9:00), with follow (9:30 through 11:30), and with draw (6:30 through 8:30).

Left-handed (stance) - Reverse stance of right-handed shooting. Bridge hand is the right hand, stick hand is the left hand. Some players are naturally left-handed shooters. Also see *Right-handed*.

Legal shot (games) - A shot that does not cause or create a foul. Generally, this means that the cue ball contacts a legal ball, and then any ball contacts a cushion or is pocketed.

Legal break (games) - The number of balls that must contact a cushion or moved above the center string (depending on the rules of the game).

Level (table) - The closeness to perfect horizontal conditions of the table bed. When a table is not level, the balls will roll off their natural line and make it difficult to properly practice or play any game. Any table with a pronounced roll off is universally condemned.

Lights (equipment) - The set of lights above a table. These are designed to eliminate shadows and provide equal illumination over the entire table.

Line (balls) - (1) The line drawn from the cue ball to a target object ball. A direct line means the object ball can be hit without kicking. (2) The aiming line that is calculated from the cue ball to the target object ball.

Line (table) - A drawn or imaginary line on the table bed cloth, includes the lines for the head string, foot string, center string, and long string.

Live ball (balls) - A ball still in motion. No shot can be made on a table until all balls are completely motionless.

Lock (games) - A game that cannot be lost except by extreme carelessness.

Long miss (balls) - When the object ball misses the pocket on the far side (i.e., A shot with a right angle and the object ball misses on the left of the pocket.

Long rail (table) - The side rails on each side of the table with the side pockets.

Long shot (balls) - Any shot where the combined travel distance is more than a half table.

Long string (table) - This is an imaginary line from the center diamonds of the foot cushion and head cushion down the center of the table.

Loop bridge (stance) - The index finger of the bridge hand is looped over the cue shaft. Also see *Closed bridge*.

Loose (player) - When a player is able to easily make shots and move from position to position.

Loose pockets (table) - When pockets are at or exceed width standards.

Lose (games) - To lose the game or match and pay the agreed penalty (anything from bragging rights to money).

Loser (games) - The individual who loses the game or match.

Loser breaks (games) - The loser of the previous game must break the balls to begin the next game.

Loser's bracket (tournament) - In double elimination, the loser of a match goes to the loser's ladder. The winner continues up to the next level in the winner's bracket.

Loss of game (games) - A penalty when a specific foul occurs. For example, in 8 Ball, sinking the eight ball early, or scratching on the eight ball is a loss of game.

Luck (games) - The ball rolls that benefit (good) or restrict (bad) the shooting player. Usually occurs on a cycle of a series of good rolls followed by a cycle of bad rolls.

Lucky roll (balls) - The roll of one or more balls that stops in near perfect position for the incoming shooter.

Lucky shot (stroke) - A comment by a player when a ball goes in a pocket apparently disregarding physical laws and the shooter's skills. This is a common blessing for the shooter or an injustice for the opponent – often assigned to direct intervention by the billiard gods.

M

Make (balls) - Make the shot - shooting the shot. Make the ball - pocketing a ball.

Mark (games) - Add a scored point to the totals. (i.e., mark the point.)

Mark (gambling) - An easy victim who easily loses money.

Mark the pocket (games) - Identify which pocket the target object ball will be made.

Marker (games) - Any object used to identify or mark a pocket.

Marker (gambling) - An acknowledgement of a debt or obligation.

Masse (stroke) - Extreme English is applied by elevating the butt of the cue stick (greater than 30 degrees) and drive the tip downwards into the cue ball. (Some masse affect is possible whenever the cue butt is raised above the table and the cue is driven downwards.)

Match (games) - A series of games that begins with the players lagging for the break and completed when the final game win is marked.

Mechanic - See *Table mechanic*.

Mechanical bridge (equipment) - A flat device attached at the end of a long stick which has a series of different height groves into which the cue stick rests. Used to reach down table when a normal stance is physically impossible (also known as: crutch, rake, granny).

Miscue (stroke) - This happens when the cue tip does not "grab" the cue ball. The reason is usually because there is not enough chalk on the tip, or because the cue ball contact was too far out from center. The result is an easily recognizable sound and the cue ball traveling in totally unanticipated paths. It is also embarrassing.

Middle pocket (table) - Either side pocket on the table.

Misrack (games) - A rack that is poorly assembled. It contains balls that are loose and not touching other balls. It can be positioned off the foot spot or slightly angled.

Miss (games) - On the stroke, when a ball or point is not made, which ends the players turn and allows the other player to shoot.

Mixed doubles (games) - A female and male partner.

Money ball (games) - The ball that must be pocketed in order to win the game.

Motion (balls) - Any ball still moving or spinning. A shot cannot be made until all balls in motion have come to a complete stop.

Mouth (table) - The opening entrance of the pocket.

Mud table (table) - A table that plays very slowly, as if the balls were rolling through mud. Mud tables usually have thick cloth. They are also noticeable in days with high humidity. All shots will require greater speeds to be successful.

Mushroom (cue) - When the cue tip material spreads out over the edges of the ferrule.

N

Nap (table) - The direction of the cloth weave. It is most noticeable in thick table clothes.

Natural bank (balls) - An alignment of the cue ball and object ball that makes a bank shot easier to make.

Natural English (balls) - The spin of the cue ball as it rolls around the table. Any English is picked up by rolling contact with the cloth and cushions.

Natural roll (balls) - The natural path of a cue ball after contact with the target object ball.

Near side (table) - The side of the target pocket closest to the target object ball.

Negative score (games) - In some games (14.1), it is possible to go to minus (below zero) in the scoring.

Nip draw (balls) - A quick downward strike just below the horizontal center line into the cue ball. Used when the cue ball and object ball are too close for a normal horizontal stroke.

Nose (table) - The edge of the cushion that juts out over the table bed.

Nudge (balls) - (1) Very minor movement when the tip touches the cue ball. Usually an accident which results in a foul because a legal shot is not made. (2) A close-in shot where the cue ball travels a very short distance with a rail contact for a legal shot.

Numbered ball (balls) - Any ball on the table with a number on the surface, aka object balls.

Nurse (game) - The process of shifting object balls into advantageous positions, usually with soft rolls.

O

Object ball (games) - All balls other than the cue ball.

Obstruction (balls) - Any interfering object ball between the cue ball and the target object ball.

Off stroke (games) - When a player cannot make shots that are normally easy to accomplish.

Off the table (balls) - Any ball that is no longer in play because it was pocketed. Can also mean any ball knocked

Offensive shot (games) - A shot that is intended to be made in order to progress towards winning the game.

On stroke (games) - When a player is making shots successfully.

On the hill (games) - During a match, when one player needs one more game win to win the match.

On the snap (games) - Pocketing the winning ball (i.e., the 9 in 9-ball) on the break.

One-handed (stroke) - Using only one hand to make a stroke.

One-piece cue (cue) - A cue stick made as a single piece. (See House cue)

Open bridge (stroke) - The cue shaft slides through a "V" formed with the thumb tight up against the index knuckle. Height is controlled by spreading and gathering the fingers.

Open table (games) - When no group of balls has been selected. As in eight ball, when no shooter has pocketed a ball to determine which player will have which group of balls.

Opening break (games) - The first shot of the game.

Outside English (games) - English is applied on the cue ball on the opposite side as the angle that the object ball will travel.

Over-cut (balls) - The cue ball contacts the object ball too far on one side and the object ball misses the pocket on the long side. (aka *too thin*)

P - Q

Paper cut (games) - A cut so thin that the object ball barely moves.

Parking the cue ball (games) - Very precise position play or stopping the cue ball in the middle of the table.

Pattern (balls) - Layout of the balls. Also the planned paths for a run out, i.e., a run out pattern).

Peas (games) - Small numbered beads (plastic or wooden) used with a bottle for various games (i.e., Kelly Pool).

Penalty (games) - The cost of any violation of the games rules. This can range from loss of turn at a minimum to loss of points and up through loss of game or match for a serious violation.

Pills (games) - see *Peas*.

Play safe (games) - The shooter makes a shot that is defensive in intention.

Play position (games) - The art of making a ball and then causing the cue ball to move into a table location that makes the next shot easy to pocket (and continue getting position).

Player (game) - The person who in turn, uses a cue to shoot balls on the table according to game rules.

Pocket (table) - The six openings around the table where balls can be made to advance the game. These are located at the four corners, and at the two mid-points on the long rails.

Pocket billiards (games) - A slightly more upper class name for pool. The term differentiates the pocket table from the carom table.

Pocket liner (table) - An addition that reduces the size of the pockets. Used during practice times when learning accuracy is important to match success.

Pocket speed (balls) - Sufficient ball roll to get to and barely fall into the pocket.

Point (games) - A single score in a game.

Point of contact (balls) - The location on the cue ball and target object ball where the two balls come together.

Polish (equipment) - A liquid used to clean and shine up the pool balls.

Pool (games) - The generic reference to any games played on a pocket billiards table.

Pool ball (balls) - The object balls and cue ball used to play pocket billiards.

Pool cue - See *Cue*.

Pool hall - A commercial location where pocket billiards, carom billiards, and snooker tables are kept and maintained. The tables are rented out to players by the game or hour.

Pool player - Anyone who picks up a cue stick and attempts to pocket balls.

Pool shark - See *Hustler*.

Pool table (table) - The pocket billiards table upon which all pool games are played.

Position (games) - Location of the cue ball for the shot on the next target ball. (aka Shape). Good position means the shot is easy to make and move into position for the next shot. Bad position means the shot is difficult to make and move into position for the next shot.

Pot (game) - Making a ball. This is an old term now coming back into common use.

Powder (equipment) - Talk or baby powder, used on the bridge hand to allow easy back and forth movement of the cue shaft.

Power draw (balls) - Stroke that uses a combination of speed and lower contact on the cue ball to pull the cue ball back (a lot).

Practice (games) - Any defined time period when the player works to improve skills through repetition.

Practice room (tournament) - Any area of tables which are set aside specifically for tournament entrants to warm up and get comfortable with the match tables.

Pre-shot analysis (games) - The review of the table layout to determine which ball to shoot and how to play the shot to advance towards the win. All of this is done while standing at or walking around the table.

Pre-shot routine (games) - A set of actions taken by a player while setting up on a shot. These are all done while bent over the table.

Professional - Any player to participates in the top level tournaments around the world. Generally, the player will also have one or more sponsors who will cover the travel expenses.

Proposition bet (gambling) - An offer (for money) to perform a seemingly impossible shot.

Push (balls) - A very slow illegal stroke that contacts the cue ball multiple times in one movement. Can also mean *Push out*.

Push out (games) - A legal shot used in 9 Ball (when rules allow). The player shoots the cue ball to any part of the table with or without contact of an object ball that allows the next player to accept or decline to shoot.

Pyramid (games) - The triangular positioning of the object balls on the foot spot to begin a game.

Quarter-ball (balls) - A contact between the cue ball and target object ball where only a quarter of the two balls overlap.

Quarter table (table) - A method of identifying 1/4 of the table surface. On way is to use the head string, center string, and foot string to divide the table into quarters. Another way is the division of the center string and long string.

R

Race (games) - An agreed upon number of games between two opponents needed to win a match. A race to five means that the first person to win five games wins the match.

Rack (equipment) - (n) The tool used to arrange object balls for the game. (v) To arrange the balls using a rack in preparation for the beginning of a game.

Racking (games) - The process of collecting all the balls into the rack and positioning correctly on the table according to game rules.

Rack 'em (games) - An informal command given by the breaker to the other player to get the balls racked up so that the game can get underway. Usually the player was doing something that was wasting time, such as carrying on a conversation with a rail bird.

Rails (table) - The top area around the table that the cushions are attached to. Short rails are the head and foot, long rails along the sides.

Rail birds - Spectators to a match.

Rail bridge (stance) - A bridge formed that allows the cue shaft to ride on the rail while being guided by an open V or finger looped of the shaft.

Rail first (balls) - A shot where the cue ball goes into the cushion first and then comes out to make contact with the target object ball.

Rail shot (stance) - A shot where the cue ball is on or very close to the cushion.

Rake - See *Mechanical bridge*.

Rattle the pocket (balls) - When a ball contacts and bounces between the jaws of the pocket and either stops in the jaws or is kicked out of the pocket.

Read the table (tactics) - The process of analyzing the table layout to determine the most effective action to take for the next shot.

Rearrange the furniture (tactics) - Shooting a shot that makes significant changes to the table layout and which will complicate the process of winning the game.

Referee (tournament) - A person designated to make decisions on the validity of shots and who can call out and enforce rule violations.

Re-rack (games) - On an illegal break, setting up the balls for a fresh break shot.

Re-spot (games) - Placing an object ball on the foot spot or if covered, in a line towards the foot rail center diamond.

Reverse English (balls) - See *Draw*.

Rhythm (stroke) - The routine amount of time used for consecutive shots. This includes regular repetition of the amount of time to select the shot, pre-shot routine, stroke, post-shot routine. As long as the inning lasts, the amount of time to execute each segment stays about the same.

Ride (balls) - A term used to send the balls for an unplanned trip around the table with the hope that something will drop into a pocket and allow the shooter to make another shot.

Right English (balls) - Occurs when the cue ball is hit on the right side of the vertical center line. The spin can be horizontal (3:00), with follow (12:30 through 2:30), and with draw (3:30 through 5:30).

Right-handed (stance) - The stance with a bridge formed with the left hand and the cue stick gripped with the right hand. Most players are naturally right-handed shooters. Also see *Left-handed*.

Ring game (gambling) - A game where multiple players each put up a specified amount of money (stake). The person who sinks the final ball wins a specified amount of money from each player. Players drop out as they run out of the stake money. The game ends when one player has won all the money from each of the other players.

Road player - Any player who travels from town to town to look for gambling opportunities in local bars and pool halls.

Road map (games) - A table layout where all object balls are easy to make.

Rob (gambling) - The process of winning money from a player who has no chance of winning.

Rock (balls) - slang See *Cue ball*.

Roll (balls) - The lucky/unlucky roll of an object ball or cue ball into a good/bad position for the next shot.

Roll-off (balls) - In an area of the table which is not level, the balls roll off the normal travel line.

Round robin (tournament) - Each contestant in a tournament plays every other contestant.

Round the world (games) - A shot that sends an object ball or cue ball to a long rail, then short rail, then a long rail, then to or near a pocket.

Rules (games) - The restrictions and choices available to players for the game being played.

Run (games) - The consecutive points made by a player during one turn at the table. Can also be the consecutive games won in a match.

Run the rack (games) - The process of shooting every ball in the rack during one turn.

Run the table (games) - See *Run the rack*.

Running English (balls) - When the cue ball comes into a cushion at less than 90 degrees, the rail imparts some angled side spin on the rebound. When a ball with running English contacts a cushion, the ball speeds up slightly more than if no angled spin.

Runout (games) - The process of a player pocketing all remaining balls to win.

S

Safety (games) - The defensive effort by a player to place balls in positions that reduce the chances of the incoming player to win.

Safety break (games) - A slower break that limits the spread of the object balls.

Sandbag (games) - The process of playing at a lower ability in order to maintain the appearance of a lower skill level.

Score (games) - (v) The process of marking points. (n) The comparative points made by each player during and at the end of the match.

Score sheet (games) - A paper record of the games and matches being played, usually in a league.

Score string (games) - See *Counting string*.

Scotch doubles (games) - A competition between two sets of partners. Instead of shooting in a regular doubles sequence (Team A, player 1; Team B, player 1; Team A, player 2; Team B, player 2) , the partners alternate shots in an inning.

Scratch (balls) - Occurs when the cue ball falls into a pocket.

Screw tip (cue) - A cue tip that screws into the ferrule. Found only on the cheapest of cues.

Seam (table) - The joint where two pieces of slate meet. When a table is assembled, this small space is hidden by leveling with a compound.

Seeding (tournament) - Pairing up of competitors based on known handicaps to allow competitive matches.

Sell-out (games) - A missed shot that allows the opposing player to run out the table to win the game.

Semi-masse (games) - An elevated shot (about 45 degrees) designed to cause the cue ball to make a tighter arc of travel then a curve shot, but less than a masse shot.

Session (games) - One or more matches played during without leaving the pool hall.

Set (games) - The number of games played until a match is won.

Setup (games) - A perfect position to pocket a ball. Often done with a ball in hand.

Shaft (cue) - The upper narrow part of the cue stick that ends in the cue tip. A two-piece cue contains the shaft and butt.)

Shake bottle (games) - Bottle used to hold the 16 numbered beads for various games.

Shape (games) - Position (good shape or bad shape) of the cue ball for the target object ball

Shark (games) - (v) Doing antics and actions that are expected to distract an opponent and cause a miss or misplay of the shot. (n) See *Hustler*.

Sharp (games) - See *Shark*.

Shim (table) - A pocket facing that is added to the sides of the pocket which narrows the pocket width. A table can be single-, double-, or triple-shimmed. (A triple-shimmed table is commonly used for one pocket.)

Shoot (games) - A stroke made on the table.

Shooter (games) - See *Player*.

Shooting off the rail (stroke) - See Rail shot.

Short (games) - A shot where the ball roll does not reach a pocket or rail.

Short miss (balls) - When the object ball misses the pocket on the near side (i.e., A shot towards the right with the object ball missing on the right of the pocket.

Short rack (games) - Any rack of balls that is less than the standard 15. For example, 9 Ball or 10 Ball.

Shot (stroke) - The ball action on a table caused by a stroke with a cue stick.

Shot clock (games) - When a limited time is available to complete a shot, this timer sets the limit. Used commonly in time chess matches, is occasionally used in some pro tournaments. A side referee starts the clock when the balls have stopped rolling for the incoming player. The clock is stopped when a shot is made. If the time is exceeded, a foul is called and the incoming player has ball in hand.

Shot library (skills) – These are all the shots that you know. To prove it, set up the shot, get ready to shoot, and then close your eyes as your make the shot. If the result is successful and consistent, you own it.

Short rack (games) - A rack which contains less than 15 object balls.

Shot (balls) - The stroke that sends the cue ball off to accomplish your intentions.

Shot diagram (equipment) - A table sketch that shows how balls are positioned. Can also show ball paths.

Side pocket (table) - The two pockets on the table in the middle of the long rails.

Side rail (table) - See *Long rail*.

Side spin (balls) - The spinning of the cue ball or object ball to the left or right side.

Side shot (balls) - Any shot where the target object ball is aimed into a side pocket.

Simultaneous hit (balls) - A situation where the cue ball contacts two object balls at the same time. This is a legal shot.

Single elimination (tournament) - A tournament format where the loser of each match is eliminated from the competition.\

Sink (balls) - Pocket a ball.

Skid (balls) - Occurs when a ball slides across the table before it interacts with the cloth.

Skirt (table) - The siding around the table underneath the rails.

Slate (table) - The material used to create the bed of the table. This is a heavy, stone material that has proven to be dimensionally stable and able to maintain the level necessary for table billiards.

Slide (balls) - See *Skid*.

Slop (game) - Any shot where a ball is pocketed because of luck.

Slow cloth (table) - A thicker cloth installed on a table. Ball rolls are less because the nap of the cloth increases resistance.

Small ball (games) - Any target object ball that is out towards the middle of the table and is thereby difficult to kick towards. Also see *Big ball*.

Snap (games) - The break. The term "win on the snap" means the game is won on the break.

Sneaky Pete (cue) - A house cue that has been cut into a two-piece cue. Originally designed so that a hustler could use this customized stick while appearing to be an ordinary stick.

Snookered (games) - A slang term meaning that the incoming player cannot directly shoot at the proper target object ball.

Solids (balls) - The 1 - 7 balls, used as a group in the game of 8 Ball.

Speed (balls) - The velocity of balls moving during a shot.

Speed (player) - The skill level of a player.

Speed control (balls) - See *Cue ball control*.

Spin (balls) - The sideways rotation of a ball applied by the cue tip. A ball can spin when it interacts with other balls and the rails.

Split double elimination (tournament) - A modified double elimination tournament where the field is split into two or more sections which must play through with the winners of each section then competing for the tournament first place.

Split hit (balls) - When the cue ball contacts two balls simultaneously, it cannot be determined which ball was first contacted.

Split the pocket (balls) - The path of a ball entering the pocket so that both sides are equal distance from the ball.

Sportsmanship - An implied, rarely documented standard of behavior by players and spectators. Basically, it is a gentlemanly courteous and honorable behavior that respects the players and the game. Any tricks or tricky behavior is to be considered below the dignity of the players.

Spot (equipment) - The location on the table where a ball can be placed according to game rules. There are three spots on a table - foot spot, center spot, head spot.

Spot shot (games) - The cue ball is shot from behind the head string to a ball on the foot spot.

Spot (gambling) - The handicap that one player gives another to try to make the game more competitive.

Spot a ball (games) - A ball replaced on the table determined by game rules.

Squirt (balls) - The sideways movement of the cue ball when it is hit on the left or right side of the vertical center line.

Stake (gambling) - The amount set aside for the match being played.

Stall (games) - Intentionally delaying the game.

Stance (stance) - The position of various body parts moved into position so that the shooter can make a stroke.

Steering (stroke) - The process of attempting to correct a bad stroke by swinging the cue to the side and twisting the wrist at the same time.

Stick (cue) - Slang. See *Cue*.

Stick hand (stance) - The hand that grasps the butt of the stick when the shooter gets down on the shot.

Stop shot (balls) - The cue ball, on contact with the object ball stops dead with no side movement. (aka Stun shot)

Straight up (games) - Playing the game with no handicaps.

Stripes (balls) - The 9 - 15 balls, used as a group in the game of 8 Ball.

Stroke (stance) - The forward movement of the cue stick which contacts the cue ball.

Stun (balls) - Shooting the cue ball so that it slides across the cloth directly at the object ball and stops dead on contact.

Sucker shot (games) - Attempting an almost impossible shot that only a beginner would attempt (it does work sometimes).

Swerve (stroke) - A very slight curve the cue ball travels with side spin is added to the cue ball.

Swing (stroke) - The movement of the forearm of the stick hand to drive into the cue ball.

T

Table (table) - The raised, flat surface, bounded by cushions, upon which a cue ball is maneuvered with the tip of a stick to the purpose of pushing object balls into various pockets.

Table cloth (table) – the cloth that covers the table and the cushions. The balls roll on the cloth.

Table cover (equipment) - A thin sheet used to cover the table to keep it free from dust while not in use.

Table time (games) - The costs of using the table in a pool hall.

Table mechanic - A person who knows how to take down, move, and install pool tables. They will also know how to replace cloth and rubber on request.

Talcum powder (equipment) - A powder used to dry hands and make it easier for the cue shaft to slide through the stick hand.

Tangent line (balls) - The perpendicular line to the contact point between the cue ball and object ball.

Taper (cue) - The thickness of the cue shaft on the top 12-18 inches.

Target object ball (games) - The object ball that will be (or must be) hit as the next shot for the player.

Target pocket (games) - The intended pocket for the target object ball.

Thin (games) - When shooting an object ball, hitting it with too much of an angle and missing the shot. Also see *Fat*.

Three foul rule (games) - If a player makes three consecutive three fouls and no legal shot was made in between those fouls, in addition to the 1 point penalty for each foul, an additional 15 point penalty are charged. The violator MUST be warned if he has two consecutive fouls.

Throw (balls) - The modified path of the target object ball caused by another ball contacting across the ball which imparts a slight spins the target object ball off its natural path. Usually done when two balls are frozen.

Tied-up (balls) - When the balls are grouped such that no easy way can be identified for a run out to a win.

Tight pockets (table) - See *Shim*.

Time shot (balls) - A shot that sends the cue ball into an object ball, then later in the ball rolls both balls contact again, attempting to pocket the object ball.

Timing (player) - The rhythm of the player (slow or fast) in which they are most comfortable shooting shots.

Tip (cue) - The part of the cue at the top, mounted on the ferrule that is used to hit the cue ball.

Tit (table) - The corners of the cushion on the edges of the pocket.

Top (balls) - See Follow.

Top cushion (table) - The short cushion at the head of the table.

Top-spin (balls) - See *Follow*.

Tournament (tournament) - A competition among multiple players to determine who will be the top winner. A director determines the individual matches and any handicaps. An entry fee usually is combined into the top money places.

Triangle (equipment) - The rack used to arrange the object balls prior to the break.

Trick shot (games) - Interesting shots, usually to impress and amaze an audience.

Two piece cue (cue) - A cue with a joint that connects the butt and the shaft.

Two way shot (games) - A shot where the cue ball is in position for the next shot if the target object ball is pocketed and, if missed, does not leave the incoming player in a bad position.

U-V

Under-cut (balls) - The cue ball contacts the object ball too soon on one side and the object ball misses the pocket on the short side. (aka *too fat*)

Unsportsmanlike conduct - Any effort that interferes, interrupts, distracts, or disrupts normal play. In tournament play, this can cause a player to forfeit and be removed.

Up and down the table (balls) - Movement of one ball (cue or object ball) that travels the long way on the table at least twice.

Up table (balls) - Aiming or sending balls towards the head of the table.

W-X-Y-Z

Warm-up (games) - (n) A practice stroke as part of a pre-shot routine. (v) Practice games before a competition (match or tournament).

Weight (gambling) - A handicap given to a weaker player by a better player to equalize the skills in order to place a bet on the game or match.

White ball (ball) - slang. See *Cue ball*.

Whitey (ball) - slang. See *Cue ball*.

Wild ball (gambling) - A designated ball that, if the player makes it, wins and ends the game. Used as a handicap to entice a lesser skilled player to compete.

Wing ball (games) - On a rack, these are the balls on each side of the rack that stick out the furthest from the center.

Winner (games) - The player or team who wins the game or match.

Winner breaks (games) - The player who wins the last game breaks for the new game.

Winner's bracket (tournament) - In a double or single elimination tournament, the players who have not lost a match.

Wrap (cue) - The material around the area on the butt of the stick which is grasped by the stick hand.

Wrist stroke (stroke) - The bridge distance is shorted to an inch. The wrist alone moves the cue stick back and forth. Designed for shots where the cue ball will only move a very short distance.

Wrong ball (games) - See *Bad hit*.

Z bank (balls) - The ball goes across side to side or the length of the table to hit two opposite rails.

Z kick (games) - A kick that crosses the width of the table twice in an attempt to make a legal hit.

www.ingramcontent.com/pod-product-compliance
Lightning Source LLC
Chambersburg PA
CBHW080918170426
43201CB00016B/2192

9781625050014